Roses from the Earth:
The Biography of Anne Frank
Carol Ann Lee

VIKING

VIKING

Published by the Penguin Group
Penguin Books Ltd, 27 Wrights Lane, London w8 5tz, England
Penguin Putnam Inc., 375 Hudson Street, New York, New York 10014, USA
Penguin Books Australia Ltd, Ringwood, Victoria, Australia
Penguin Books Canada Ltd, 10 Alcorn Avenue, Toronto, Ontario, Canada m4v 3b2
Penguin Books (NZ) Ltd, Private Bag 102902, NSMC, Auckland, New Zealand

Penguin Books Ltd, Registered Offices: Harmondsworth, Middlesex, England

First published 1999
10 9 8 7 6 5 4 3 2 1

Set in 11/15 pt Linotype Sabon
Typeset by Rowland Phototypesetting Ltd, Bury St Edmunds, Suffolk
Printed in Great Britain by Clays Ltd, St Ives plc

A CIP catalogue record for this book is available from the British Library

ISBN 0-670-88140-6
ISBN 0-670-88618-1

'A person is worth more than a book' Miep Gies

Contents

My interest in Anne Frank began at a very early age. I discovered a re-telling of her story when I was about six or seven years old, and read the diary when I was eight. The question I have been asked most frequently by people over the years, and particularly during the course of writing this book, is: what drew you so strongly to Anne Frank? I don't think I knew myself until someone asked me another question: having written the book, has anything you discovered led you to change your opinion of Anne Frank and the person you perceived her to be? I answered instinctively, 'No, not at all. I liked her very much at the beginning; I like her still.' It really is that simple.

There is no doubt, however, that since I first read the diary, my interest has grown into a fixation which has its culmination in this book. Without the aid of many people, writing it would have been a far more difficult task. The list is too long to be indulged here, but it includes all those who were kind enough to share their time and memories with me. Among them are Eddy Fraifeld, Jetteke Frijda, Dr Trude K. Hollander, Bernard Kops, Herbert Levy, Jacqueline van Maarsen, Edmond Silverberg, Eva Schloss, Alice Schulmann, Lotte Thyes, and Betty C. Wallerstein. To Hanneli Pick-Goslar, with whom I corresponded, but was unable to meet due to circumstance, I'd also like to offer my thanks. I apologize to those whose testimonies I have not been able to include.

I received inestimable help from a number of archivists, librarians and individuals, particularly: Horst Hoffman of the Frank-Loeb'sches House in Landau, Dr Appel of the Landau town archives, Joan Adler,

Wolf von Wolzogen of the Frankfurt Historical Museum, the staff of the exhibition *Anne Aus Frankfurt*, Gillian Walnes and Barry van Driel of the Anne Frank Educational Trust, Jan Erik Dubbelman of the Anne Frank Stichting, Fama Mor of the Simon Wiesenthal Centre, the Shoah Foundation and Michael Engel, the staff of the Wiener Library in London, David Barnouw and Manon Wilbrink of the Netherlands State Institute for War Documentation, the staff of Yad Vashem in Israel, Aaron T. Kornblum of the United States Holocaust Memorial Museum, and the staff of the Belsen and Westerbork museums and remembrance centres.

For source material and advice on research I would like to single out Jon Blair, Gerrold van der Stroom, Dick Plotz and John Francken. I must also thank Christoph Knoch for his assistance with the photographs.

I am grateful to Rosalba Venturi, Liz Kim and Anthony Tisbury of K. International for translations from Dutch into English, and to David Nuth for translations from German into English.

There are a handful of people whose patience I have tried more than most. In England, my agent, Jane Judd, and my editor at Penguin, Andrew Kidd, have provided guidance, enthusiasm and staunch support. In the Netherlands, Françoise Gaarlandt-Kist and Jan Geurt Gaarlandt of Balans have done likewise. I would like to thank Jan Michael for all of the above, and for her hospitality in Amsterdam. For reminding me that I live in the present as well as the past, I must thank my family and friends, all of whom have been there for me when I needed them.

Finally, there are four people without whom, for various reasons, this book truly could not have been written. They are: my mother, Buddy and Gerti Elias, and, of course, Anne Frank. To these four, I dedicate *Roses from the Earth*.

I have drawn on a wide range of literary sources in my attempt to understand the past and the central figures of this book. Grateful acknowledgement is made to those authors and publishers who have granted permission to quote copyright material. While every effort has been made to trace all the copyright holders, I apologize for any oversights. Anyone believing they are entitled to exercise rights over these omissions are requested to contact the author.

All photographs, and quotations from Anne's diary, are under copyright of the Anne Frank-Fonds, Basel, Switzerland. The letters of the Frank family, and Otto Frank's memoir, are used by the kind permission of Buddy Elias.

On 10 September 1997 the office of the Anne Frank-Fonds forwarded Carol Ann Lee's first letter to me. I am Anne Frank's last living direct relative, the cousin she called Bernd in her diary, and I am president of the Foundation. I read the first line: 'Dear Sirs, I am writing to ask whether you would consider giving your approval to a book I am writing about the life of Anne Frank.' My first thought was: another writer trying to make money out of Anne Frank. But I kept on reading and, line by line, my first impression changed. I saw that this was different, this was promising, interesting: a dedicated young lady whose life since early childhood was affected by Anne Frank, her diary, her short life, her destiny. I was moved.

I was even more moved by her first letter to me personally, telling me that her planned biography of Anne was of such importance to her that, should she not succeed, she would consider her career as having failed. Melodramatic? No, credible to me – especially after having received and read her first two chapters: remarkable evidence of meticulous research, of visible talent.

And then I met Carol when she came for an interview to answer a few questions. It turned into a conversation that lasted almost three hours as we exchanged questions and answers and discussed Anne, her family, her life, my life, my family. In short, Carol knew so much already that it was clear to me she was more than capable of telling the world about the phenomenon of Anne Frank. Not only was her knowledge astonishing, but her love and dedication to this cause warmed my heart.

Foreword

This book will be an enrichment to all those interested in Anne Frank, her short life, her family and the circumstances that led to her terrible destiny. But more so, this book is a must for all those with only a vague idea about the Holocaust, and especially for those who still believe that it never happened.

Buddy Elias

Karl Josef Silberbauer, the man who arrested the Frank family, interviewed by Dutch journalist Jules Huf in 1963:

JH: *Aren't you sorry for what you did?*

KJS: *Of course I am sorry. Sometimes I feel positively like an outcast. Each time I want to take a tram, I have to buy a ticket now, just like anybody else. I can no longer show my police card.*

JH: *And what about Anne Frank? Have you read her diary?*

KJS: *I bought the little book last week to see if I was mentioned in it. But I'm not.*

JH: *Millions of people read the diary before you did. But you could have been the first to do so.*

KJS: *That is quite true. I never thought of that. Maybe I should have picked it up after all . . .*[1]

It was 4 August 1944, mid-morning in Amsterdam, warm and still. In the main office at 263 Prinsengracht, ripples of light, the reflection of the sun shining on the canal, cast distracting patterns across the ceiling. The only sound to be heard was muted: the rumbling of the spice-mills in the warehouse below. The occupants of the office were each engaged in some routine task; Bep Voskuijl, 25-year-old typist, pored over the receipts book, while Miep Gies, aged thirty-five, and Johannes Kleiman, forty-eight, were likewise engrossed in their work. None of them noticed the slow purr of a car pulling up outside. Vehicles of all kinds parked alongside the canal every day. There was nothing unusual about it, even when the car stopped directly in front of the warehouse.[2]

Bep: 'The front door opened, and someone came up the stairs. I wondered who it could be. We often had callers. Only this time I could hear that there were several men . . .'[3]

The office door opened. A tall, thin man in civilian dress stood in the corridor. He had a 'long, dried-up, yellowish face',[4] and in his hand a gun. Pointing the pistol at them, he warned, 'Just sit there quietly and don't move.' Then he went out, leaving the three of them sitting motionless, in utter shock. Miep suddenly said, 'Bep, we've had it.'[5]

In the adjoining office, Victor Kugler heard footsteps in the corridor. Then his door, too, opened. He started at the sight of the men before him.

Kugler did not know their names then, but one was Karl Josef Silberbauer, a stocky man in his forties, unremarkable but for his Gestapo uniform. He was accompanied by three or four plain-clothed Dutch Nazis who behaved 'rather like detectives in a movie thriller'.[6] One of them was Maarten van Rossum, a notorious collaborator.

The Gestapo official stepped forward. 'Who is the owner of this house?' He had a distinct Viennese accent. Kugler gave him the name and address of the landlord.

'That's not what I mean. Who is in charge here?'

'I am,' Kugler replied.

One of the Dutch Nazis approached the desk. 'We know *everything*. You've been denounced.' He paused, then said, 'You are harbouring Jews. They're in this building. Take us to them.'

Kugler flushed to the roots of his hair. It was over. He got up, and led the way upstairs.

Miep fiddled with her bag, extracting the illegal ration cards needed to feed eight people in hiding. She held them in her lap as she dipped into the bag again, taking out money and her husband Jan's lunch. Some time had passed since Jan had left them. When he came back it was about quarter to twelve. Miep stopped him at the office door, thrust the money, food and ration cards at him, and whispered urgently, 'It's wrong here.' He knew exactly what she meant. Quickly and quietly, he left the building.

Miep: 'Afterwards, there seemed to be another Dutch man present and a German-speaking man (who later appeared to be an Austrian, born in Vienna like myself). This one was in charge. I heard them going upstairs, whereupon Mr Kugler had to accompany them . . .'[7]

Kugler, Silberbauer and the Dutch Nazis were in the small corridor connecting the front house to the annexe at the back, on the floor above the offices. There was a bookcase at one end of the hallway, a diamond-patterned door at the other, and a pair of windows side-on, partially obscured by stiff paper.

Kugler: 'Outwardly I showed great calm, but inwardly I was terrified . . . We had come to the crucial place.'[8]

He pointed to the bookcase, its shelves packed with old office files bearing the titles 'Opekta' and 'Pectacon'. The men in civilian dress rattled it violently, but the bookcase stood firm.

Kugler: 'The bookcase did not yield an inch. Again and again they tried to move it but failed. Finally, they found the hook which kept the bookcase in its place. The hook was unfastened and they moved the bookcase . . .'[9]

It swung open to reveal a plain grey door. One of the Dutch Nazis turned the doorknob; a row of well-trodden, steep steps led up into darkness. At the foot of the staircase, to the left, was a narrow corridor. To the right was a small washroom.

Kugler: 'The moment I had dreaded for two years had arrived. I knew we had been betrayed. The eight in the secret annexe were doomed; a terrible fate awaited them all.'[10]

Silberbauer now drew his gun. He pushed Kugler in front, his pistol pressed against his spine, and ordered: 'In.'

Kugler walked slowly along the corridor to the left of the closed staircase and entered a low-ceilinged room. It was unpleasantly humid, as always during the summer months. The window was never opened, the thick, yellowing curtains never moved aside to allow the wind to sweep through the stale rooms. Wallpaper peeled from its moorings, discoloured with age, and the dark paint on the woodwork had flaked away.

Kugler raised his eyes to the dark-haired Jewish woman standing beside the table, her expression at once anxious and confused.

'The Gestapo are here,' he said.

Downstairs, one of the Dutch Nazis strode into the office where Bep, Miep and Kleiman were still waiting. He told Kleiman to accompany him into Kugler's office. After ten minutes, Kleiman reappeared alone, having been ordered to give Miep the keys to the building. He handed Bep his wallet and told her to take it to his friend, who had a pharmacy on nearby Leliegracht. 'Tell him to pass it on to my wife,' Kleiman said, and so Bep was able to escape. Before returning to the rear office, he pressed the keys into Miep's palm and whispered, 'See that you stay out of this, Miep – you can't save us now, but make the best of a bad thing here.'[11]

Miep carried on sitting there in silence. When asked after the war whether there had ever been a plan for this eventuality, she replied, 'No, no. We were so sure that it would never happen.'[12]

In the small, damp garret space beneath the attic, Otto Frank was giving English dictation to Peter van Pels, a boy of eighteen. He was correcting Peter's mistakes when he heard someone racing up the stairs, making no effort to be quiet. Otto jumped up, astonished. The door flew open and a man pointed a pistol at them: 'Raise your hands.'

They were searched for weapons. Finding nothing, the man indicated with his gun: 'Step forward.' They walked past him and into Peter's parents' room, where Mr and Mrs van Pels and Fritz Pfeffer, who shared their hiding place, stood with their hands above their heads. Another Dutch Nazi guarded them.

'Downstairs.'

In the Franks' room, Edith Frank and the two girls, Margot and Anne, stood with raised hands. Margot wept softly. Kugler was there, together with a third Dutch Nazi and Silberbauer, who had drawn his pistol. The sun glittered through the thick curtains.

Otto: 'I had not imagined for so much as a moment what it would be like when they came. It was simply unthinkable. And now here they were.'[13]

Silberbauer watched them intently. There were no hysterics. He looked at Otto Frank. 'Where are your valuables?'

Otto pointed to a cupboard. Silberbauer lifted out a small cashbox. Inside were a few pieces of jewellery and a roll of banknotes. He glanced about, and his gaze fell on Otto's briefcase. He picked it up and shook it open: notebooks, loose papers and a check-covered autograph album fell to the floor. He emptied the cashbox into the briefcase, along with some silverware and a brass menorah. 'Have you any weapons?' he asked, snapping the briefcase shut.

All heads shook in succession.

'Good.' Silberbauer thought for a moment, then said, 'Get ready. Everyone back here in five minutes.'

The group dispersed. The van Pelses headed upstairs for their knapsacks. During their two years in hiding, the fugitives' greatest fear, aside from being discovered, was of fire breaking out in the wooden-structured house. For that reason, they each had an 'emergency bag' in case they needed to evacuate the annexe. Of course, they had no idea where they would have found new shelter.

Anne and Pfeffer went into the room they shared, leaving Otto, Edith and Margot with Silberbauer and the Dutch Nazis. Otto took down his bag from a hook. Silberbauer paced about the room. A map of the Allied advance hung on one wall; little red pins marked their progress. Others were stuck in the faded, flowered wallpaper, waiting to be used. Beside the map there was a column of horizontal pencil lines with letters and dates: 'A, 1942', 'A, 1943', 'A, 1944'. At some point Otto told Silberbauer how long they had been in hiding.

'*Two years?*' Silberbauer was genuinely amazed. 'I don't believe you.'

Otto pointed to the pencil marks: 'That's where we've measured the height of my youngest daughter while we've been here.'

Silberbauer was further surprised when he noticed a grey army footlocker standing between the neatly made beds and the window. 'Where did you get this?' he asked sharply.

'It belongs to me,' Otto said. 'I was a lieutenant in the German army during the Great War.'

Silberbauer reddened. 'Why on earth didn't you report your status?'

he demanded. 'You would have been sent to Theresienstadt, you would have been treated decently!'

Otto did not reply. Silberbauer evaded his steady gaze.

Kugler: 'I was watching Silberbauer struggling with his mixed feelings . . . He had come to attention in front of Mr Frank and I had the feeling that a sharp command would make him salute.'[14]

Silberbauer spun round and ran upstairs. He came back a moment later, calling, 'There's no rush, take your time, take your time!' He told his subordinates the same thing.

Otto: 'Perhaps he would have spared us if he had been by himself.'[15]

The Dutch Nazi who had first threatened the three in the office reappeared downstairs and seated himself at Bep's desk. Miep listened to him telephoning for a car, until Silberbauer entered and stood before her. 'Now it's your turn,' he said.

She decided to take a chance. 'You're from Vienna,' she said. 'So am I.'

Silberbauer stared at her, then asked for her papers. Miep handed him her identity card. His eyes flickered over it, registering that her name was 'Gies'. One of the businesses in the building was Gies & Co. He swung round and yelled at the civilian, 'Get out of here!' The man scuttled to the door.

Silberbauer threw down the card and screamed, 'Aren't you ashamed? You're a traitor to your country! Helping Jews! You deserve the worst punishment!' Miep kept silent. Suddenly, Silberbauer regained his composure. 'What should I do with you?' he said thoughtfully. Reaching down, he took the keys from her and said, 'Out of personal sympathy, you can stay here. But God help your husband if you disappear. Because then – we will take him.'

Miep shouted, 'Leave him alone! He's got nothing to do with it!'

Silberbauer snorted. 'Don't be stupid, child. He's in on it, too.' He went out, saying, 'I'll be coming back.'

Miep: 'I had no idea what was going on in the rest of the house. I was in a terrible mental state. I felt as though I was falling . . .'[16]

*

In the annexe Anne tapped her father on the shoulder. She held out a bundle of objects. Otto sorted through them quickly, telling her what she should and should not take.

Otto: 'Anne walked back and forth and did not even glance at the briefcase where she kept her diary. Perhaps she had a premonition that all was lost now.'[17]

No one showed any emotion. Eventually they were all ready, and then, one by one, for the way was very narrow, they walked along the corridor to the swinging bookcase. When everyone was in the hallway, one of the policemen locked the door and shoved the bookcase into place.

Alone in her office, Miep heard them coming down the wooden stairs, 'like beaten dogs'.[18]

They gathered in the private office, amongst the elegant furniture that Otto Frank had chosen with pride years before. Kugler was already there and Kleiman entered shortly afterward. A Dutch Nazi stood between them while Silberbauer fired questions first at Kugler, then at Kleiman. Their answer was always: 'I have nothing to say.'

'All right,' Silberbauer snapped, his colour rising, 'then you'll come along too.'

Jan Gies stood with Kleiman's brother on the other side of the canal. They saw a windowless police van park outside 263 Prinsengracht, and a crowd of onlookers gather around it.

Kleiman and Kugler were the first to step out of the building. They were followed by the occupants of the secret annexe, to whom fresh air and direct sunlight seemed an anomaly after two years of constant confinement.

Otto: 'Our two warehouse clerks stood at the front entrance as we came down, van Maaren and the other one, but I did not look as I passed them, and in memory I can only see their faces as pale, blank discs which did not move.'[19]

Inside the van Kleiman sat down on the bench just behind the driver, and as his eyes grew accustomed to the gloom, he noticed another man sitting opposite. The others were climbing in and finding seats. The driver whispered to Kleiman, 'Don't talk now – he's one too.'[20] He inclined his head slightly towards the man in the corner as the bells of the Westertoren pealed out. Then the doors slammed shut and darkness fell around them.

Sunlight came into the room in an arc, spilling on to the debris left behind by clumsy hands. Scattered across the floor, exactly as the Gestapo had abandoned them, were the contents of the briefcase. The same slanting handwriting covered everything – long, pointed strokes, like accusatory fingers, on coloured papers, school-books, under photographs in a battered old album: 'This is a photograph of me as I wish I looked all the time . . .'; 'This is June 1939 . . . Margot and I had just got out of the water and I still remember how terribly cold I was . . .'[21] and beneath a faded photograph of a young girl leaning over a balcony, her dark hair fluttering in a spring breeze: 'Granny was supposed to be on the photograph. Margot pressed the shutter and when it was developed we saw that Granny had disappeared . . .'[22]

In the middle of the mess lay a cardboard-covered book, and then another and another, all shaken open, all bearing the distinctive script: 'The atmosphere is so oppressive, and sleepy and heavy as lead; you don't hear a single bird singing outside, and a deadly sultry silence hangs everywhere, catching hold of me as if it would drag me down deep into an underworld . . . I don't even feel a response any more; I go and lie on the divan and sleep, to make the time pass more quickly, and the stillness and the terrible fear, because there is no way of killing time.'[23] On the last book of all, that same curious, slanting hand had written: 'Secret Annexe. Diary of Anne Frank. From 17 April 1944 to . . .'[24]

To 4 August 1944. The diarist had gone.

We Were Still Part of Ordinary, Everyday Life 1929–40

Part One

Chapter One

'Blurry, why did you run away?'
'I wanted to discover the world,' was his answer.
'And did you discover it?'
'Oh, I have seen very, very much. I have become a very experienced bear.'
'Yes, I know all that; but I asked you if you had discovered the world.'
'No, no . . . not really; you see, I couldn't find it!'

Anne Frank, *Tales from the Secret Annexe*, 'Blurry the Explorer'

'Pim is a great optimist,' Anne Frank once said of her father, 'but he always finds a reason to be . . .'[1] Growing to adulthood in Frankfurt's affluent Westend, Otto Frank, his two brothers and younger sister had little reason to believe that life had anything other than goodness to offer. It was a neighbourhood steeped in familiarity and warmth, populated mainly by Liberal Jewish families who had worked hard to make their homes there. Otto's mother, Alice Betty Stern, could trace her family back to the turn of the sixteenth century in the city archives; many of her forebears had distinguished themselves in German society and commerce. However, both of Alice's parents had ancestors who had lived on the notorious Frankfurt Judengasse. Alice's paternal great-grandfather, Abraham Süsskind Stern, was born at the 'Golden Sword' on the Judengasse, while one of her mother's relatives, Nathan Michel Cahn, had been the almshouse scribe. The Judengasse was a tapering half-circle, 'a narrow lane, more slum-like and overcrowded than any other tenements in Frankfurt. A closed compound, it was shut off from the rest of the city by high walls and three heavy gates. The gates were guarded by soldiers and were locked at night, all day on Sundays and Christian holidays and from Good Friday until after Easter. In it lived the largest Jewish community in Germany in conditions of almost total isolation, or apartheid.'[2]

Such humble beginnings notwithstanding, when August Heinrich Stern and Cornelia Cahn wed on 3 March 1865, they were without financial worries and the Judengasse was behind them. Alice, their only child, was born on 20 December 1865 at the family home on Langestrasse.

She was twenty years old when she married, not into another eminent local German-Jewish family as expected, but instead to a man from outside Frankfurt circles, and one who had made his money largely by himself.

Michael Frank had arrived in Frankfurt with confidence, determination, and perhaps a little pecuniary aid from his father. He came from Landau, in the Rhineland-Pfalz, a town whose Jewish community had been expelled bloodily several times before achieving full civic status in 1851, the year of Michael's birth. His father, Zacharias Frank, was a banker who bought a number of substantial vineyards in Albersweiler and was famous for his post-harvest parties. In 1870, he bought the beautiful fifteenth-century galleried tavern, Zur Blum, in Landau's centre. The property remained in the family's possession for almost eighty years, but fell into disrepair during the Second World War and its aftermath. It has recently been restored and opened to the public as 'The Frank-Loeb'sches House'. A photograph of Michael Frank stares down from its walls, but in fact Michael, and most of his siblings, had left Landau by the time Zacharias bought the house.[3]

Born on 9 October 1851, Michael was the seventh of eleven children. Of the eleven, only two stayed in Landau, and when two of Michael's sisters, Rosalia and Caroline, married prosperous men from Frankfurt-am-Main, he decided it was there that he should try his own luck.

Frankfurt was a logical destination for a young man who wanted to better himself. The central position of the city, on the banks of the River Main, made it an ideal setting for trade, although when Michael Frank arrived there in 1879, the Jewish population had only recently acquired the right to participate fully in commercial life. There had been a Jewish ghetto in Frankfurt for centuries. Following a pogrom in 1614, in which all Jews were repelled from the city, those who returned were compelled to distinguish themselves with a circular badge sewn on their clothing. In the eighteenth century, the tiny houses packed tightly along the Judengasse and Konstablerwache were so squalid that even the usually unsympathetic French press devoted an article to their plight. On certain days Jews were prohibited from the streets, and their freedom to trade was strictly limited to those businesses which the Nazis would later accuse them of monopolizing. Only twelve marriages were allowed annually and girls were banned from walking outside the ghetto by the Frankfurt kehillah. Finally, in the early nineteenth century, as a result of dogged lobbying by Jews and some non-Jews, the laws were progressively relaxed and Jews were granted equal rights. When Michael Frank arrived in Frankfurt, the hated ghetto was in the process of being torn down. Even so, a strain of anti-Semitism continued to pulse under the surface of the new liberalism.

Following his marriage on 3 January 1885 to Alice Stern (whom Anne describes in her diary as 'a very dear and clever woman, who gets on well with all her acquaintances friends and relatives and would do anything for them'),[4] Michael Frank began dealing in stocks and shares, foreign currency and bills of exchange. He invested in various companies, including a cigar manufacturer, a baby food firm, a printing works, and the producer of a brand of throat pastilles. Aided by French war repatriation payments, the German economy thrived, and joint stock companies flourished. By 1900 Michael was a contented man, having very profitably sold all his shares except those in Fay's pastilles. Although her grandparents were never as rich as Anne liked to claim (in her diary she writes, 'Michael Frank owned a bank and became a millionaire'[5]), their future seemed assured. Michael's private bank concern moved to a smart address to accommodate swelling trade, and the Franks themselves needed a larger home: by now they had four children.

Anne's father, Otto Heinrich, was the middle son, born on 12 May 1889. Robert was born on 7 October 1886 and Herbert on 13 October 1891. Helene, nick-named Leni, followed on 8 September 1893. As the only girl, tiny and fragile-looking, Leni was very protected, particularly by Otto, who affectionately called her Lunni, or Lunna. In 1902 the family moved into a splendid house at 4 Jordanstrasse in the Westend. The house had been built the previous year and, though not ostentatious, its balconies and grand cupola gave it an air of noble comfort. In common with their neighbours, and approximately 80 per cent of German Jews, the Franks belonged to the Liberal Jewish congregation, with friends of varied faith and background. Otto said he could not recall 'ever having encountered an anti-Semite in my youth in Frankfurt. Certainly there were some, but I never met any of them.'[6] Shortly before his death, however, Otto showed a friend a photograph of his childhood playmates and admitted, 'They all became Nazis.'[7]

Anne described her father's youth as 'a real little rich boy's upbringing, parties every week, balls, festivities, beautiful girls, waltzing, dinners, a large home, etc, etc . . . Before the war they still had quite a few rich relatives, such as Olga Spitzer in Paris and Milly Stanfield in London. And Jacob and Hermann in Luxembourg couldn't complain of lack of money either. Daddy was therefore extremely well brought up . . .'[8] A photograph of the Franks at a stylish Black Forest health resort in 1900 shows them all exquisitely dressed. Michael Frank, with moustache and bowler-hat, and Alice Frank, stout and handsome, pose behind Otto, Helene and Herbert. Robert stands to the right, his hair a mass of bohemian black curls, and looks older than his fourteen years. Eleven-year-old Otto, wearing a fashionable sailor suit and holding a straw boater, sits on the front row next to Leni. There is a marked resemblance between Otto and his future daughter Anne at the same age; they share narrow, sharp faces and slight overbites, but there is also something of Leni in Anne when she became a teenager – the same long, watchful prettiness, high cheek-bones and deep-set, clever eyes. A photograph taken of Leni sitting on Otto's shoulders when she was in her mid-teens cannot help but make one wonder just how strong the similarity would have been.

Otto's schooldays were spent at the Lessing Gymnasium, and he received the Abitur (leaving certificate) with honours when he graduated. His passions were the arts, archaeology, and Greek and Roman antiquity, but he knew that he and his brothers would eventually be expected to administer the bank business. Yet Michael Frank did not push his sons single-mindedly in that direction; he invested in a Frankfurt art business, and appointed Robert (then studying art history) as deputy manager. Perhaps inspired by his father's understanding of Robert's inclinations, in 1908 Otto enrolled on an art history course at Heidelberg University. There he struck up a friendship with a recent arrival from Princeton University in America, Nathan Straus.[9] The relationship was to be one of the most important in Otto's life, lasting through two world wars and their aftermath. Straus was the son of Nathan Straus Senior, who owned Macy's in New York. According to the family historian, Nathan Junior was 'very scrappy, like his father . . . capable of grand gestures but mercurial'.[10] One of his grand gestures was to offer Otto a job at Macy's, which Otto accepted, leaving Heidelberg after only a single term's study.

Otto fell in love with New York's brashness, pace and breathtaking volubility. New York *was* the new century, and through working in its biggest and best department store, Otto learned much about modern business practice. In September 1909, however, he learned that his father had died.[11] Otto sailed home immediately.

Ownership of the bank passed to Alice, Michael's widow, but it was largely Otto who assumed control of the business. A year later he took on a full-time administrative job with a Dusseldorf metal engineering firm. He was still working in Dusseldorf and juggling his duties at the family bank with frequent trips to New York when the First World War broke out.[12]

Some 100,000 Jews served in the German army during the Great War. Otto, Robert and Herbert Frank were all drafted into the military. Otto joined the ranks of the artillery as a range-finder attached to the infantry. The majority of men in his unit were surveyors and mathematicians. In August 1915 Otto was training at a depot in Mainz, and wrote home full of enthusiasm, convinced that Germany would triumph: 'I got into my straw-bed at 11 o'clock. Nineteen men in a room made for eight! Today we've been told which units we're in and given clothes. Afterwards there was a big "house" clean-up. I had to clean the windows and polish my boots, etc ... I'm glad to have reached this place, as apparently this was the last transport here; everything further has been cancelled. Many have asked to come and join in the victory too.'[13]

A year later the Somme offensive was launched. When the campaign was over, Britain had lost 400,000 of her troops, France 200,000, and Germany 450,000. Otto Frank was amongst those who participated but somehow survived. A handful of Otto's letters from the Western Front still exist.[14] In them, Otto rarely mentions his experiences as a soldier; no doubt he wished to spare the recipient of the letters – his young sister – from the grim aspects of his daily life. Instead, Otto counsels Leni on her problems growing-up, her interest in boys, and her slightly less harmonious relationship with their older brother Robert. It is easy to draw comparisons with Otto's future relationship with Anne. He repeatedly refers in his letters to the importance of communication between families and, prefiguring the years in hiding when his would be the calm voice of reason, he tries to resolve the quarrels between Leni and Robert, telling her: 'I like to act as mediator if it helps clear up misunderstandings . . . I also get the feeling that mothers, brothers and sisters are the only trustworthy people. At least that's how it is in Jewish families like ours.'[15]

His reference to his religion is an interesting one, for throughout the war Otto felt very strongly that he was fighting for his country, and there was no sense of a dichotomy between being German and being Jewish. In a letter of 1917 he hungers for a German victory: 'I'm salivating at the stuff in the newspapers, hoping that the Russians feel the full might of Germany! Russia isn't able to come through another winter again, so I'm staying optimistic.'[16] In retrospect he explained, 'Born in Germany into an assimilated family that had lived in that country for centuries, I felt very German';[17] and in another letter: 'I cannot claim that I did not feel Jewish at the time. But somehow I was quite consciously German. Otherwise, I would never have become an officer during World War I, nor would I have fought for Germany. But later on, as we know, this made not the slightest difference in the eyes of our persecutors.'[18]

The Germans withdrew to the Hindenburg Line in February 1917, and the head of Otto's unit, whom Otto judged 'a decent, enlightened man who handled his unit with the utmost fairness',[19] put him forward as an officer candidate. He was accepted, and photographs from that year show him plotting manoeuvres on a large board, or seated behind a desk. Towards the end of 1917 his unit moved up to Cambrai. They were there on the morning of 20 November, when 321 British tanks rumbled unexpectedly out of the dawn mists and attacked the Hindenburg Line. Otto's was the first range-finding unit to deal with tank warfare. In 1918 he was promoted to lieutenant for his part in a courageous reconnaissance action. He was transferred to the heavily barraged St Quentin sector of the front. In her diary Anne often writes of him suffering badly with his nerves, which might have been a consequence of his military service, but there are no records of any serious injury befalling him. In that respect he was highly fortunate; Otto and his brothers were amongst the few to return to their homeland physically unscathed when the war ended on 11 November 1918.

Although the Franks withstood no loss of life during the war years, their wealth was gone. Whilst she and her daughter were volunteer nurses at a Red Cross army hospital, Alice had made an ill-fated investment in war loans which, together with inflation, led to the downfall of the family bank business. Even the partnership formed after the war by Otto, Herbert and Leni's husband Erich Elias was unable to revive it. The only possible means of rescuing the business seemed to be foreign expansion, and in 1923, trading under the name 'Michael Frank & Sons', Otto opened a branch of the bank in Amsterdam at 604 Keizersgracht.

Two men joined the Dutch bank in its first year: Jacques Heuskin from Luxembourg, and Johannes Kleiman. Kleiman, born in 1896 in Koog aan de Zaan, was to play a vital role in Otto Frank's life in the years to come. Miep Gies, who subsequently became just as important, remembered him as 'a frail-looking, pale-faced man, with large, thick glasses, a pinched nose and a delicate look. He was a quiet person whose personality immediately inspired feelings of trust and kindness.'[20] Kleiman and Otto immediately hit it off, although their friendship would not begin in earnest until ten years later. Despite the efforts of all concerned, in 1924 'Michael Frank & Sons' of Amsterdam went into liquidation.

Otto was the last of his siblings to marry. Leni had been the first, marrying Erich Elias in Frankfurt on 16 February 1921. The couple lived with Leni's mother in the house on Jordanstrasse, together with their first son Stephan. In July 1922 Robert married Charlotte Witt. The fact that Charlotte was not Jewish made no difference to the Frank family, as Otto declared to a friend, 'My older brother married a non-Jewish girl. Both are not at all religious, but anyhow my sister-in-law offered to become Jewish, but my brother did not think it necessary, the more as they had no children.'[21] Herbert had managed to extricate himself from a disastrous three-year relationship with an American lady named Hortense Schott. Otto seems to have had at least one serious attachment before his marriage (there are oblique references in Anne's diary to a love affair Otto had either during or soon after the Great War), but by 1924 any romantic liaisons were over, and he began courting a businessman's daughter from Aachen, Edith Hollander.

Edith was the youngest of four children born to a wealthy manufacturer and his wife. Her great-grandfather, Levy Elkan, had married twice, and there were children from both marriages.[22] Edith's grandfather, Carl Benjamin Hollander (known as Benjamin), was the son of the second marriage and the creator of the Hollander fortune, dealing in scrap metal and opening a number of metalworks factories. Edith's father Abraham was born on 27 October 1860 in Eschweiler, a city on the edge of the Eifel Mountains. Not a great deal is known of Abraham's eight brothers and sisters, most of whom emigrated to the Netherlands, America, Spain or Russia. He was closest to Karl, five years his senior, and Emanuel, one year older. It fell to Abraham to run his father's business, since Emanuel was, according to a family source, 'a drinker and a gambler, and spent his money on women. He was banished to America – a form of banishment in those days.'[23] He married an Irish woman, and died, childless, in New York. Karl was killed in action on 28 December 1915.

Abraham, it would appear, was steadier than his brother Emmanuel. He directed his father's business and was a committed family man. His wife, Rosa Stern, was born on 25 December 1866 in Langenschwalbach, and bore their first child, Julius, on 11 December 1894 while they were living in Eschweiler. Thereafter they moved to Aachen, on the borders of Belgium and the Netherlands, and either bought or rented the house at 1 Pastorplatz. A second son, Walter, was born in 1897, and a daughter, Bettina, in 1898. Edith was their youngest child, born on 16 January 1900. Her childhood in the middle-class region around Pastorplatz was tranquil but for one incident: the sudden death, from appendicitis, of her sixteen-year-old sister Betti in 1914. In later life Edith never mentioned this incident and chatted to friends and family about the happiness of her youth, remembering especially the company of her brothers, and the sumptuous dinner parties her parents would throw for up to two hundred guests.

Edith's rather plain looks and large-boned frame were tempered by warm, appealing eyes and masses of sable-coloured hair which she wore in a fashionable bob until her early thirties. Naturally shy, but gracious and good-natured, Edith was twenty-four when she met her future husband. Exactly how they met is not known, beyond that it was through the Franks' bank business. The Hollander family today believe that the marriage was one of convenience for Otto, who, they contend, used Edith's considerable dowry to 'clean up long-standing debts . . . Otto Frank was obviously the master of the household.'[24] It is impossible to say for certain whether this was the case. Unquestionably the relationship was not without difficulties, but Otto and Edith also had much in common: their backgrounds, their love of art and nature, their mutual respect and, later, their children.

They married on Otto's thirty-sixth birthday, on 12 May 1925, at the Aachen synagogue. The ceremony was conducted by Rabbi Davin Schoenberger and attended by both families. Edith, eleven years younger than her groom, looking genuinely beautiful on her wedding day. She wore a stylish, low-waisted white dress, just below the knee in length, and decorated with real flowers on the skirt. A long, embroidered veil and white T-bar shoes completed the outfit. Otto wore a dark suit with a cream waistcoat and matching bow tie. Photographs of the day show the wedding party in formal pose, Edith's mother and father to her right, her father's hand protectively on her mother's shoulder, and Alice Frank, very elegant and proud, sitting at Otto's side. The honeymoon was spent touring Italy, and various photographs illustrate the couple's evident happiness, and Edith's innate, up-to-date taste in dress, whether lounging on a beach or walking amongst the lush palms of San Remo.

Returning to Germany, they moved in with Otto's mother, Leni, Erich and little Stephan. Leni and Erich's second child, Bernhardt, was born on 2 June 1925. Stephan nicknamed his feisty baby brother Buddy, after a boxer, and from then on Bernhardt became Buddy to everyone except his uncle Otto, who always called him Berndt, and his aunt Edith, who addressed him as Bernd.[25] There were now two small children in the house on Jordanstrasse, and the following year they were joined by a third.

Margot Betti was born on 16 February 1926, her second name honouring Edith's sister. Otto's previous interest in photography now became a much-practised hobby, as he captured his new daughter on camera when she was just a few hours old, in her mother's arms. From then on, photographs of every stage of Margot's life were carefully pasted into leather-bound albums, along with those of cousins Stephan and Buddy, her constant playmates. Edith assiduously recorded Margot's progress in a baby book, noting the gifts commemorating her birth ('a golden coin and a baby carriage'),[26] how she woke every day at 6 a.m., and how well-behaved she was when taken on the sleeper-train to Aachen in May 1926. Her first toys ('a white toy ape and a teddy-bear')[27] are registered, along with her first tooth, her first play-suit and her first time outside. Margot was quite a weak baby, gaining weight and strength slowly, and she reacted badly to her vaccinations; Edith notes that months later 'the child pointed to the scar, saying "au".'[28]

By the time Margot was a toddler, it was obvious that she resembled the Hollander side of the clan, and had inherited her mother's thoughtful, lucid eyes and abundance of dark hair. She was very photogenic, as scores of surviving pictures attest, although her baby book maintains, 'Margot is afraid of being photographed.'[29] Margot was gentle and kind, and her shyness did not prevent her from playing with the neighbourhood children. The friendships she made during the first years of her life lasted even when time and circumstance took her away from Germany. In autumn 1927 Otto, Edith and eighteen-month-old Margot moved into an apartment in a large modern house at 307 Marbachweg, in one of the city suburbs. They rented the spacious apartment on the first two floors of the house, which had shutters at every window and a gabled roof. A rear balcony, which Edith filled with potted flowers, overlooked the adjacent houses and gardens, and they had room at last for the many fine pieces of antique furniture that had formed part of Edith's dowry. A tall, nineteenth-century French secretaire and an Ackerman grandfather clock, made locally, took pride of place amongst the other highly polished, dark wood pieces. Otto concentrated on building up his already extensive library.

Despite his languishing businesses, Otto always managed to keep his family afloat financially, although this was their leanest period before the war. Their life was not frugal, and there were many weekends in Aachen and day-trips to local beauty-spots, as well as a holiday with the Strauses at Otto's cousins' luxury villa in Sils-Maria. Nathan no longer worked at Macy's. After his uncle Isidor drowned in the *Titanic* disaster of 1912, the store passed to Isidor's sons, while Nathan and his brothers ran the company Abraham & Straus.[30] Nathan sent a postcard to Otto's sister Leni from the Spitzers' villa, telling her that he and his family were 'very happy here with Otto and Edith'.[31] There was no mention of Margot, but she had been ill with an ear infection, so it is possible she had stayed behind with her grandmother, or even with her parents' domestic help, Kathi Stilgenbauer, a young woman in her mid-twenties.

In the winter of 1928 Otto and Edith divulged that they were about to become parents again. Six months later, on the evening of 11 June 1929, Edith went into labour. It wasn't until the next morning, after an exhausting and difficult delivery, that the child was born. Otto had been at the hospital throughout, and telephoned Kathi shortly after half-past seven to tell her proudly that the baby was a girl and everything was fine – although the hospital register had mistakenly recorded the 'birth of a male child'.[32]

Annelies Marie Frank (thereafter known as Anne) was photographed by Otto that morning. The picture shows a crumple-faced infant with eyes tightly shut against the world. A few days later, when she was allowed home and a maternity nurse, Mrs Dassing, had been engaged to help out, everyone assembled for photographs on the balcony. It was a warm summer's afternoon, and the windows were thrown open wide, the flowers blooming in their pots on the ledge behind the small group, composed of Kathi with Margot on her knee, Mrs Dassing with Anne on hers, Edith smiling down at them, and their young neighbour Gertrud Naumann standing nearby with two other little girls. In honour of her birth, Anne had been given an infant's silver necklace, on which hung a triangular pendant. It was engraved on one side with a Hebrew inscription, and on the other, 'Lucky Charm, 12.6.1929, Frankfurt-am-Main'.

By the time Anne Frank was born, Frankfurt had become the scene of frequent political agitation. Not least, the National Socialists were beginning to make their presence felt, having risen from the ashes of the turbulent 1920s on a kindling of resentment. Their increasingly common attacks on the city's 30,000-strong Jewish population, the second largest in Germany after Berlin, caused considerable anxiety over what the future might hold if they were ever to gain absolute power. The Nazis' targets included Jews, black people, Romanies, homosexuals, the handicapped and the mentally ill. But Hitler reserved his greatest spleen for the Jews, whom he cited as the epitome of the sub-human non-German. As the Nazis' popularity grew, the tributaries of anti-Semitism that had always existed in Germany began to merge into a single, powerful torrent.

Only 20 per cent of Jews living in Germany were born elsewhere. Most German Jews, many of whom had fought for their country in the First World War, had been assimilated into the mainstream and were prominent in the economic and cultural life of Germany. Jews formed just 1 per cent of the total population, and very few had actually accumulated the kind of wealth that Hitler claimed, but the Nazis, with their profound love of both German history and German myth, and their talent for combining the two until they were indistinguishable, succeeded in creating an apocalyptic vision of Jewish domination. One of their earliest triumphs was the popularization of *The Protocols of the Elders of Zion*. This rancorous leaflet was discussed at length at Nazi Party meetings, even though the 'document' was a forgery. It was the perfect springboard for converting people to Nazism, boasting that plans for world domination by Jewish capitalists had been uncovered in Russia. The magazine of the NSDAP (National Socialist German Workers' Party), *Der Stürmer*, edited by Julius Streicher, referred to it repeatedly, and spread tales of Jews as sexual deviants and child-killers, in terms that harked back to Martin Luther: 'It is the practice to entice non-Jews to Jewish celebrations and then to murder them. At the Passover in particular, the Jew prefers to murder non-Jewish children. He trusses the child up, stabs it and tears the flesh to pieces. He opens the child's veins and catches the blood. He mixes it with the wine which he drinks and adds to the Matzen (unleavened bread), which he eats . . .'[33]

On New Year's Day 1930 members of the SS murdered eight Jewish persons in Berlin, and the Nazi war cry went up: 'Death to Judah!' From that moment on, for the 500,000 Jews residing in Germany, the future would become a nightmare of unprecedented horror.

Otto and Edith were acutely aware of the madness gathering pace in Germany. Kathi, their housekeeper, was without their foresight and it was with puzzlement rather than alarm that she told them about a local incident involving the National Socialists: '. . . the washerwoman came early in the morning, and was in a temper . . . she said, "I didn't get a wink of sleep all night. There was a big racket in the street again." "What was up?" I asked. And she said, "The Brownshirts were fighting and making a row again." '[34] During lunch that day, Kathi asked her employers who the Brownshirts were. 'Mr Frank just laughed and tried to make a joke of the whole thing, and although it wasn't very much of a laugh and not much of a joke, he did try. But Mrs Frank looked up from her plate, she did, and she fixed her eyes on us, and said, "We'll find out soon enough who they are, Kathi." And that was no joke and it wasn't said like a joke . . .'[35]

Otto may have feigned laughter, but he was clearly very concerned about the political situation, and confided his unease to his English cousin, Milly Stanfield. She recalls, 'I remember talking to Otto about politics. He said, "I don't like it. I don't know what's going to happen. I'm scared of the Right." He saw it coming – at a time when I don't think many of the Jews were particularly worried.'[36]

Milly did not see her cousin again until after Anne's birth. 'Mother and I were in Frankfurt for a short time. I can still remember the day well. Anne was lying in a crib. She couldn't talk yet, naturally. But she kept trying to sit up and look at us all. Even in those days she was terribly interested in everything. Her facial expressions said, "I'd like to know what they're talking about."'[37]

Anne and Margot's cousins, Stephan and Buddy, visited often, and the girls were taken to their grandmother's house, where they all played together. One day out ended in mischief, as Buddy recalls: 'My brother and I took the baby pram that Anne was in and went out outside. We went racing around and around the street but we couldn't get the curb right and the pram tipped up. Anne flew out of the pram! We told no one of course, and Anne was OK.'[38] It was safer when Stephan stuck to his impression of Charlie Chaplin, which was a great favourite with Anne and Margot. Otto's two brothers were also very popular with the children. Buddy remembers Robert as 'so full of humour . . . I still have at home a book he made for my brother filled with drawings and poems. It was beautiful. He was so much fun.'[39] Herbert, too, Buddy says, was 'full of fun, a wonderful man'.[40] The children's grandmother, Alice, was a much adored figure whom Buddy likens to 'a queen, very cultured, very quiet. I loved her. We were great friends. Every Sunday morning at seven I was allowed to creep into her bed and we turned on the radio and listened to a concert and she told me a story about a little mouse. I remember that. And every Sunday it was another mouse. The kitchen mouse, and the church mouse, and the field mouse. That was my weekly adventure, to creep into Oma's bed and to hear the story about the mouse.'[41]

Buddy was not the only one to be regaled with nursery stories. Otto amused his daughters with tales about two sisters, Good Paula and Bad Paula. Margot knew that she preferred Good Paula, but Anne never quite managed to decide between them. Later on, when times were particularly frightening in the Secret Annexe, Otto would keep Anne calm with new stories about the two Paulas. In the book she entitled 'Tales and Events from the Secret Annexe', Anne wrote one of the stories down, prefixing it with an explanation: 'Long ago, when I was little, Papa used to tell me stories about "naughty Paula"; he had a whole collection of stories and I was crazy about them. And now again, when I'm with Papa at night, he sometimes tells me about Paula, and I've written down the latest story.'[42] This is 'Paula's Plane Trip', set in the Great War and telling the story of how Paula finds herself trapped in an aeroplane destined for Russia. When the plane touches down, she is taken in by a farmer and his wife. For a little over two years, she lives on a farm in Minsk and earns money dancing in cafés, before going back to Germany. In Berlin she finds a boyfriend and becomes a performer in a cabaret, where she bumps into her own father, who is overjoyed to see her. Together they return home and walk into 'the station at Frankfurt on the Main, arm in arm'.[43] The story is simple, improbable in parts, but served its purpose of deflecting Anne's terror from the planes flying over the house on Prinsengracht, and took her back instead to her first home in Frankfurt when, like Paula, she was 'a German girl'.[44]

From her high-sided cot on the balcony of the house, curious little Anne could gaze at other houses, trees, streets and people passing by. Anne was as affable as Margot was shy; like the two Paulas, they were already classic cases of the sensible, reserved older sister and the naughty, spoiled younger one. Margot was always immaculate, 'the little princess', Kathi called her,[45] while if Anne was not watched with a careful eye, anything could happen. Writer Ernst Schnabel recounts, 'One morning, Kathi found [Anne] sitting on the balcony in the rain, in the middle of a puddle, chortling with delight. A good scolding left the little girl unaffected. She did not even offer to get up out of the puddle. She wanted Kathi to tell her a story right there and then, and it made no difference that Kathi had no time. The story could be a short one, she said. She picked Anne up, carried her into the nursery and set her firmly down on the table to change her clothes. Above the nursery table hung a handsome lamp. It was very big, and Mr Frank had had it painted with animals. A regular zoo it was, and Anne would always look up at it. She had all sorts of stories about the animals.'[46]

The lengthening shadow of Nazism first touched the lives of the Frank family in March 1931, when their landlord developed Nazi sympathies. It is not known if he asked them to leave or if they did so of their own accord. Their new apartment, 24 Ganghoferstrasse, was not far from Marbachweg, in the developing district known as the Poets' Quarter. It was smaller than the previous one, but it boasted a yard and large garden ideal for Anne and Margot to play in. Opposite the house was an overgrown field offering limitless possibilities to imaginative children, and there were hills nearby, perfect for tobogganing when the snows came. This particularly appealed to Margot, who had a little sleigh in which to pull her baby sister around. Initially Anne was too young to go outside the garden, and played instead in the generously proportioned sandpit, or, on very hot days, in a huge old metal bath filled with water. There were plenty of other children in the neighbourhood too, besides those they already knew from Marbachweg, and there would often be a noisy group of them at play.

Otto and Edith encouraged their daughters to take an interest in the diverse religious celebrations of friends. At the home of their young friend and neighbour, Hilde Stab, Margot and Anne would pretend to be servers at Hilde's make-believe mass, watched with amusement by their mothers. Margot attended Hilde's first Holy Communion ceremony, and amongst her prized possessions was a photograph taken of Hilde for the occasion, which Margot captioned, 'In commemoration of Hilde's most beautiful day'.[47] Their own religion was a source of open discussion; the children could ask any questions and expect a considered reply. Otto and Edith viewed Judaism with differing degrees of importance, but for both, it was more peripheral than it might have been. Otto was a progressive thinker, and believed his daughters' education was immensely important. As Margot and Anne grew older, they began to make increasing use of his extensive library. Margot tended to keep her thoughts and opinions to herself, but when Anne learned to talk she was quite the opposite and whatever popped into her mind also popped out of her mouth. She once shocked everyone at her friend Gertrud Naumann's home when, aged three, she fixed her penetrating gaze on Gertrud's father and exclaimed, 'Why, you have eyes exactly like a cat!'[48]

The apartment on Ganghoferstrasse served them well for a year and a half, but the dwindling fortunes of the family bank meant another cut in their income. The Great Depression, the closure of the Dutch branch, Herbert's arrest for a mistaken case of fraud, and the closure of the Frankfurt Stock Exchange for an indefinite period in the summer of 1931 had all contributed to its failure. Business was directed from a more modest address which they shared with another company, probably on the Boersenplatz, from where Otto wrote to a friend or relative,[49] 'Business is poor. You can't see straight when nothing seems to be going right.' He ended his letter, 'Only the children seem to be enjoying themselves, as no doubt your children are.'[50] The expense of the flat on Ganghoferstrasse was beyond their means. At the end of December 1932 Otto gave notice, and in March 1933 they moved in with his mother again.

Life went on much as it always had, with visits to and from friends and family, and days out. Edith's interest in fashion extended to her daughters, and she often took them into the city centre to browse around the shops, choosing a fluffy white coat for Anne one day, and a pair of patent shoes for Margot the next. These expeditions inevitably included a visit to one of the cafés on the Hauptwache, where Edith would meet her friends and treat her daughters to coffee and torte. When work permitted, Otto accompanied them. Photographs record one such day out, on the Hauptwache, in March 1933. Walking home that day through the cold streets, neither Otto nor Edith can have failed to notice a pernicious new form of graffiti: damning anti-Semitic slogans daubed in white paint across Jewish-owned shop windows.

There is a school named after Anne in Frankfurt now, and a memorial plaque fixed to the wall of 24 Ganghoferstrasse. Standing before the house in 1957, Ernst Schnabel came under scrutiny from an elderly resident: 'I clapped my notebook shut and we looked at one another. "Do you live here?" I asked. "No, but nearby." "You've lived here long?" I asked. "Yes, but I did not know her." He tilted his head to one side. "There are too many children in this neighbourhood. See." He pointed to a nearby pavement where a band of schoolchildren involved in some game were trotting by. "I have been thinking about it ever since I first heard," he said. "But there were always so many children . . ." '51

In January 1933 the Nazis were duly elected as the majority party in the Reichstag and on 23 March 1933 Hitler seized absolute power, using the previous month's Reichstag fire – supposedly started by a young Dutch Communist – as a convenient excuse to punish political opponents. One of the arrested men was given 100 whiplashes because he was a Communist *and* a Jew. Hitler announced 'the beginning of a great new epoch in German history . . .'52

Otto Frank's decision to leave his homeland was motivated in part by the phlegmatic response of acquaintances to the news that Hitler had been made Chancellor. He recalled, 'On January 30th we happened to be visiting some friends. We were sitting at the table and listening to the radio. First came the news that Hitler had become Chancellor. Then came an account of the Stormtroopers' torch parade in Berlin, and we heard the shouting and cheers, and the announcer said that Hindenburg was standing at the window, waving. At the end, Hitler made his "Give me four years" speech. Our host said in good spirits, "Why don't we just see what the man can do? Give him a chance!" I could not reply, and my wife sat as if turned to stone.'53

    The Franks were living, like many families, as normally as they could in a country that no longer recognized their citizenship. Otto's war service for Germany meant nothing now. In the centre of Frankfurt after the elections for the municipal council, which the Nazis won outright, there was a demonstration on the steps of the Town Hall. Uniformed Nazis, brandishing the swastika and raising their arms in the Hitler salute, screamed, 'Juden raus! Juden raus!' The red-white-and-black party flag was unfurled across the building. The anti-Semitic chanting continued, and supporters on the streets joined in. Otto and Edith knew the time had come for them to leave, before it was too late. A new decree stating that Jewish children were unwelcome at schools attended by non-Jews cemented their decision. Anne had been enrolled in a nursery school for September 1933, but, as a Jewish child, the arrangement was void. Margot would have to leave the Ludwig-Richter school, which she loved, and find another. Their parents found this latest measure too outrageous to ignore. Otto reflected, 'You cannot bring up children like horses with blinkers, ignorant of the social landscape outside their small group . . . The world around me collapsed. When most of the people of my country turned into hordes of nationalistic, cruel, anti-Semitic criminals, I had to face the consequences, and though this did hurt me deeply I realized that Germany was not the world and I left forever.'[54]

Other family members had already left Germany. In the summer of 1929 Otto's brother-in-law Erich Elias had been invited to open a Swiss branch of Opekta (of which he was a founder member), a subsidiary of the Frankfurt-based company 'Pomosin-Werke', which dealt in pectin, a substance used in jam preparation. Erich took up the offer, moving to Basel in Switzerland, where he was joined by Leni and Buddy in 1930, and Stephan in 1931. Buddy wasn't upset by the change, 'I felt absolutely fine. It was an adventure, somewhere else. I went to kindergarten right away in Basel. Pulled little girls' pigtails. I remember I got scolded for that.'[55] The Eliases stayed in a pension for several months before renting a place of their own.

Otto's younger brother Herbert had emigrated to France after his arrest in April 1932 on charges of disregarding the Trade in Securities in Foreign Countries Act. He was accused of accepting foreign shares and selling them to various banks at a profit. He was released on 14 May and his trial set for October 1933. Although he refused to appear in court due to 'material and mental injury',[56] he won his appeal. Herbert never fully recovered from the shock, but he was fortunate to have escaped a fine. Buddy recalls, 'He was very independent and the black sheep of the family. He loved life and he was always after the girls; even in his seventies and eighties he was always after the girls!'[57] Eva Schloss, whose mother married Otto Frank after the Second World War, used the same phrase about Herbert: 'He was very jolly. He was very lively and never really worked. He was sort of the black sheep of the family. Very friendly . . . but he could never *cope*.'[58] Herbert put down new roots in Paris, where he had relatives living near by.

Otto's older brother Robert, and his wife Lotti, left Frankfurt in 1933, travelling by ship to England. Buddy remembers, 'Robert was so funny, he became *so* British, what he thought being British meant. When he went to England, right away he got a bowler hat and an umbrella. And his wife Lotti, she was German too, she became *so* British too. They both lost their accents completely and spoke English perfectly. They loved it there.'[59] Robert and Lotti lived at 39 Roland Gardens in South Kensington, and set up a successful art dealership in St James Street. Buddy remarks, 'You know, if you go to the Tate Gallery today, there are two wonderful paintings by John Martin bequeathed by Mrs Robert Frank. John Martin was forgotten then, but Robert rediscovered him and collected his works.'[60] The paintings originally hung in the Franks' home. Eva Schloss echoes Buddy again: 'Robert was just the opposite to Herbert. He was a very distinguished-looking gentleman, very precise, very accurate. He could have been English. Pre-war English! And in St James, he mixed with all those people in clubs there . . . Lotti also became very discreet, and when I phoned her I always had a tummy-ache because you were not allowed to speak loudly and you had to be so polite! But she was very nice.'[61]

In Germany the Franks' bank business was gradually being wound down and all trading ceased in January 1934. When Erich suggested that Otto open a Dutch offshoot of Opekta, Otto considered the offer in light of the situation in Germany, his familiarity with the Netherlands and the friendships he had made there, and the fact that the Dutch policy on refugees was more lenient than most. Otto was originally to have become manager of the Utrecht branch of Pomosin, but problems arose with their managing director, and he set up in business in Amsterdam instead. Erich (then manager of Opekta, Switzerland) provided the financial backing with an interest-free loan of 15,000 guilders repayable over ten years. Otto acquired the rights to Opekta on the understanding that he purchased pectin exclusively from Opekta, Cologne, and 2.5 per cent of his profits were given to Pomosin. He could repay the loan whenever he wished by giving up his shares in Opekta, Amsterdam.

The children's friends called round to elicit promises that Anne and Margot would stay in touch. Gertrud, a little older than the rest, remembered how Otto's habitual merriness seemed to have deserted him. 'Mr Frank never spoke about anything that troubled him. But . . . you could see the way it was worrying him and working inside him.'[62] Otto departed in June 1933 to find a suitable home for his family while Edith and the children moved in with her family in Aachen. Alice Frank closed up the house on Jordanstrasse and emigrated to Basel. A photograph taken on her arrival at Basel station shows Alice with her daughter, son-in-law and grandsons, all of them smiling in the October sun.

The Franks were among 63,000 Jews who left Germany in 1933, a watershed year for Hitler and his supporters. Some 150,000 'political opponents' were seized for 're-education' and 10,000 active members of the labour movement were arrested. Every household was issued with a Nazi flag, which had to be prominently displayed at all times. The Nazi stormtroopers and élite corps, the SA and SS, infiltrated the German police, using violence and propaganda to establish a new system of terror. Hitler bargained for the loyalty of a select number of judges who accepted the new discriminatory laws, placing the Gestapo, SS and SA in supreme control of German society.

Between 1 and 3 April Jewish-owned shops were boycotted and vandalized. People with the most tenuous blood relation to the Jewish faith were dismissed from their jobs, regardless of ability or duration of service. New laws deposed Jews and political opponents from teaching and governmental offices. Jews lost their academic titles. The number of Jewish and female students of any background in higher education was kept to a minimum. Nazi textbooks promoting extreme nationalism and portraying Jews as monsters replaced standard educational material. One of the most widely used textbooks was *The Poisonous Mushroom*, which informed children that 'just as a single poisonous mushroom can kill a whole family, so a solitary Jew can destroy a whole village, a whole city, a whole people'.[63] At break-times, children were encouraged to play the latest board game, *Jews Out!* The Hitler Youth, formed in 1926 for 'Aryans' between the ages of ten and fourteen, continued to attract members. It eventually became compulsory (from 1939), and all other youth groups were banned.

On 10 May 1933 all unions were liquidated to form the German Workers Front, and every employee was induced to join. Strikes were outlawed. In Berlin books by Jews, homosexuals, Communists and other 'forbidden' writers were ripped apart page by page and flung on to a huge pyre. Artists who failed to depict the Aryan ideal were prohibited from buying materials. Jewish artists were excluded from the annual Academy exhibition and banned from working. On 25 July 1933 an anti-Semitic group calling themselves 'The German Christians' were given a majority vote in the Evangelical Church elections.

Four months earlier, Heinrich Himmler, Provisional Police President of Munich, made an announcement that presaged the horror still to come. The grounds of a disused gunpowder factory near Munich were now ready for use. In a grim area where high barbed-wire fences had been erected and watchtowers built, Dachau concentration camp opened to receive its first victims.

Soon after the Franks' arrival in Aachen, Kathi received a card. She recognized Edith's elaborate handwriting straightaway, and correctly attributed the huge pencilled scribble decorating it to Anne. Gertrud Naumann also found a letter in her post from Edith on behalf of Margot and Anne, with the postscript, 'Anne reminds me of you in her fondness for babies. She peeks into every pram we pass. If she had her way, she would take every toddler she sees for a walk.'[64]

Across the border in the Netherlands, Otto Frank was proving an innovative businessman and had already attended his first Rotterdam stock exchange on behalf of Opekta. He had taken rooms on the second floor of an apartment block at 24 Stadionkade, a twenty-minute tram ride from Amsterdam's centre. The Opekta offices were at 120–26 Nieuwe Zijds Voorburgwal, a tall building instantly noticeable for its modern and unusual sea-green mirrored façade. Inside, two rooms and a tiny kitchen were assigned to the company. One room served mainly as Otto's office, the other as a cluttered dispatch room. The kitchen had regulation work-tops under which were stacked various fruit. The workforce included several chatty, efficient representatives who traversed the country promoting and selling the latest products.

Due to the long-term absence through illness of one of his regular office workers, Otto took on Miep Santrouschitz, a fashionable, Austrian-born woman in her mid-twenties. Miep was born Hermine Santrouschitz in Vienna on 15 February 1909. Due to a shortage of food in Vienna following the Great War, she had grown weak and undernourished, and a welfare organization arranged for her to spend three months with a Dutch family, where she would receive wholesome food and return home revitalized. Miep arrived in the Netherlands in December 1920 and settled in quickly with her foster family in Leiden, who gave her the Dutch nickname 'Miep'. Her stay was lengthened indefinitely, and she moved with her adoptive family to Nieuwe Amsterdam-Zuid (New South) in 1922. She visited her parents in Vienna in 1925 and 1931, but elected to stay with her foster family permanently, because she was 'now a Dutch girl through and through'.[65] At Opekta, Miep learned how to make jam before moving on to the Complaints and Information desk, where she dealt with customers' problems and enquiries. Her job included typing and book-keeping, and she was kept on when the typist whose position she had stepped into returned. She liked Otto instinctively. 'I felt immediately his kind and gentle nature, stiffened somewhat by shyness and a slightly nervous demeanour . . . he wore a moustache and when he smiled, which was often, he revealed quite uneven teeth.'[66]

Supervising all of the employees was Victor Gustav Kugler. Miep describes him as 'a husky, good-looking man, dark-haired and precise. He was always serious, never joked . . . always quite formal and polite . . . he liked things done his way and his way alone.'[67] Despite his slightly off-putting manner, Kugler was both straightforward and essentially kind. Born in Hohenelbe, Austria, in 1900, he was conscripted into the Imperial Navy at the age of seventeen, but a year later, whilst serving in the Adriatic, he was injured and dismissed. After a few months' recuperating, Kugler moved to Germany for two years, where he worked as an electrician, a trade he had learned in the navy. In September 1920 he emigrated to Utrecht, where he worked for the company Otto should have joined. He was given the responsibility of overseeing the Amsterdam branch of Opekta, but was unsuccessful at it, and resigned from his position to work under Otto. Kugler lived in Hilversum with his wife.

Otto was desperately lonely without his family and spent every spare minute searching for a suitable home for them. His quest took him to Nieuwe Amsterdam-Zuid, where Miep lived, and he finally found the perfect family apartment there. Edith and Margot boarded the train for the Netherlands on 5 December 1933. Anne remained with her grand-mother, whom she adored, in Aachen until February 1934, when she was

– as she later phrased it – 'put on Margot's table as a birthday present'.[68] She was not quite five years old. Edith wrote to a friend, 'Both children are full of fun. Anne a little comedian.'[69]

Chapter Two

'If I think back to the Merry,[1] my girlfriends, school, fun, it is just as if
another person lived it all, not me . . .'

Anne Frank, *Diary*, 8 November 1943

In the early 1930s increasing numbers of Jews in flight from the Nazis
settled in the Netherlands. The Dutch coalition government had no real
policy on refugees, other than requiring proof that they could support
themselves. The sudden influx caused friction amongst Jews already living
in the Netherlands (approximately 113,000 in 1930), who hoped to
maintain the good relations that existed between themselves and non-Jews.
In 1933 the Minister of Justice advocated new laws on asylum seekers.
These were never enforced, but reception camps were introduced for
'aliens' and the flow subsided.

Many refugees were attracted to the developing districts of
Amsterdam-Zuid. The Frank family rented the apartment at 37
Merwedeplein, in the area known as the River Quarter. Their new flat
was spacious; there was a large upstairs room which they rented out to
a succession of lodgers, male and female. They had brought all their
furniture from Frankfurt, and Edith's beloved secretaire stood between
the two windows in the sitting room, joined by the grandfather clock in
another corner and a couple of fine modern sculptures and some pieces
of crystal. At the rear of the apartment a wide gravel balcony overlooked
the gardens and houses in the street behind. Buildings were streamlined
and uniform: five-storey blocks of flats in dark brown brick with white-
framed windows soaring up to the roofs in neat rows. Narrow corridors
and stairwells led down from the first floors on to unusually wide streets
laid out around grassy squares. The neighbourhood had an energetic,
contemporary air. On the eastern side was the River Amstel, with its
painted, converted barges, and the tree-lined Jozef Israelskade canal separ-

ated the New South from the Old. Waalstraat, which ran past Merwedeplein, housed bakeries, butchers' and coffee shops, where the smell of warm bagels drifted across the air. Pickle shops had carts outside proclaiming 'The Best Pickles in Amsterdam!' and were always packed with gossiping clientele.

The Franks were instantly at ease in their new surroundings. Margot was enrolled at an elementary school on Jekerstraat, opposite Merwedeplein. She made a few close friends and quickly established herself as a gifted pupil. Anne attended the Montessori kindergarten on nearby Niersstraat. The Montessori system allows children more freedom in the classroom, encouraging them to talk to each other while they work. Edith and Otto had chosen the school specifically, knowing Anne could not bear to sit still for long and loved to chat. On her morning walk to school, Anne was often accompanied by her teacher, Mr van Gelder, who had noticed how garrulous she was: 'Sometimes she told me stories and poems which she had made up together with her father when they went out for strolls. These were always very jolly stories. She told me a great deal about her father, and very little about her sister or her mother . . . she was no prodigy. She was likeable, healthy, perhaps a little delicate, although I believe that showed up later on. She certainly was not an extraordinary child, not even ahead of her age. Or perhaps I should put it this way: in many things she was mature, but on the other hand, in other things she was unusually childish. The combination of these two characteristics made her very attractive. There are many potentialities in such a mixture, after all.'[2]

Anne's best friends, Hanneli Goslar and Sanne Ledermann, also attended the Montessori school. Anne wrote in her diary, 'people who saw us together always said there they go Anne, Hanne and Sanne.'[3] Sanne was the second daughter of Franz and Ilse Ledermann of Berlin. The family originally intended to emigrate to Palestine, but Franz was disappointed by a visit there, and instead they arrived in Amsterdam's River Quarter shortly after the Franks. They lived at 37 Noorder Amstellaan. Hanneli was also from Berlin, and her family emigrated to Amsterdam in 1933, moving into the flat 'kitty-corner' below the Franks at 31 Merwedeplein. Hanneli (Lies) and Anne instantly became firm friends. Lies's mother had been nervous about her daughter's first day at school, but Lies remembers: 'My mother brought me to school. I couldn't speak Dutch yet and my mother was very anxious, how it would turn out, how I would react. But when I went in, there was Anne standing across from the door, ringing the bells. She turned around and I flew into her arms, and my mother was able to go home reassured. I had dropped my shyness and forgotten my mother in the same instant!'[4]

Certain games and patterns of behaviour were prevalent amongst the neighbourhood children. Poetry albums were a craze: friends wrote pages of sentimental verse about each other and decorated their stanzas with pictures of animals and flowers. In the holidays and at weekends friends called for the others by whistling their signature tune through the letterbox. To her great disappointment, Anne could not whistle. So she sang instead – five notes up, five notes down – and thus hers was the most distinctive call in the neighbourhood. Hopscotch, cartwheels and handstands against walls were popular games. Anne herself admitted she was hopeless at them all, but joined in regardless. When her friend Toosje tried to comfort her by pointing out that she was shorter and younger than everyone else, Anne disagreed: 'That's still no reason not to be able to do a handstand.'[5] After a particularly boisterous game of hopscotch, Lies remembers she and Anne arrived home to 'a report on the radio that there had been an earthquake somewhere. We laughed a lot about that!'[6] Photographs of Anne from the early 1930s usually show her at play, whether digging in sandpits, skipping, or writing with chalk on the pavement. Edith wrote to a friend, 'Margot is happy at school and Anne loves her kindergarten.'[7]

Otto, Margot and Anne soon learned to speak Dutch. Edith found it more difficult, but persevered with the help of friends. She met Miep at the Opekta offices in 1934 and their friendship deepened over the years, despite Edith's natural reserve. In her autobiography Miep writes, 'Mrs Frank presented herself as one would who came from a cultured, wealthy background, aloof but sincere . . . Mrs Frank missed Germany a great deal, much more than Mr Frank. Very often in conversation she would refer with melancholy to their life in Frankfurt, the superiority of some kinds of German sweets and the quality of German clothing. Mrs Frank liked to reminisce about the past, about her happy childhood in the small city of Aachen, her marriage to Mr Frank in 1925, and their life in

Frankfurt.'⁸ Edith's misgivings about her new life were shared by thousands of refugees, most of them German, who lived in the area. For more observant Jews, the transition was doubly difficult because in the early 1930s there was no proper place of worship locally, and therefore no real community centre. Jewish religious leaders resolved the situation mid-decade, when building commenced on a synagogue for the neighbourhood.

The Franks spent the summer of 1934 visiting Aachen and taking day-trips to Zandvoort, a popular coastal resort. Otto's secretary from Frankfurt, Mrs Schneider, accompanied them on one occasion, and a photograph shows them all eating ice-creams, surrounded by the usual holiday paraphernalia. On 12 June Anne celebrated her fifth birthday with a party at home. One of the guests was three-year-old Julianne Duke, whose family lived in the flat above the Franks. She was too young to remember the party, other than that 'each guest gave a gift and in turn received one. I was given a child-sized tin tea service.' She liked living in the River Quarter: 'Relationships with the Franks and other neighbours developed easily because many of the residents were linked together by a similar background – the German language, the experience of being rejected by their homeland and the uncertainty of the future.' In the afternoons Julianne's mother took coffee with Edith Frank. Julianne enjoyed the visits: 'I could have one of Mrs Frank's cream-cheese sandwiches covered with chocolate sprinkles and could play with Anne. I will always remember her energy and laughter. She often buttoned my coat, hugged me, took me by the hand . . . In the winter, if there was snow on the ground, Anne pulled me around our horse-shoe shaped street on a small wooden sled. I remember hanging on and both of us laughing when we went over a bump. When the weather was better, we played in the small park in the centre of Merwedeplein. At other times, I sat on the steps in front of the apartment and watched Anne as she and her friends played their pavement games . . . Each morning I stood by the window in our living room overlooking the street and waved goodbye to my father . . . Soon after his departure, I would wave to Anne and Margot, longing to be included in their sisterhood and to go to school with them. One day, my wish came true. I was invited to spend the day at the Montessori kindergarten. Anne was so proud of the large sun-drenched room framed with windowsills supporting red flowers in clay pots. She moved comfortably among the beehive of children working . . . and, like all the members of her family, was a sociable person.'⁹

Julianne and her family left the Netherlands for the USA before war broke out, and on the day of their departure Anne went outside to see the removal van being loaded. Julianne remembers: 'Anne asked me to come downstairs and stand on the pavement to watch our possessions tumble like a waterfall out of the living-room window. Everything was lowered to the street by a metal cable because the staircase up to our apartment was very narrow. All of a sudden, Anne pointed up to the window and laughed. The object of her mirth was my little white enamel chamber pot descending ever so slowly to the street. I was so embarrassed. I wanted to run away and hide.' Julianne's mother and Edith Frank exchanged letters regularly until 1938. 'My mother told me that she always ended her letters with the plea, "Come to America". Mrs Frank wrote that she wanted to emigrate, but Mr Frank saw no need to leave Holland. He trusted in man's basic goodness, rather than focusing on the darker, irrational side of human nature.'¹⁰

In 1934 things were going well for Otto. Business was good enough to justify larger premises, and Opekta moved to 400 Singel, in a gabled building above the colourful floating flower market. Otto wrote cautiously to his cousin Armand Geiershofer in Luxembourg, 'Though my income remains fairly modest, one must be satisfied to have found some way of earning a living and getting on.'¹¹ He found the work tiring, though, and confessed in a letter to Gertrud Naumann, 'I am travelling almost every day, and only get home in the evening. It's not like in Frankfurt, where one eats at home at lunchtime – and where one can relax a little too. It goes on all day . . .'¹²

In Germany, on the evening of 30 June 1934, Ernst Röhm, Erich Klausener, and a priest, Bernhard Stempfle, along with 200 members of the Nazi SA, were shot. Hitler announced that the murders were 'a matter of national security'.¹³ In truth, he had arranged the killings because he feared the SA would undermine his authority. In March 1935 he publicly denounced the Versailles peace treaty of 1919 (which had imposed heavy reparation payments on Germany and limited her military capability), and introduced conscription for all non-Jewish German males, securing an oath of loyalty from every serviceman. Britain and France, increasingly nervous, signed a treaty with Russia declaring mutual assistance. Germany began to re-arm, and in a bid to limit her resources, Britain signed a naval treaty which allowed Germany possession of submarines and a navy equal to a third that of Britain. The action broke up the treaty of mutual assistance and an atmosphere of uncertainty and suspicion hung over Europe.

At the NSDAP Congress in Nuremberg on 15 September 1935, the Reichstag passed two new laws. Designed to 'protect German blood and German honour',[14] they defined German citizenship as a matter of 'German or kindred blood'.[15] Under the laws, Jews could not declare themselves German, fly the German flag, employ a German woman under forty-five years of age as domestic help, marry or have sexual intercourse with Aryans.[16] In October Jewish-owned cinemas were forcibly sold to Aryans and Jewish film producers had their licences confiscated. As rumours of the brutality towards Jews in German internment camps became more widespread, more than 50,000 Jews left the country.

On 26 March 1935 Edith sent a wistful note to Gertrud in Frankfurt: '. . . That we hope to see you again, you can rest assured. But we don't want to make any plans just yet. Margot and Anne speak often of you.'[17] Margot added briefly, 'Dear Gertrud! I hope you're well, I am. I'm really sad that I don't see you anymore. I like it very much at school. Greetings, Margot, and Anne.'[18]

Schoolwork was proving a slight problem for Anne, as Edith informed Kathi Stilgenbauer: 'Anne is not so well behaved as Margot and does not like to buckle down to things . . .'[19] A few months later, she wrote again, 'Anne is struggling with her reading lessons. Margot has a great deal of schoolwork . . .' As if to prove her mother wrong, at the bottom of the letter Anne diligently wrote: 'hello anne'.[20] In another letter to Kathi, Edith writes, 'Our big girl, Margot, is very hard-working and already thinks of going on to college. Little Anne is somewhat less industrious, but very droll . . . witty and amusing. The children are always playing in the street.'[21] A photograph of Anne at the Montessori school in summer 1935 shows her seated at the back of the class, a diminutive figure in white. The classroom is bright and airy, filled with children counting large numbers on a blackboard. Otto described the contrasts between his

daughters: 'Anne was always gay, always popular with boys and girls . . .
a normal, lively child who needed much tenderness and attention, and
who delighted us and frequently upset us. Whenever she entered a room,
there was a fuss . . . Margot was the bright one. Everybody admired her.
She got along with everybody . . . But Anne, you couldn't see her talent.
She always wrote good essays at school and she used to sometimes read
to us what she had written, little stories . . . She was ebullient – and
difficult.'[22]

In an effort to revive the children's health, the summer holidays were
divided between the beach and the Spitzers' villa in Sils-Maria. Margot
suffered from stomach-aches and was prone to illness, while Anne had a
weak heart and rheumatic fever. Her arms and legs had a tendency to
dislocate as well, a source of much amusement to Anne herself, who
thought it great fun to crack her shoulder in and out of its socket before
horrified friends. Otto explained: 'Anne wasn't a strong girl. There was
a particular time when she was growing very quickly, and she had to rest
every afternoon because of her health problems. She wasn't allowed to
do any demanding sport, but had lessons in rhythmic gymnastics, which
she really loved. Then later she learned to ice-skate with great enthusiasm.
She was very upset when a law came out in winter 1941/42 prohibiting
Jews from ice-skating. Of course she had a bicycle, like everyone else in
the Netherlands, but she only used it to go to school, not for trips out.
She preferred to stay in town rather than be out in the country, and she
wasn't interested at all in the trips we took around Amsterdam. She
enjoyed going to the beach where she could play with other children.'[23]
The sea air rejuvenated her, and Edith wrote to German friends, 'During
the school holidays I was at the seashore with the children . . . Anne is
learning to swim with great pleasure. Her health is much better this year.'[24]
The improvement was substantial; Anne won two medals for her prowess
in the public baths in Amsterdam.

In her diary Anne referred to this time as 'ordinary life'. Despite the
troubles in Germany and elsewhere, in Amsterdam Anne and Margot
could still enjoy their childhood. Alice, Herbert and Stephan came to stay
occasionally, and there were frequent visits to Switzerland, where the
Eliases had rented a four-room apartment. In Amsterdam the Franks had
become good friends with the Goslars. Lies's father, Hans Goslar, had

been Chief of Press in Germany and Deputy Minister of the Interior of the pre-Nazi Prussian Cabinet in Berlin. Lies's mother, Ruth Judith Klee, was a teacher and the daughter of one of Berlin's most distinguished barristers. They emigrated to England, but Hans was unable to find decent employment there, and in 1933 they moved to the Netherlands, where Hans set up in business with Sanne's father, a lawyer, helping asylum-seekers with financial difficulties.

The Goslars were deeply religious and Hans was a founder member of the pro-Zionist German Mizrachi. Until she was twelve, Lies would eat with the Franks on Yom Kippur, leaving her parents free to fast and attend synagogue with Edith and Margot, whilst Otto and Anne prepared the evening meal. The Franks usually shared the Goslars' Friday-night Sabbath repast and they also celebrated the Passover together. Lies recalled, 'Mrs Frank was a little religious and Margot went in that direction too. Margot always said that after the war, if she could choose, she wanted to be a nurse in Palestine.'[25] Edith became very involved with the Liberal Jewish congregation and often read to her daughters from Martin Buber's children's Bible, but Otto's attendance at the synagogue was sporadic. Of the two girls, Margot was clearly the more interested in religion. The Franks celebrated Christmas, which Lies's parents did not, although they allowed Lies to participate in the school party and the Franks' celebrations. New Year's Eve would find either the Franks at the Goslars' apartment, or the Goslars at the Franks'. On Wednesday afternoons and Sunday mornings, Lies studied Hebrew. Margot also took classes in the language, but Anne preferred to spend Sundays with her father at his office. Lies went along, too, in the afternoons and they pretended to be secretaries, ringing each other on the office telephones and getting up to mischief. Their favourite trick, particularly at Merwedeplein, was throwing buckets of cold water from the high windows on to passers-by. Lies did not attend school on Saturday, since it was the Jewish Sabbath, but went to synagogue in the morning with a girl who was a pupil at Margot's school. Anne was jealous of the friendship; it is this 'Sabbath friend' of whom she writes in her diary on 27 November 1943: 'I . . . was too young to understand her difficulties. She was attached to her girl friend, and to her it seemed as though I wanted to take her away.'[26] Apart from this one issue, Anne and Lies remained very close until their teens.

Above her bed in Merwedeplein, Anne had pinned a photograph of one of the hotels she stayed in with Lies's family (the same picture would later hang above her bed in the Secret Annexe). They had nicknamed the hotel, a black and white thatched cottage close by the North Sea, 'The Tomato House' because of its strict vegetarian menu. Lies remembers that holiday for their first encounter with a Hall of Mirrors at an amusement park, watching piggy banks being made and each receiving one afterward, and for an evening thunderstorm when her parents were out and Anne had cried for her own parents and sister.[27] Although Anne frequently teased Margot and was sometimes jealous of her, both she and Lies looked up to her, envying her 'grown-up eyeglasses that made her prettier and intelligent-looking. Margot was bright, obedient, quiet and serious. She was good at mathematics and everything else.'[28] The Franks were a close family, but Lies was aware that Anne was 'a bit spoiled, particularly by her father. Anne was her Daddy's girl; Margot was more like her mother. It's a good thing there were only two children.'[29]

When Lies is asked to describe Anne, she can only say honestly, 'At the time of our childhood she really was a girl like other girls her age, only her development was much quicker and [later] her writing very mature.'[30] She remembers how Anne loved little secrets and she loved 'to chat. And she collected pictures of movie stars . . . I was never very interested in that. But both of us collected pictures of the children in the royal families of the Netherlands and England. We traded for those. And she began to write. She was always game for a prank. She was a stubborn girl. She was very good-looking . . . She liked being important – that isn't a bad quality. I remember my mother, who liked her very much, used to say, "God knows everything, but Anne knows everything better." '[31] Lies and Anne were inseparable. They confided their secrets, teased each other, shared the same dentist on the Jan Luykenstraat, called for each other with their special tune, and even, in 1936, caught a number of illnesses from each other. The worst of these was measles. Lies was sick from 6 December and Anne from 10 December. They spoke every day on the telephone, but were not allowed to meet until they were fully recovered. On 18 December Anne felt well enough to send her grandmother in Switzerland a short letter: 'Dear Omi, I wish you all the best on your birthday. How are Stephan and Bernd? Thank Aunt Leni for the beautiful ski gloves. Did you get some nice presents? Please write back. Kiss, Anne.'[32] By Christmas she was back to normal, but the nickname she had been given during her illness – 'Tender One' – remained.

In March 1936 Hitler's troops advanced into the demilitarized area of the French/German south-west frontier and established fortifications along it. At the end of the month, the German election results were announced: 99 per cent of the plebiscite had voted for Hitler. In August the Olympic Games were held in Berlin and the Nazis' talent for the spectacular was shown to full effect. In September a 25 per cent tax was put on Jewish valuables. In the past two years 69,000 Jews had left Germany. Palestine had also received 11,596 Jewish refugees from Poland.

July 1936 saw the start of the Spanish Civil War. France and Britain were determined to keep their distance, but they did allow volunteers to fight for the Republicans. Mussolini and Hitler intervened on the Nationalists' behalf, contributing arms and men. The war continued until 1939, when Madrid surrendered to Nationalist rebels, making their leader, General Franco, head of the government. For the Nazi Party, the war had been an invaluable exercise in testing aeroplanes and methods of attack. The Germans were gaining strength in both arms and allies: in 1936 Hitler and Mussolini created the Rome–Berlin Axis, and Hitler signed the Anti-Comintern Pact with Japan.

The Dutch subsidiary of Opekta was proving a success. Adverts for pectin, written by Otto or Miep, were placed in women's magazines under the slogan, 'Jams and Jellies in 10 minutes . . . Make your own jam with Opekta – success is guaranteed.'[33] Otto introduced a complete kit for jam-making, an Opekta Journal, a promotional film and an advertising van. Rival companies kept Otto on his toes, but he borrowed funds from his cousin Armand Geiershofer and the business continued to prosper.

Otto had noticed a relationship growing between Miep and a 34-year-old Dutchman named Jan Gies. He invited them to dinner at Merwedeplein one evening. Jan also lived in the River Quarter and, like Miep, he was not Jewish, but was as disgusted by events in Germany as she was. He worked for the social services and reminded Miep of her employer, for they were 'of similar build, tall, thin, but Jan was somewhat taller . . . Mr Frank's dark hair was fine and receding. They were similar in character as well: men of few words with high principles and ironic senses of humour.'[34] The evening at the Franks' apartment passed pleasantly. The flat was welcoming, and a charcoal sketch of a mother cat with her kittens caught Miep's eye. 'The Franks were cat lovers,' she noticed, and saw, too, that 'everywhere were signs that children dominated this house: drawings, playthings'.[35] The children ran in from their bedroom. Margot, at ten years old, was a serene, beautiful child. She had the same hairstyle as her sister, and wore similar clothes, but looked neater than seven-year-old Anne, who was talkative and confident. All Anne's energy and verve seemed to be in her eyes – quick, darting eyes that were grey with electric green flecks. Both girls had excellent manners. Miep approved of their hearty appetites and how, 'after dinner, the children excused themselves, first saying good-night. They went back to their room to do their homework. As she left, I noticed Anne's thin little legs encased in white ankle socks and little pumps. The socks drooped slightly around her ankles in a tender, comic way.'[36]

Returning to school in autumn 1937, Anne found her first 'boyfriend', Sally Kimmel. He lived in the River Quarter, and he and his cousin were in Anne's class. Seven years later, Anne recalled him in her diary: 'He had lost his father, I believe his parents were divorced and he lived with his mother at her sister's. One of Sally's cousins was Appy [Ab] and the two of them were generally together and generally dressed the same way. Appy was a slender, good-looking dark boy and Sally a short, fat, fair friendly boy, with a great sense of humor. But looks did not count with me and I was very fond of Sally for years. We used to be together a lot for quite a time, but for the rest, my love was unreturned.'[37] Kimmel survived the war and emigrated to Israel. In his memory, he sees Anne as very girlish, popular and sensitive, but not an outstanding student. 'We often visited each other's homes,' he recalls. 'They had brought many beautiful possessions from Germany and there was a sense of opulence. It was a cultured home with books and music.'[38] The two friends lost touch when, in 1941, the laws forced them to change schools.

Anne's circle of friends now included a number of boys. Lies was amused by Anne's flirtatious nature and her habit of curling and twirling her hair around her fingers. 'Boys really liked her. And she always liked it a lot when all the boys paid attention to her . . . Everyone generally liked her, and she was always the centre of attention at our parties. She was also the centre of attention at school.'[39] Her sentiments were echoed by Otto, who noticed his daughter becoming 'a real problem child. A great talker and fond of nice clothes.'[40]

Relations between the immediate members of the Frank and Hollander families remained close-knit, despite the physical distances. There were always birthday cards and little notes, though Buddy cannot recall Anne's gift for writing showing up then. 'I had no idea that she could *write*! I mean, I had seen her letters and so forth but she could write letters and there was nothing special in it. It was amazing to see it afterwards. Of course this occurred in the Secret Annexe . . . I never dreamed that the lively girl who visited us on holidays had the depth Anne developed in the two years in exile.'[41] Margot was 'the serious one, always reading books and marking crossword puzzles . . . She was very different to Anne. I had very little contact with Margot. Not that I didn't like her, I liked her very much, but she was no fun, very quiet.'[42]

Buddy looked forward to his cousins' visits to Switzerland because he and Anne were such good friends. 'As a boy, I adored her because she was such a good sport – always ready for fun and games. We used to dress up and play film stars. Anne had a very keen sense of fairness and justice. Whenever we got dressed up and acted out our scenes, Anne never took the best garments for herself. She always gave them to me, and the funnier I looked, the better she liked it.'[43] He remembers another aspect of Anne's personality that only emerged during the period in hiding: 'Anne didn't like nature then. Not at the beginning, no. She didn't ever want to go for walks and things like that. She was a city girl. She loved the seaside, she loved to go swimming, she would love to be on the beach, but she didn't like nature. Until she went into hiding – that changed her . . . the tree in the garden and the sky . . .'[44] He finishes, 'Anne carried her heart in her hands – she was never very good at covering up her feelings. Margot was always kind and sweet, but I have to admit it – I liked Anne better.'[45]

In 1937 Otto visited Germany for the last time before war broke out. He was painfully aware of how his homeland now viewed him. Having met Gertrud, he remarked quietly, 'If they saw us together now they would arrest us.'[46] At the end of the year Edith wrote to Gertrud again, and her mood was disconsolate: 'My husband is hardly ever at home. Work is getting harder and harder . . .'[47]

Following Hitler's occupation of the Rhineland, tension spread throughout the Netherlands; no one discounted the threat of invasion, although the German Foreign Office continually assured the Dutch that their neutrality was not in danger. In Germany itself, the Gestapo, now the country's Supreme Police Agency, took 385 black children to hospital for sterilization. All Jews had to carry identity cards and have their passports stamped with the letter J. They had to prefix their own names with 'Sara' for women and 'Israel' for men. In 1937 3,601 German Jews emigrated to Palestine, along with 3,636 Jews from Poland; 25,000 Jews fled Germany in all that year. The country was awash with propaganda. At the Nuremberg Carnival in 1938, one of the carts featured men in concentration-camp uniforms holding aloft a banner, 'Away to Dachau!', and a windmill with puppet Jews hanging from the sails was paraded through the streets. Magazines with anti-Semitic overtones swamped the market. *Der Stürmer* declared: 'The Jews are Our Misfortune.'[48]

On 12 March 1938 Vienna was stormed by German troops and Austria was incorporated into the Reich. Austrian Jews immediately suffered as a result, being forced to scrub streets and clean lavatories under the jeering supervision of the Hitler Youth. Crushing decrees were enforced: Jews were forbidden to frequent public baths, parks, cafés and restaurants, they could not practise their professions and had to surrender any property they owned. During the first two months of Austria's occupation, 500 Jews committed suicide.

The assassination of Ernst vom Rath, a Third Secretary of the German Embassy in Paris, by a desperate young Polish Jewish student was used as an excuse to launch 'spontaneous demonstrations' across Germany.[49] During 9 and 10 November 1938, 7,000 Jewish businesses were ruined, 191 synagogues burned, 91 Jews killed and 30,000 Jewish men deported to the concentration camps of Buchenwald, Dachau and Sachsenhausen. The Aachen synagogue where Otto and Edith Frank were married in 1925 was burned down, and its rabbi, Davin Schoenberger, and the majority of his congregation were arrested. The Schoenbergers were spared further torture, mainly because the rabbi's wife had foreign nationality. They escaped, via Luxembourg, Paris, and England, to America. The rest of the congregation were deported. In Berlin 8,000 Jews were expelled from their homes. Torah scrolls and sacred Jewish books were burned on immense bonfires lit in the middle of Jewish neighbourhoods. Twenty per cent of Jewish-owned property was confiscated and remaining businesses were expropriated. A fine of one billion marks was placed on the Jews of Germany. The 'spontaneous demonstrations' became known as 'Kristallnacht' (Crystal Night), after an estimation that the amount of shattered glass from Jewish-owned shops equalled half the annual production of glass imported from Belgium. News of the latest pogrom flashed around the world and the trade boycott on German goods was stepped up, but it failed to discourage the Nazis. Jewish businesses were sold to Aryan retailers and Jews themselves were banned from a vast number of public places. Those who disobeyed faced internment in a prison camp or, in some cases, execution.

Panic reigned in Germany as people made arrangements to leave quickly, knowing that refugees were being refused entry to many countries. Some 250,000 Jews had emigrated to other lands by then, including cities as distant as Shanghai. In December 1938 thousands of German Jewish children arrived in Britain with no knowledge of when, or indeed if, they would see their families again.

During 1938 Miep and Jan often discussed politics over dinner at the Franks' flat in Amsterdam. They all shared a deep loathing for the Nazi Party. Miep's Austrian passport had been confiscated and replaced by a German one. Otto spoke reticently about events abroad, feeling that his country was going through a phase of madness, but would come to its senses before long. Edith openly disputed her husband's theory and maintained a more pessimistic outlook. All talk of politics stilled whenever Anne and Margot appeared. They seemed to be growing up very quickly. Miep noticed 'the colour in [Anne's] cheeks was bright; her conversation came in a rush. She had a rapid, high-pitched voice . . . Margot was getting even prettier, approaching adolescence; quiet, sitting with a straight back, hands folded in her lap . . . Margot got remarkably high marks at school.'[50] Anne's studies were improving too, and she was 'turning into a social butterfly'.[51] Miep admired how tidy the two girls looked: 'They always wore freshly starched and ironed little print dresses, many with hand-embroidered white linen collars. Both girls' dark hair was always freshly washed and combed to a sheen.'[52] After dinner Anne and Margot went into their bedrooms to finish their homework before Otto joined them for his evening story-telling session. 'Anne was always very happy about that,'[53] Miep remembers.

The year passed quickly, with many trips beyond Amsterdam for the Frank family, and visits from relatives who were eager to see them. In March the Franks 'made the Viermerentocht' (a tour of the lakes);[54] they returned to greet Otto's cousin Milly, who was in town. 'I stayed for a few days in a room opposite their home in Amsterdam,' she recalls. 'Anne came to fetch me breakfast. She was perfectly sweet. Then Otto and I and the two girls went out for a walk. I remember not being able to talk with them. The girls were not allowed to talk a word of German in the streets. Otto and I talked English. The children talked Dutch.'[55] Milly does not explain why the children were forbidden to speak German, but it was the last time she ever saw them.

After the summer holidays Otto turned his attention to finding a means of compensating for the seasonal wane in trade. He established a new company, Pectacon, listed in the Amsterdam telephone directory as a 'wholesale herb merchant, manufacturer of pickling salt and mixed spices'.[56] Pectacon became official in November. Otto appointed himself director and his old friend Johannes Kleiman as supervisory director and book-keeper for both Pectacon and Opekta. Goods were imported from Hungary and Belgium and exported to the latter. As an adviser for the company, Otto chose a man he had often met on business trips abroad, Hermann van Pels.

Van Pels was born on 31 March 1898 in Gehrde, Germany, and was one of six children. After completing his education, Hermann represented the family trade in Osnabrück and dealt in flavourings, particularly those used in sausage manufacturing. He married Auguste Röttgen on 5 December 1925. Like her husband, Auguste was German-Jewish by birth, and also had a grandfather who ran his own business. In Anne's diary she comes across as cheerful, selfish, irritable, kind, easily upset and inclined to gossip. Her cousin, Hermann Röttgen, described her as 'a very brave, somewhat homely, middle-class person, who would never hurt

anybody else'.[57] The couple moved into an apartment on Martini-
strasse, Osnabrück, and had one son, Peter, born on 8 November 1926.
Anne would later characterize him as being 'honest and generous . . .
modest and helpful'.[58] Like his father, he was of large build, with thick
brown hair and pale blue eyes. Peter's young life changed dramatically
in the mid-1930s, when the Nazi boycott led to the sale of the family
business and Peter and his parents emigrated, in June 1937, to
Amsterdam.[59]

Hermann van Pels was well liked within Pectacon, where he took
the orders from the sales representatives and discussed recipes for
combining seasonings with Kugler. His recipes were ground and mixed
on the premises and sold to butchers all over the country. Miep was very
impressed: 'There was nothing about spices that van Pels didn't know;
with one sniff of his nose he could name any spice.'[60] She remembers him
as having 'a manly, plain-looking face . . . Mr van Pels always had a
moment for a joke . . . never could he start his work without strong coffee
and a cigarette.'[61] The van Pelses initially rented a flat at 59 Biesboschstraat,
but in 1939 they bought a flat directly behind the Franks, at 34 Zuider
Amstellaan. About sixty other Jews from Osnabrück arrived at that time,
and they became a community within a community, organizing their own
'Osnabrück evenings'.

Max van Creveld, who lodged with the van Pelses during 1940 and
1941, recalls that they and the Franks were 'good friends, the men as well
as the women. I had my own room and every evening we ate together.
Mrs van Pels did her own cooking. I was not a close friend of the van
Pelses. I didn't know, for instance, that they were going to go into hiding.
But you kept that sort of thing to yourself during those years. It was a
perilous time. Mr van Pels was very charming, and Mrs van Pels was
too.'[62] He remembers Peter only vaguely as 'a fine young man'.[63]
Hermann's cousin, Bertel Hess, knew Peter rather better: 'I saw a great
deal of Peter. He came to visit Aunt Henny and his grandpa . . . He was
a very sweet boy, and shy, very shy. He was very good with his hands.
He often went to Henny's if she had small chores to be done, carpentry
and that sort of thing. He wasn't very talkative.'[64]

Peter and his parents often attended the Franks' Saturday afternoon
gatherings. Otto's aim was to bring German Jews together, to help them

and introduce them to 'Dutch people who were interested in their lot, why they had fled and in their welfare here in Holland'.[65] The conversation usually worked its way round to the situation in Germany, and angry words would fly across the large, circular, oak table. The gatherings generally included Miep and Jan, the van Pelses, the Baschwitzes, a Jewish pharmacist named Lewinsohn, who had a shop on the corner of Prinsengracht and Leliegracht, his non-Jewish wife, and the newly arrived dentist Fritz Pfeffer and his fiancée, Charlotta Kaletta, from Berlin.

Pfeffer, who would later share the secret annexe with the Franks and the van Pelses, was born on 30 April 1889, in Giessen, Germany. When Pfeffer left school, he trained as a dentist and became a talented jaw surgeon. After a brief, failed marriage to a woman named Vera (who also emigrated to the Netherlands before the war and was deported), he devoted himself to his career and his young son, Werner Peter. In spring 1936, aged forty-seven, Pfeffer met nineteen-year-old Charlotta Kaletta. Despite the differences in their ages, Pfeffer and Lotte had much in common. Not least, Lotte, too, had a broken marriage behind her, and a son, Gustav.

After Kristallnacht, Pfeffer knew they had to leave Germany. Werner Peter was sent to England, where he lived with his uncle Ernst, also a dentist. Pfeffer made an agonizing decision not to join them there on practical and economic grounds. Instead, on 8 December 1938, having left Lotte's son in Germany, where his father insisted he stay with him (and where they were both subsequently killed by the Nazis), he and Lotte emigrated to the Netherlands.[66] Lotte found life in Amsterdam difficult at first because 'many of the Dutch did not believe the stories we told them about Germany. Not even the Jews in Holland could believe it.'[67] They met the Franks very soon after their arrival in Amsterdam, and soon became part of their circle, though no one had any idea then just how closely entwined their lives would become.

Otto's new business venture, Pectacon, was doing extremely well. Kugler – who had taken Dutch citizenship in May 1938 – was learning how to treat and mix herbs under van Pels's expert tutelage, and a full-time typist had been taken on in 1937, Bep Voskuijl. Bep was Dutch, born in 1919, the eldest of nine children, and lived at home with her parents. Tall and bespectacled, she was kind-hearted and painfully shy, but everyone liked her and she and Miep became good friends. Bep met her employer's family and in time became like another sister to Anne. She noticed that the relationship between Otto and Kleiman was based on a strong friendship: 'they used to play cards every week, I believe.'[68] She thought it 'only natural for Anne to be most closely attached to her father . . . the two of them were alike. Mr Frank too . . . was a person with the kind of understanding one mostly only finds in writers. He could be as affectionate as Anne, and he too, was as unsparing with himself . . . Sometimes [Anne] was bad and nasty-tempered. Then only her father could bring her to her senses, but he could do it with a single word. "Self-control" was the magic formula and he needed only to whisper it to her. It took immediate effect, for Anne was as keenly sensitive as her father, upon whom a soft word always made far more impression than any shouting.'[69]

In 1938 Otto took his daughters to Switzerland.[70] Buddy distinctly remembers the visit: 'That was the last time I was with Anne. Our grandmother was living in an apartment because there wasn't enough room for her with us then. And the last time Anne was there, I remember we played at my grandmother's with my puppet theatre. We took it in turns. Then we went to my grandmother's wardrobe and got dressed up. With hats and everything! We imitated the grown-ups – we had an awful lot of fun. We laughed ourselves sick, I remember that . . . She had such a sense of comedy.'[71] It was the last time Buddy ever saw Anne and Margot. From then on, communication was by letter alone.

In March 1939 Edith's mother, Rosa Hollander, joined her daughter and family in Amsterdam, bringing with her only 'a spoon, a fork, a knife, and some food'.[72] Edith's father had died in Aachen on 19 January 1927, but Rosa was not alone in the house at Pastorplatz until the end of 1938. Her two sons remained with her until then. A 1935 Nazi register of Jews living in Aachen lists the family:

Julius Hollander, b. Eschweiler 11.12.1894, Merchant, unmarried, Pastorplatz 1.

Rosa Hollander, née Stern, b. Langenschwalbach 25.12.1866, widowed, Pastorplatz 1.

Walter Hollander, b. Aachen 06.02.1897, Merchant, unmarried, Pastorplatz 1.[73]

Both Julius (who was married briefly in Germany to a woman named Anna Haymann) and Walter had taken over the administration of the family business, but a second Nazi-compiled register of firms 'Aryanized and otherwise removed from Jewish control, 1938–1942' lists the Hollander business and mistakenly records Julius and Walter as having emigrated to Amsterdam. In fact, after Kristallnacht, one of the brothers emigrated to America (having had his affidavit for immigration signed by a relative already living there), and arranged for the other to join him soon afterward. Several members of the Hollander family had emigrated to America. One of Edith's cousins, living in Peru, tried to organize the Franks' passage but the scheme collapsed. Julius and Walter settled in Boston, where they 'found inferior employment in the firm of a cousin – Ernst Hollander – who had his own financial difficulties stemming from lack of knowledge of the language and of established American business methods. Both brothers remained together and moved to another Massachusetts factory town (Leominster), where they were employed as blue collar workers, since that was all they were brought up to know. They lived frugally.'[74]

Their mother, meanwhile, was happy in her new home on Merwedeplein. Anne was ill with influenza when her grandmother arrived, bringing her a special gift: a beautifully crafted fountain pen, wrapped in cotton wool in a red leather case. It later became Anne's favourite pen for writing in her diary. Rosa was then seventy-three, but could always spare time to listen to Anne's stories about school and friends.

Otto had to go abroad on business in May 1939 and, knowing how much Anne missed him when he was away, he sent her a letter, written in German, which she kept, to serve as 'a support to me all my life'.[75] It reads:

My dear little Anne,
When you were still very small, Grandma used to call you:
'Little woman'. And that you have remained, you flattering little
kitten.

You know we often have secrets from each other. It's true, things
haven't always gone as smoothly for you as they did for your sister,
though in general your sense of humour and your amiability allow

you to sail through so much so easily. I have often told you that you must educate yourself. We have agreed the 'controls' with each other and you yourself are doing a great deal to swallow the 'buts.' And yet you like to spoil yourself and like even more to be spoiled by others.

All that isn't bad, if deep in your little heart you remain as lovable as you always have been. I have told you that as a child I, too, often rushed into things without thinking twice and made many mistakes. But the main thing is to reflect a little bit and then to find one's way back to the right path.

You are not obstinate and so, after a few tears, the laughter is soon back again.

'Enjoy what there is' – as Mummy says.

May this happy laughter stay with you, the laughter with which you enhance your, our and other people's lives.

Your Pim. [Pim was the nickname Anne and Margot used for their father].[76]

Anne later wrote about the letter in her diary: 'Jacque [a school-friend] thought this was a declaration of love by some boy and I didn't try to enlighten her.'[77]

In the summer, Rosa Hollander accompanied Margot, Anne and Edith on day-trips to the beach, despite her increasing ill health. Anne had a severe cold, but insisted on going swimming. A photograph shows her looking thoroughly miserable, clutching the folds of her striped robe. She captioned the picture, 'This is June 1939 . . . Margot and I had just got out of the water and I still remember how terribly cold I was, that's why I put on my bathrobe, granny sitting there at the back so sweetly and peacefully. Just as she was wont to do.'[78]

Anne's tenth birthday was celebrated with a special party to mark her entry into double figures. She was allowed to invite her favourite girlfriends. A photograph taken by her father that day shows them all standing in the sun on Merwedeplein, linking arms and wearing their best dresses. Anne gave a copy of the picture to Lies, having written on the back, 'Anne Frank's birthday party, 12–6–39'.[79] Lies was there, of course, and so was Sanne, along with six other girls: Lucie van Dijk, Juultje

45

Ketellapper, Kitty Egyedi, Mary Bos, Rie (Ietje) Swillens, and Martha van den Berg. The young revellers picnicked in Amstelrust Park, where Anne had her photograph taken holding a rabbit. Of the nine girls who attended the party that day, only six were still alive six years later: Anne, Sanne and Juultje Ketellapper were all killed in the Holocaust.

In January 1939 Hitler told his followers at the Reichstag that: 'If international finance Jewry within Europe and abroad should succeed once more in plunging the peoples into a world war, then the consequence will be not the Bolshevization of the world and therewith a victory of Jewry, but on the contrary, the destruction of the Jewish race in Europe . . .'[80] On 15 March his troops invaded the remainder of Czechoslovakia.

In the Netherlands that summer, food rationing was introduced. D. J. de Geer, the head of the Christian Historical Union, had become prime minister and continued to rule a coalition government. Rumours of a possible German invasion made the Dutch jittery, but the Germans issued another declaration of respect for their neutrality.

On 23 August Germany and Russia signed a non-aggression pact and agreed to the partition of Poland. On 1 September Germany invaded Poland, and annexed the town of Danzig on the same date. Two days later, France and Britain declared war on Germany. Russia's Red Army penetrated Poland's eastern borders on 17 September. Under the might of the Blitzkrieg, Poland admitted defeat and was subsequently partitioned under the terms agreed on 23 August in a treaty signed by the Russian and German foreign ministers, Molotov and Ribbentrop. German troops entered Warsaw on 30 September. Russia took control of Estonia, Latvia and Lithuania, and invaded Finland on 30 November. Hitler's announcement that he still wanted peace was dismissed outright by Neville Chamberlain. In an attempt to fragment Polish society and extinguish the Polish ruling class, five 'Einsatzgruppen' (German special-duty paramilitary police) were given orders by Hitler to murder as many intellectuals, officials and priests as possible.

For Jews in Germany, Austria and now Poland, life was becoming unendurable. Jews in Austria were subjected to humiliating restrictions, forced to wear a yellow star, and made to leave their ransacked homes for ghettos. Adolf Eichmann's first assignment as head of the Centre for

Emigration of Austrian Jews was to organize the 'forced emigration' of every Austrian and Bohemian Jew. In order to leave, each person had to pay a set amount, plus a sum in foreign currency. The money went towards so-called 'emigration funds'. To enter another country, a fee was required for visas and foreign money for admittance. Some 60,000 Jews left under the system until 1941, when all emigration stopped. Many headed for Palestine, but faced opposition there from Arabs, and were given little support by Britain. In 1940 refugees aboard the ships *Patria* and *Salvador* were refused entry into Palestine by the British government. Both ships mysteriously sank, with the combined loss of 450 lives. Neville Chamberlain wrote in a letter: 'No doubt the Jews aren't a lovable people . . .'[81]

On 17 October 1939 more than 1,000 Jews were sent to Poland from Czechoslovakia and told to build themselves a camp. The first Jewish Councils of the war (groups of prominent Jewish citizens directly responsible to the Nazis) were set up in the eastern sector of Poland known as the General Government on 28 November. German authorities issued new decrees through the councils evicting Jews from government offices, forbidding them to have business dealings with Aryans, and to give or receive medical treatment to or from Aryans, amongst numerous other restrictions. Some 600,000 Jews were sent in cattle trucks to the General Government between December 1939 and February 1940. When the governor of that area, Hans Frank, complained about the dwindling food supplies, the transports stopped. In the first two months of Poland's occupation, 5,000 Jews were murdered. As 1939 drew to a close, 40 per cent of the Jewish population remained in Austria; 150,000 had escaped, while 200,000 Jews still lived in Germany.

On 12 March 1940, after a fierce battle lasting three months, Finland succumbed to the Russian Army. Denmark, Norway and Luxembourg were conquered by Germany in quick succession during April and early May; Luxembourg's government promptly took flight after the occupation. Finland was home to 2,000 Jews, Norway to 1,800, Denmark to 8,000, and Luxembourg to 5,000. Among this last group were relatives of the Frank family.

1940 was Anne's last full year at the Montessori school. From the first year to the fourth, her teacher had been Mr van Gelder. Towards the end, he noticed that Anne had a new ambition. 'It is correct that she wanted to be a writer. That I remember. It started early with her, very early . . . and I imagine she might very well have become one. She was able to *experience* more than other children . . . I might almost put it that she heard more, the soundless things too, and sometimes she heard things whose very existence we have almost forgotten. That happens with children.'[82] He remembered her in class as 'very hard-working and very intelligent . . . She loved to draw, and in other subjects she showed great diligence and understanding . . . She was always occupied and she wanted – this was always noticeable in her – she always wanted to know all the subtleties about everything. Whenever something was explained to the class, she always asked for further clarification; she wasn't satisfied until she fully understood the matter and it had become her own mental property.'[83]

In the fifth year Anne was taught by Miss Gadron, and in her final year by the headmistress, Mrs Kuperus. She remembered Anne vividly: 'Anne was a lovely girl, not conspicuous, but always active and spontaneous . . . she was intelligent, but I had more intelligent children in the class. I do know that she loved reading and drama too, she revelled in drama . . . she was a very good pupil, and she took a great interest in school. She always had lots of friends, she was a girl who was easy to get on with. She was certainly not introverted. She had a great team spirit and really enjoyed working in groups . . . I was so anxious to keep Anne another year. She was still very young for the class, and very frail also. She had been ill for a while but she recovered very nicely and during her last years here she was in good health. Anne and Lies were always together, of course. But I cannot recall that the two chattered so much during class as Anne describes in her diary. Perhaps it attracted attention over at the Lyceum, but here in the Montessori school they had no reason to be talking. We don't require the children to sit still . . . The last year was particularly nice. We had started to do theatricals. The children wrote plays in one class and in the following class we put them on. Anne was in her element. Of course she was full of ideas for the scripts, but since she also had no shyness and liked imitating other people, the big parts fell to her. She was rather small among her schoolmates, but when she played the queen or the princess, she suddenly seemed a good bit taller than the others. It was really strange to see that.'[84]

The school had served Anne well, just as her parents had hoped. In a memoir written many years after the war, Otto reflected, 'It was good for Anne to go to a Montessori school, as every child was treated individually . . . Anne was never a very good schoolgirl. She hated maths. I practised her times tables with her countless times. She only excelled in those subjects that interested her, particularly history. One day, she came to me and said that she had to give a short speech to the class about Emperor Nero, "Everyone knows what's in the history books about him, what is there for me to say?" To help her, I took her with me to one of my friends who had a large library. There she got some specialist books, which she took home with pride. A while later I asked her about her speech. "Oh," she said, "my classmates didn't want to believe what I told them, because it was so different to what they knew about Nero." "And what about the teacher?" I asked. "He was very pleased," she answered.'[85]

In spring 1940 Anne and Margot began writing to two pen-pals in America. The exchange was arranged by Birdie Matthews, a young teacher from Danville, Iowa. Birdie visited Europe almost every year and always took with her a list of children who wanted to start up an international correspondence. In 1939 she visited Amsterdam and met another teacher who was interested in the scheme. They exchanged names and addresses, and on her return to Danville, Birdie asked her pupils to choose their correspondents from a list of Dutch children. Juanita Wagner, who lived on a farm in Danville, chose Anne Frank. In her letter, she told Anne about her home, her family, and her older sister Betty Ann, who also wanted a pen-pal. Anne wrote back immediately, enclosing a postcard, photos and a letter from Margot for Betty Ann. The letters were written in English, but Otto probably translated them from Anne and Margot's originals. Margot's letter to Betty Ann read:

27 April 1940.
Dear Betty Ann,
    I have only received your letter about a week ago and had no time to answer right away. It is Sunday today, so I can take time to write. During the week I am very busy as I have to work for school at

home every day. Our school begins at 9.00 a.m. Til noon, then I go home by bicycle (if the weather is bad I go by bus and stay at school) and return for the class beginning at half-past one; then we have clas [sic] until three o'clock. Wednesday and Saturday afternoon we are free and use our time to play tennis and to row. In the winter we play hockey and go skating if it is cold enough. This year was unusually cold and all the canals were frozen; today is the first really spring day, the sun shining bright and warm. Generally we have a lot of rain. In summer we have a two months holiday, then a fortnight at Christmas and so on Easter; Whitsuntide only four days. We often listen to the radio as times are very exciting, having a frontier with Germany and being a small country we never feel safe.

In our class most of the children communicate with one or the other so I do not know children who would want to take up corres-pondence. I only have two cousins, boys living in Basel Switzerland. For American ideas this is not far but for us it is. We have to travel through Germany which we cannot do or through Belgium and France and in that we cannot either. It is war and no visas are given.

We live in a five room flat attached to the only sky scraper of the city being twelve storeys high! Amsterdam has about 200,000 inhab-itants. We are near the sea shore but we miss hills and woods. Everything being flat and a great part of the country lying below sea level, therefore the name Netherland.

Father is going to business in the morning and returns home about 6 p.m.; Mother is busy at home. My grand-mother is living with us and we rented one room to a lady. Now I think I have told you quite a lot and I am expecting your answer.

With kindest regards,

Your friend

Margot Betti Frank.

P.S. Many thanks for Juanita's letter, as Anne is writing to her I need not write myself.

Margot.[86]

Anne's letter to Juanita read:

Amsterdam, 29 April, Monday,
Dear Juanita,

   I did receive your letter and want to answer you as quick as possible. Margot and myself are the only children in our house. Our grandmother is living with us. My father has an office and mother is busy at home. I have not far from school and I am in the fifth class. We have no hour classes we may do what we prefer, of course we must get to a certain goal. Your mother will certainly know this system, it is called Montessori. We have little work at home.

   On the map I looked again and found the name Burlington. I did ask a girl friend of mine if she would like to communicate with one of your friends. She wants to do it with a girl about my age not with a boy.

   I shall write her address underneath. Did you yourself write the letter I received from you, or did your mother do it? I include a post-card from Amsterdam and shall continue to do that collecting picture-cards I have already about 800. A child I used to be at school with went to New York and she write [sic] a letter to our class some time ago. In case you and Betty get a photo do send a copy as I am curious to know how you look. My birthday is 12 June. Kindly let me know yours. Perhaps one of your friends will write first to my girl friend, for she also cannot write English but her father or mother will translate the letter.

   Hoping to hear from you
   I remain
   Your Dutch friend
   Annelies Marie Frank.
P.S. Please write me the address of a girl. The address of my friend is . . . [Sanne's address followed.]

On the postcard Anne had written:

Dear Juanita, This picture shows one of the many old canals of Amsterdam. But this is only one of the old city. There are also big canals and over all those canals are bridges. There are about 340 bridges within the city. Anne Frank.[87]

Juanita recalls, 'Needless to say, we were both thrilled to have established communications with a foreign friend, and we both wrote again immediately. However, we never heard from Anne or Margot again . . . We assumed their letters could not get through because of censorship.'[88] Betty Ann continues the story: 'We often talked and wondered about the family. Did they have enough food? Were the bombs dropping nearby? . . . To be very honest, we grew up in a small country town. There were some Jewish people there but it was no big deal. It never dawned on me that the other girls were Jewish. If we had known, we would have prayed and done more.'[89] The girls had no further contact with the Frank family until after the war.

Communication with friends and relatives abroad would become problematic, but in 1940 there were no difficulties with post to and from the Netherlands, as Otto's cousin Milly remembers: 'During the first months of the war, Otto was virtually our only link to the continent. We couldn't write to relations in Germany, for England was at war with Germany. But Otto could write to Germany because he was doing so from neutral Holland. I got a letter from him saying how terribly unhappy he was because he was sure that Germany was going to attack. He said, "I don't know what to do about the children. I can't talk to Edith about it. There's no use worrying her before she has to be worried. Forgive me, but I just had to write it." I took the letter straight to my mother and said, "Don't you think we should let him know at once that if he'd send the children to England we'd look after them for the duration of the war?" She said, "Of course." I did that, straight away. I wrote back, "I know it sounds crazy, because we're at war and you're not. But if you think it's the least bit safe, please send the children here." The next letter I got back from him was the last before Hitler invaded. It said, "Edith and I discussed your letter. We both feel we simply can't do it. We couldn't bear to part with the girls. They mean too much to us. But if it's any comfort to you, you are the people we would have trusted." Then the lights went out in Holland.'[90]

On 4 March 1940 Anne wrote in her schoolfriend Henny Scheerder's poetry album. Her verse, illustrated by a sticker of daisies, roses and forget-me-nots on the same page, reads, 'It is of little worth, what I offer you, pick roses on earth and forget-me-not.' In one corner she identified herself: 'By myself written, by myself done, Anne Frank, so is my name,' and in the other, having read a previous entry in the book which was dated upside down, she wrote in rhyme, 'Tip tap top, the date stands at the top.' On the facing page, she glued in an embossed design of a basket of red roses, white flowers and greenery. A dove carries a letter in the midst of the colourful blooms. And in each corner of the page, she repeated her plea: 'for - get - me - not'.[91]

On her visits to the Franks' apartment that spring, Miep was astonished by the rate at which Margot and Anne were growing up: 'Margot Frank turned fourteen . . . we realized we were seeing a young lady rather than a girl. Her figure had filled out quite a bit. Thick eyeglasses now covered her serious dark eyes, and her attentions were always on bookish matters and never on frivolity. Regardless of the glasses, Margot continued to grow prettier, her skin smooth and creamy . . . Anne clearly looked up to her older sister. Anything Margot did or said was sponged up by Anne's darting eyes and quick mind. In fact, Anne had developed the skill of mimicry. She would mimic anyone and anything, and very well at that; the cat's meow, her friend's voice, her teacher's authoritative tone. We couldn't help laughing at her little performances . . . Anne loved having an attentive audience, and loved to hear us respond to her skits and clowning. Anne had changed too. Her thin legs seemed to be stretching longer and longer from beneath her dress, her arms too. She was still a small, thin girl, but seemed to be entering a pre-adolescent spurt, the arms and legs suddenly too big for the body. Still the baby of the family, Anne always wanted to get a bit of extra attention.'[92]

The Franks went to a professional photographer every year to record their children growing up. The photos taken of Anne in 1940 were appropriated by the subject herself. In them, she sits hunched up, her arms folded, with her hair pinned up at the sides. She smiles on most, looking above or to the side, and has captioned them: 'Things are getting more serious, but there's still a smile left over from the funny bits'; 'Oh, what a joke'; 'Whatever next?'; 'That's a funny story'; 'Nice one, as well'.[93] On one photograph, she lifts her head slightly and seems to be deep in thought. She wrote on it in black pen: 'This is a photograph of me as I wish I looked all the time. Then I might still have a chance of getting to Holywood [*sic*]. But at present, I'm afraid, I usually look quite different.'[94]

On 10 May 1940 Germany invaded the Netherlands.

When the Sufferings of Us Jews Really Began 1940-42

Part Two

Chapter Three

'Now that the Germans rule the roost here, we are in real trouble . . .'

Anne Frank, *Diary*, Thursday, July 1942

For four days, near hysteria reigned in the Netherlands. A mood of desolation swept the country at the news that the Dutch royal family, together with the prime minister and his cabinet, had flown to London. The Germans issued an ultimatum: either the country's forces surrendered or Rotterdam would be destroyed. Two hours before the deadline was due to expire, Rotterdam was bombed. Its centre was virtually annihilated, 900 people were killed, 78,000 made homeless and over 24,000 buildings reduced to rubble. Rotterdam surrendered on 13 May 1940. The Netherlands capitulated the following day.

In a massive convoy the Germans entered Amsterdam. Reich Commissioner Arthur Seyss-Inquart's proclamation was displayed throughout the city: 'I have today taken over civilian authority in the Netherlands . . . the magnanimity of the Führer and the efficiency of German soldiers has permitted civilian life to be restored quickly. I intend to allow all Dutch law and general administration to go on as usual.'[1]

At the time of the German invasion 140,000 Jews lived in the Netherlands, 60 per cent of these in Amsterdam; 14,381 were German/Austrian refugees who had arrived after 1933, 117,999 were Dutch and 7,621 were Jews of other nationalities. The Dutch NSB (National Socialist Movement) had been formed by Anton Mussert in 1931. In its early days the party was ardently nationalist, but there was no 'race' policy; the NSB advocated religious freedom and counted Jews among its ranks. As German influence on the party increased, Jewish members were forced out. The NSB gained 7.9 per cent of the vote in the 1935 States General

57

elections, but their increasingly blatant anti-Semitism lost them considerable support. At the beginning of 1940 there were only 33,000 NSB
members remaining. After the invasion Dutch Nazis took over the central
Netherlands' news agency and all Jewish staff at ANP (the Dutch Press
Agency) were dismissed. Jews were also compelled to resign from the
Dutch Cinema Union. The WA (NSB defence corps) attacked Jews
physically and fought in the streets with anti-Nazi citizens, yet the Burgemeester of Amsterdam assured Jewish dignitaries that the German military
commander had given his word that their communities were safe.

At first, life in Amsterdam continued much as it always had, despite the
black-outs and the air-raid sirens. Margot's friend Jetteke Frijda remembers, 'The day after the invasion was a school day. We were called into
the large assembly hall and were told that we were at war with Germany.
We were sent home and didn't come back until after the capitulation.'[2]
Eva Schloss adds, 'During the invasion there were aeroplanes coming over
from both sides. We were terrified by all the bombing and shooting. It
was the first war *we* encountered, and it was extremely frightening. But
with the surrender, things almost became normal again. We went back
to our schools and it wasn't too bad for us Jewish people or anybody
else. Enough food and so on. It came gradually . . .'[3]

Eva was then Eva Geiringer, and had recently arrived with her
parents and brother from Brussels. They lived directly opposite the
Franks on Merwedeplein, which was, Eva recalls, 'Perfect for children.
We played rounders and skipping, or sat talking on the steps in front
of the flats, boys and girls together. There was a real affinity amongst
people because so many Jewish families lived there. Unfortunately, we
moved to Merwedeplein in February 1940; we only had a few months of
freedom. In May we had the war, but, as I said, things didn't change
immediately.' Eva met the Frank family in March: 'I was out playing and
told Anne that I couldn't speak Dutch very well. She said, "Oh, well, my
father can speak German with you," and she took me up to see her
parents.'[4]

In navy raincoat and wellington boots (the 'required uniform'[5]
for the local children), Eva sometimes tagged along to the Franks' apartment, making a bee-line for Anne's cat, Moortje: 'The Franks had a large

cat that purred appreciatively when I picked it up . . . I would wander into the sitting-room to cuddle the cat and find Mr Frank watching me with amused eyes. He was . . . very kind. He always made a point of talking to me in German. Mrs Frank would prepare lemonade for the children and we would sit drinking together in the kitchen.'[6] Eva wanted to be near Anne's friend, Sanne Ledermann: 'I had sort of a crush on Suzanne. She was very sweet. She lived on Noorder Amstellaan on the second or third floor, then there were the gardens in-between, and we lived opposite, on the first floor of Merwedeplein. Our balconies were opposite each other. We had a rope between them and we sent messages to each other. Even when we had to be in before eight [when the curfew was instituted], we still communicated across the balcony. I liked her a lot.'[7]

Anne, Sanne and Lies had begun to distance themselves from the other children, preferring to sit in the square reading fashion magazines, discussing film stars, and giggling about boys. Eva reflects, 'Anne was definitely an early developer . . . They were an inseparable trio, each of them a little more sophisticated than the rest of us – more like teenagers . . . One warm Sunday afternoon when I was sitting with Sanne on the steps of our apartment, she confided in me how much she admired her friend Anne Frank because she was so stylish.'[8] Eva had already noticed that 'Anne looked after herself, she was very vain, which was unusual for that age, eleven or twelve. She was very interested in clothes and I was not at all.'[9] As an example of Anne's stylishness and self-possession, Eva cites the day she and her mother, Fritzi Geiringer, visited the dressmaker's on Merwedeplein to have Eva's coat altered. In her autobiography Eva writes, 'We were sitting waiting our turn and heard the dressmaker talking to her customer inside the fitting room. The customer was very determined to have things just right. "It would look better with larger shoulder-pads," we could hear her saying in an authoritative tone of voice, "and the hemline should be just a little higher, don't you think?" We then heard the dressmaker agreeing with her and I sat there wishing I was allowed to choose exactly what I wanted to wear. I was flabbergasted when the curtains went back and there was Anne, all alone, making decisions about her own dress. It was peach-coloured with a green trim. She smiled at me. "Do you like it?" she said, twirling around. "Oh, yes!" I said breathlessly, in great envy. I was not up to that standard . . . Anne had to have it more sophisticated. For me, that was unimaginable. Anne appeared so much more grown-up than me, even though I was a month older.'[10]

Fritzi Geiringer knew the Franks only casually, but she recognized Anne's confidence and her growing interest in the opposite sex: 'She seemed like any other girl her age. Except a bit more extroverted . . . and boy crazy! Her one flaw was her vanity.'[11] Eva recalls that Anne 'flirted with boys and had boyfriends. She walked with them and flirted with them. I wasn't interested, but then I had a brother, so boys were not a big thing to me.'[12] Eva did not share Anne's other interests either: 'I wasn't one of her best friends because we had such different interests. I was a tomboy; she was a real *girl*. So although we played together, we were not close, and her serious side, which she shows in the diary – I never knew that. She really was a terrible chatterbox, though, and Margot was partly suppressed by her because Anne always had to be the centre of attention. Anne looked very modern and kind of flirtatious, sexy nearly. Margot was more . . . stiff. She had the same colouring as Anne, but Anne was definitely prettier. That was partly because she was lively in her expression, and if people smile, it makes them more attractive. Anne was always the smiling one. She was the great personality. Margot, I suppose, was deeper. She didn't push herself forward. Edith was the same, very friendly, but not the sort to make an impression. Otto *did* make an impression on me, though. He was very outgoing and you could feel a warmth coming from him, but not from the mother.'[13]

Of course the older children, such as Margot's friends, took much less notice of Anne and regarded her as they did all the younger girls. One such friend was Laureen Klein, who had emigrated from Frankfurt in 1936 with her parents and two sisters. The Kleins were near-neighbours of the Franks in the River Quarter and often met socially. On Wednesday afternoons Laureen and her elder sister Susi would meet Margot on the street corner and walk together to the synagogue for religious education classes. 'Anne never went,' Laureen remembers. 'She didn't want to go. And her father never forced her.'[14] Laureen thought Anne was 'just a shrimp'.[15] She was infinitely more taken with Margot.

In summer 1940 Otto Frank received his first inkling of what lay ahead. He watched a German Army car heading down Scheldestraat on the edge of the River Quarter. It stopped at a street-corner stall brimming with bright flowers. The driver asked the flower-seller a question, then continued on his way. Suddenly the car spun round and headed back along Scheldestraat. When it reached the corner again, one of its passengers, a young soldier, flung open the door, jumped down, and struck the flower-seller savagely across the face. Otto would always say afterwards that 'that was how it all began'.[16]

In August the Franks visited Zandvoort again. A photograph shows Margot, aged fourteen, laughing and pushing her dark hair away from her face as she stands above Anne, who lounges on the beach, grinning and holding a rubber ring. Anne pasted the picture into her diary two years later, and her caption reveals both her desire to emerge from girlhood to womanhood, and an element of competition between the two sisters: 'This is in 1940, Margot and I again. I console myself with the thought that on the photograph above taken in 1939 Margot was not all that well-developed either. She was 13 at the time, the same age I am now or even a little older. So she's got no cause to look down on me.'[17]

Anne was embroiled in her first adolescent love affair, with a local boy, fourteen-year-old Peter Schiff. She recalled him in her diary four years on: 'Peter crossed my path, and in my childish way I really fell in love. He also liked me very much and we couldn't be parted for one whole summer. I can still see us walking hand in hand through the streets together. Then I went into the 6th Form of the Lower School and he into the First Form of the 4th-3. I would often fetch him from school, or he would fetch me and I often went to his house. Peter was a very good-looking boy, tall, handsome and slim, with an earnest, calm, intelligent face . . . When he laughed a naughty glint came into his eye.'[18] The friendship inevitably waned when Peter moved house and one of his new confidants laughed at his relationship with a much younger girl. Not wanting to lose face amongst his peers, Peter pointedly ignored her. Anne was miserable at first, but her home and social life were too busy for her to dwell on the broken romance.

The Franks' continuing Saturday afternoon gatherings were, more than ever, a source of solace in an uncertain environment. People did everything to ensure that the children were troubled as little as possible.

Otto and Edith were keen walkers and the family spent afternoons strolling about the city, taking advantage of the beautiful weather. Lies's father, ever the joker, used to make himself up like Hitler, sweeping his black hair back from his forehead and bristling his moustache. Lies thought this was hilarious: 'The Franks lived next door and he would ring at the door and go in and I remember the first time, they were really frightened – what had happened?! If you could imagine them thinking Hitler had come to the house! But it was very funny, when they saw who it was . . . !'[19] As autumn approached, and no significant changes had taken place in their lives since the German invasion, all that anyone could do was to pray that they might yet be left in peace.

In July 1940 Jews were dismissed from the Netherlands' Air-Raid Precautions Department, which grew increasingly inefficient as a result, and then from the civil service. A circular listed 'undesirables' exempt from labour in Germany: 'anti-social elements, e.g., people who have served long prison sentences, those with a clear communist history, and Jews'.[20] A decree announced through the Official Gazette of the Reich Commissioner for the Occupied Netherlands ordered that 'All Jews of other than Dutch nationality are required to report at once.'[21] German Jews were told to leave The Hague and the Dutch coasts, but were given no reason as to why this was necessary. The Communist Party held their meetings in secret, having been ordered to disband by the Nazis. Books which the Nazis deemed offensive to German sensibilities were removed from libraries. School and university textbooks were replaced with Nazi-approved material and Jewish newspapers were outlawed. All radio stations outside Germany and the occupied territories were banned, but daily quarter-of-an-hour broadcasts from the Dutch government and royal family in exile had begun. After his pleas for negotiated peace fell on angry ears, D. J. de Geer was succeeded as Dutch prime minister by Professor P. S. Gerbrandy of the Anti-Revolutionary Party.

At the end of September 1940 a circular to all provincial authorities outlined who was Jewish according to Nazi definition: a person was Jewish if he/she had one grandparent who was, or had been, a member of the Jewish community, and a person was Jewish if he/she was married to a Jew. Dutch professors signed a petition which stated that the country's universities considered it 'a matter of indifference whether a scholar is Jewish or not'.[22] On 18 October the Amsterdam City Council distributed two forms which all heads of education departments had to complete and return within a week. The forms asked if the recipient was a Jew or an Aryan. At the University of Leiden 1,700 students sent in a petition to Seyss-Inquart protesting against the new measure.

A curfew was instigated for all inhabitants of the Netherlands; no one was allowed on the streets between midnight and four o'clock in the morning, and travel across the borders, other than that specifically authorized by the Germans, was forbidden. Rationing was enforced with great severity, and it soon became clear that Dutch supplies were being shipped to the Fatherland. Various household goods were disappearing from the shops; soap, tobacco and alcohol were increasingly hard to find.

On 22 October the *Official Gazette* issued the 'Decree Concerning the Registration of Companies', by which 'All industrial or commercial firms owned by Jews or having Jewish partners are to be reported. Infractions of this order will be punished by up to five years' imprisonment or fines of up to 100,000 guilders.'[23] All companies which at the date of the German invasion had one or more partners or directors who were Jewish, Jewish shareholders or Jewish capital were liable and had to report to the Bureau of Economic Investigation.

On 4 November Jewish education officers were suspended from their jobs. None was ever reinstated. Two universities, at Delft and Leiden, were closed due to their persistent resistance against the Germans. Amsterdam University was shut down temporarily by its own administrators to ward off demonstrations from students, which might otherwise have resulted in complete closure. On 25 November Jews were dismissed from all government and public offices. On 19 December a decree banned Germans from working in Jewish households.

It was now clear that the treatment of Jews in the Netherlands would be no different from that elsewhere in occupied Europe. Some people had never been in doubt; during the first month of Nazi rule, 248 Jews had committed suicide. Families with sufficient finances were willing to pay anything to obtain exit permits. A few braved danger and set off on foot across France in the hope of reaching Spain and freedom. About 1,000 succeeded. Two hundred Jews escaped to England by ship from Ijmuiden, aided by a non-Jew, Gertrude Wijsmuller-Meijer, who devoted herself to this cause throughout the war.

The day after the 'Decree Concerning the Registration of Companies' had been passed, Otto registered a new company with a notary in Hilversum. Shares in the company, La Synthèse NV, were owned by the supervisory director, named as Jan Gies, and its managing director, Victor Kugler. The real owner of the company, Otto Frank, was able to hide behind this front. However, on 27 November Otto registered Opekta, admitting himself to be its sole proprietor and the investor of 10,000 guilders in capital, and Pectacon, declaring that he owned 2,000 guilders worth of share capital, while the rest had not been issued. The forms appeared to be fairly harmless on first examination. Questions concerned the name and address of the business, and the nature of its imports and exports. On a personal level, there were enquiries about the directors and managers of the company. Otto, Kugler (who had been appointed Proxy for Pectacon that year) and Kleiman gave information about their place and date of birth, positions held in the company and their current addresses. Question 9B asked baldly, 'Jew?'[24]

On 1 December 1940 the Opekta/Pectacon companies relocated to new premises at 263 Prinsengracht, in the area known as the Jordaan. The Westerkerk, the largest and one of the oldest Protestant churches in the Netherlands, stands just down the street, and the bell of its brick tower, the Westertoren, echoes over the city every fifteen minutes, exactly as it did almost sixty years ago, when Otto Frank moved his company into its shadow. Built in 1635 by Dirk van Delft, 263 Prinsengracht has seen a number of changes to its structure over the centuries. The gable was replaced in 1739 and the old annexe (the back house) was torn down and a larger one built. Isaac van Vleuten, a druggist, paid 18,900 guilders for it in 1745, and lived there despite owning a country-style house on the Haarlemmer Trekvaart. When van Vleuten died, the house remained vacant for years. In 1841 the ground floor became a stable for five horses, and was intermittently used as a business premises until the turn of the twentieth century, when a firm specializing in heaters, stoves and beds took possession of it. In the 1930s it was used as a workshop by a firm manufacturing piano rolls, and was sold to the head of the company, Mr

Kruijer. It had stood empty for one year when Opekta/Pectacon moved in, renting it directly from the new owner, M. A. Wessel.

Double doors on the right side of the building led straight into the warehouse, which was divided into three separate spaces on the ground floor. The entrance next to the warehouse doors led up to the first-floor offices. The door on the left led from the ground floor, via a steep staircase, to the second floor, where three rooms, from front to back, were used to house large mixing containers, sacks of jam-making ingredients, and spices. The attics above were also used for storage. The annexe was empty on the second and third floors, but Otto had the open space on the first converted into two rooms for his private office and the staff kitchen. The building was flanked to the right by a branch of the Zaandam Keg company and to the left by a furniture workshop.[25]

There were eleven staff at the Prinsengracht in all, five working for Pectacon and six working for Opekta. Temporary employees were taken on by both companies. Every Saturday morning, representatives handed in reports and orders from pharmacists for Opekta and butchers for Pectacon. Kugler presided over the warehousemen and the office staff, and shared a workspace with Hermann van Pels. Kleiman, Miep (now living with Jan Gies in the River Quarter's Hunzestraat) and Bep were installed in the main front office. Ostensibly, the atmosphere was as relaxed as it had ever been, but as more anti-Semitic decrees were introduced, Miep knew that Otto's apparent composure disguised his real feelings: 'Although Mr Frank gave the impression of everything being normal, I could see that he was worn out. Now, because he was not allowed on the streetcar, he had to walk many miles to the office each day and then return home by foot at night. It was impossible for me to imagine the strain that he, Mrs Frank, Anne and Margot were under. Their situation was never discussed, and I did not ask.'[26]

In December Margot wrote to her grandmother in Switzerland. There is no specific mention of the events unfolding in the Netherlands, but her references to school seem to imply that things were changing.

Dear Omi,

   Congratulations on your birthday. This year is a special one. You only have a 75th birthday once. On your 70th birthday, Daddy and

I were in Basel, and I hope that we'll be with you on 20 December.

We don't go out in the evenings for long because it gets dark so quickly, and I play cards with Mr Wronker, our lodger. Anne and I like to go and see the Goslars' baby.²⁷ It laughs already and is getting sweeter every day. Tomorrow Anne is going to the ice-rink which is now in the Apollo Hall, so it's much nearer. Is Berndt skating a lot, or does he have too much work?

At our school, some of the teachers have gone, we don't have any French lessons, and we have another teacher for maths. School now starts at quarter-past nine instead of half-past eight, and we have an hour shorter lessons. On Saturdays I go into town with Mummy and just now, before Hanukkah, we can always find something to buy.

So, good wishes to you and to Stephan for his birthday.
From your
Margot.
[Addition in Edith's hand:] *Otto will write from the office.²⁸*

The Franks did not arrive in Switzerland in time for Alice's and Stephan's birthdays; all travel across the borders of occupied territory was closed to them.

On 5 January 1941 cinemas closed their doors to Jews. In cafés, restaurants and parks signs warning Jews that they were unwelcome began to appear. On 10 January an announcement was made that 'All persons of the Jewish religion or wholly or partly of Jewish blood are to report. Failure to report will be considered a crime.'²⁹ Jews in Amsterdam were given ten weeks in which to report to the Census Office (those living elsewhere were given four weeks), where they received, for a fee of one guilder, a yellow identity card stamped with a large black 'J'.

On 11 February Jewish students were expelled from universities. On 12 February, during raids on Jewish markets on Waterlooplein and at Amstelveld, a member of the WA (the Dutch Nazi paramilitary faction) was injured in the rioting and later died; Germans claimed Jews had bitten through a vein and sucked out his blood. Higher SS and Police Leader Hans Rauter completely sealed off the Waterlooplein area and summoned leaders of Jewish communities, ordering them to form a council.[30] The Jewish Council, led by A. Asscher, President of the Council of the Great Dutch Synagogue, and Professor D. Cohen, formerly President of the Committee for Jewish Refugees, was expected to keep order in the Jewish section and to convey all further instructions to the Jewish community.

That same month at the Koco ice-cream parlour, SS men were sprayed with ammonia by the German-Jewish owner, Ernst Cahn, who was later tortured and shot at Amsterdam's Gestapo headquarters. Himmler called for the deportation of over 400 Jews, and on 22 February there was a razzia (round-up) in the Jewish Quarter. Jewish men snatched at random were lined up on Jonas Daniel Meijerplein and subjected to screams of abuse and beatings by uniformed Nazis, who baited them with their dogs. The prisoners were sent, via Schoorl and Alkmaar, to Buchenwald concentration camp. After two months the survivors were sent to Mauthausen, to be worked and thrashed to death in the stone quarries. In protest at the Meijerplein razzia, a strike began on 25 February, lasting two days in Amsterdam, Hilversum and Zaandam, and bringing business, industry and transport to a standstill, before martial law was imposed, aided by the German Army. The SS warned that more reprisals would be brought against Jews, and another 300 arrested, if people refused to co-operate. Asscher was told that if the Jewish Council could not end the strike, 500 Jews would be shot. The Germans carried out their punishments anyway: sixteen Resistance workers and three strikers were shot by a firing squad in The Hague, the Dutch were heavily fined and a decree threatened any would-be pickets with a minimum one-year prison sentence.

In March some Jewish property was forcibly requisitioned for 'Aryanization'. Jews were struck off the list of blood donors. Jews and non-Jews were segregated in their work in abattoirs. On 12 March the 'Economic Dejudification Decree' stated that any changes made between 9 May 1940 and 12 March 1941 to businesses registered under the October 1940 decree had to be declared by 12 April, subject to German approval. Another decree declared that the Netherlands was in an administrative state of siege and anyone resisting police orders would face the death penalty. *Het Joodsche Weekblad*, the Jewish weekly newspaper used by the Nazis to issue directives, made its first appearance. On 9 April Dutch newspapers reported that Jews were banned from almost every public place in Haarlem, on the orders of the city's Burgemeester. Jews in Haarlem were forbidden to move house and Jews thinking of moving to Haarlem were told they were unwelcome. A new decree was issued forbidding Jews to move out of Amsterdam. On 15 April all Jews were ordered to surrender their radios and sign a declaration that they had not procured another in its place. The radio was a lifeline for many, especially since the transmission of Radio Oranje, the mouthpiece of the Dutch government, had begun. Thousands held on to their sets clandestinely. A film entitled *De Eeuwig Jood* (*The Eternal Jew*) was released in Dutch cinemas, billed as 'A Documentary about World Jewry'. Its advertising poster depicted a twisted, hook-nosed face with the star of David on its forehead, and urged, 'You Must See This Film!'

From 1 May Jews were banned from the stock exchange in the Netherlands and Jews in certain professions were forbidden to work for non-Jews. On 23 May Jews were banned from the labour service. Jewish-owned farms were registered on 28 May with a view to selling them to Aryans by September. Jewish musicians were excluded from all orchestras funded by the government and Jewish medics were only allowed to tend Jewish patients. At the end of May edicts banned Jews from public parks, race meetings, swimming pools, public baths, and from renting rooms in hostels, boarding houses and hotels.

Anne wrote two letters to Switzerland in January and March 1941, mainly about her passion for skating. Fragments of both have survived. The first, dated 13 January, reads:

> *Dear All,*
>   *I got Bernd's letter today, I think it's really nice that he's written to us, so many thanks once again. Every spare minute I am at the ice-rink. Until now I always wore my old skates, which used to belong to Margot. The skates had to be fixed on with a key and at the ice-rink all my friends had figure-skates which had to be fixed on to your shoes properly so you couldn't get them off. I really wanted skates like these and after a long wait, now I've got them.*

I'm now taking regular lessons at the ice-rink and I do waltzing, jumping, in fact everything to do with ice-skating. Hanneli has now got my other skates and she's really happy with them, so now we're both content. Hanneli's sister is really nice, sometimes I pick her up in my arms and she laughs at me . . .[31]

The second letter is dated 22 March:

Dear Omi and dear All,

    Many thanks for the nice photo, you can certainly tell that Bernd is very funny.[32] *I have hung the photo over my bed. Mr Wronker has gone, so we've got the large room to ourselves now, which we think is terrific, and we also have a bit more space. Today Mummy and I went into town to buy a coat for me. On Saturday I was at the office with Daddy and I worked there from nine until three, then we went into town together and finally went home.*

    I know that I could start again with the skating, but I need a lot of patience. After the war, if Daddy can still pay for it then, I'll get lessons at the ice-rink. If I can skate really well, Daddy has promised me a trip to Switzerland to see you all.

    At school, we have a lot of homework. Mrs Kuperus is very nice, and so is Hanneli. Margot was on her own looking after the baby, and on Sunday I am going along with Mrs Goslar and the baby. Sanne is rarely with us, she has her own friends now. Barbara Ledermann comes tomorrow . . .[33]

While Anne contemplated her skating career, her father was preoccupied with devising a plan to prevent Pectacon falling into Nazi hands. With the decree of 12 March in mind, Otto made an application for German approval concerning changes to the business he said had been made at a board meeting on 13 February 1941, and which had resulted in Pectacon being transferred to complete Aryan control. At the imaginary meeting, the remaining 8,000 guilders-worth of shares were allotted to Kleiman and A. R. W. M. Dunselman, the city lawyer who had been appointed supervisory director of Opekta in 1935. Otto thus resigned from the board, leaving Kleiman to step into his place and Dunselman to take over from Kleiman as supervisory director of Pectacon. These moves would have meant that the business had been 'dejudified'. On 8 May, with Jan Gies's co-operation, Pectacon became Gies & Co. In reality, these changes were only on paper and business continued as it always had, with Otto at the head of the company.

Unfortunately, the Nazis saw through his smokescreen immediately, as a German report to the Bureau of Economic Investigation reveals: 'These measures were intended to create the impression that most of the capital as well as the directorship of the business were in Aryan hands. Because the decisions taken at the annual general meeting on February 13, 1941 . . . have no legal validity, the General Commissioner for Finance and Economic Affairs, Division for Economic Investigation, has, on September 12, appointed *mr.* Karl Wolters as trustee of the company under VO 48/41 and has charged him with its liquidation.'[34] Wolters, an Amsterdam attorney, advocate and Dutch Nazi Party member was, despite his political allegiances, less unreasonable than most with the Jewish businessmen placed in his charge. He gave Otto and Kleiman eight to ten days in which to wind up Pectacon. With the assistance of a broker, they were able to transfer everything – all the machinery and stock – to Gies & Co., and Otto held on to his shares.

On 12 June 1941 Anne had her twelfth birthday. She wrote to her grandmother in Switzerland at the end of the month, explaining why she had been unable to reply sooner:

Dear Omi and everybody else,

Thank you all for the lovely birthday letter. I read it on the 20th because my birthday was postponed due to Oma[35] being in hospital. I have a lot of money from Oma, f2.50, an atlas from Daddy, a bicycle from Mummy, a new school-bag, an outfit for the beach and other things too. Margot gave me this writing-paper because I had run out, and sweets and other little presents, so I didn't do too badly.

It's very warm here. You too?

I liked the little poem Stephan wrote very much. I have one from Daddy as well – I always get one from him. Soon we'll have the holidays. I'm going with Sanne Ledermann (Omi might know her) to a children's camp, which makes it not so lonely. Yesterday (Sunday)

I was out with Sanne, Hanneli and a boy. I can't complain of a lack of boyfriends.

We don't have much chance to get tanned any more because we can't go to the swimming-pool.[36] *It's a pity, but that's how it is.*[37]

The letter ends there, but a few days later Anne sent a postcard to Switzerland from a tea-house, De Weide Blik, Oud Valkeveen: 'Dearest Omi, we went out today because the weather is lovely. This is such a nice postcard. We're thinking of you, Anne, Sanne and Hanneli.'[38] Otto added his signature to the card as well. Two more letters written by Anne that summer have survived. Both are from the 'summer camp' she mentions in her letter to her grandmother, and both are addressed to her father:

Monday evening.
Dear Papi,
Many thanks for the letter and the money, I can certainly use it. I spent a lot up until now, but not on nonsense. I needed stamps to write to everybody.
f0.25 for sweets
f0.05 for envelopes
f0.10 for more sweets
f0.30 for flowers for Aunt Eva
f1.80 for more stamps
f0.05 for a little notebook
f0.73 for postcards
Altogether that comes to f3.28.
Do you want to congratulate Mr Drehrer[39] *for me, I wrote him a postcard also. Today I lay the whole day in the garden and played ping-pong too, because I want to learn it now. Uncle Heinz and Aunt Eva*[40] *are playing very well. I'm reading a lot. I had read all but one of the books I borrowed from Sanne. I haven't had post from Mother since Saturday evening and it's now Monday evening. The weather here is very nice and it doesn't rain. Ray*[41] *is a little bit of a nuisance, but nice. Will you write to me as soon as possible? Many kisses from,*
Anne.[42]

My most beloved Hunny Kungha,[43] *by that I mean my Papi,*

   Thank you so much for the film-star cards. I got two more, but I didn't have those. I was very glad to get your letter, and I've eaten the sugar, jam and rice you sent. The rice really arrived at the right moment because I have an upset stomach and so I ate the rice immediately. Today I'm up for the first time after my illness, I'm recovered apart from a little headache and the stomach upset.

   This evening we ate baked fish and potatoes and salad. I couldn't eat the salad or the bread, but afterwards we had a lovely cherry pudding with sauce. I think pudding is marvellous, but only when it's with sauce. I'm sure Mother can do this too, for example with raspberry syrup.

   I was very happy with your letter. Couldn't you make your holiday one week later, and if that's not possible, couldn't you just visit me? I'd like it so much. You could come by train at half-past nine from Amsterdam and then you could maybe take a bus from the station to Beekbergen, then you can get out at the 'Sonnenhuis' and then you have to ask for the Koningweg 5, 'Op den Driest'. [Illegible sentence] . . . please bring butter-bread with you. They like that very much here. I do hope you'll do it, I'm longing so much for all of you. Write me immediately because on Sundays we don't get mail, lots of greetings and kisses,

   Your Anne.[44]

Otto, Edith and Margot joined Anne at the house 'Op den Driest' in July. When the four of them, and Sanne, returned to Amsterdam, they were delighted to hear that Miep and Jan were getting married. All the family were invited, but Anne's grandmother was seriously ill again, and Margot, too, had an illness of some sort. Edith decided to stay with them in case they needed her. Otto and Anne, though, were thrilled to be amongst the guests, who included Miep's family, Mrs Stoppelman (Miep and Jan's landlady), the van Pelses, Kleiman, Kugler and Bep. The wedding took place on 16 July 1941 in the Town Hall close to Dam Square. Miep wore a long, fashionable coat over a pretty printed dress with a hat, and Jan wore a light suit and hat. Anne wore a new, neat little suit and a matching cloche hat with a ribbon. Her hair had been cut and styled into a chin-length bob for the occasion and she looked every inch the chic young girl her friends so admired. The weather stayed fine and a street photographer took snaps of the wedding party. The following morning, Otto gave the couple a modest reception at the Prinsengracht offices. Anne and Bep prepared the food (provided by one of the reps) and offered it around. There were presents for the newly-weds too; the Franks and the office staff had bought them an expensive silver platter, which Anne presented with a flourish.

The couple visited the Franks at home shortly afterwards, and Miep noticed how the two girls were affected by the changes taking place: 'Since the occupation, Margot's poor health had been aggravated by anxieties. She was sick quite often, but she managed not to let anything interfere with her studies. Her sweet, quiet nature covered up her fears. Meanwhile, Anne was evolving into the most extroverted person in the family . . . she was very indignant about the injustices being heaped on the Jewish people . . . In addition to Anne's many interests, like the cinema, famous film-stars, and her best girlfriends, a new subject had got her attention – boys. Her talk now was spiced with chatter about particular young people of the opposite sex. It was as though the terrible events in the outside world were speeding up this little girl's development, as though Anne was suddenly in a hurry to know and experience everything. On the outside, Anne looked like a delicate, vivacious girl, but on the inside, a part of her was suddenly much older . . .'[45]

In July 1941 some schools in the Netherlands began dismissing Jewish pupils. In August Jewish-owned finances were placed under the supervision of bankers Lippmann, Rosenthal & Co. The bank was used by the Nazis as a dipping-well to fund new schemes, and when Jews began to go into hiding, the money used to pay their betrayers often came from the vaults of Lippmann, Rosenthal & Co. On 18 August all Jewish estates were liable for take-over, either by German authorities or by Dutch non-Jews. The Netherlands Union, established on 29 July 1940, now banned Jews from becoming members and dismissed those who already were. The Germans set up a Nazi-approved society for non-Jewish creative arts in an attempt to crush resistance. Anyone not joining the 'Kultuurkamer' was forbidden by law to continue working.

On 29 August a decree dismissed Jewish children from schools attended by non-Jews. This was the first decree to have a significant impact on the lives of Jewish children in the Netherlands. Special Girls' High Schools and Boys' High Schools were established in Amsterdam and The Hague. Jewish pupils in the provinces were dismissed from technical colleges and sent to German labour camps. The move 'took the separation of Dutch Jews from the rest of the Dutch public one vast step forward'.[46]

On 15 September a mass of new 'forbidden to Jews' laws came into effect, banning them from places of entertainment and sporting activity. On 22 October a decree was issued whereby Jews in employment had to apply for special permits to continue in their jobs. Jews with short-term contracts could be fired at will by their employers (and would be subject to dismissal from 31 January 1942). In November German Jews in all occupied territories were stripped of their nationality. Those living in the Netherlands were ordered to report to the Zentralstelle and told to compile a list of everything they owned, all of which would be liable to Germany. On 5 December all Jews of other than Dutch nationality were again ordered to report to the Zentralstelle, this time for 'voluntary emigration'.[47]

At the end of 1941 the Germans drew up a balance sheet for the first full year of the occupation of the Netherlands. It concluded, 'Survivors of 900 Jews deported to Mauthausen: 8'.[48] In a letter to Arthur Seyss-Inquart, Bohmcker, the German delegate in Amsterdam, confided, '. . . all Dutch Jews are now in the bag . . .'[49]

For Anne and Margot Frank, the second half of 1941 was devastating, as they were turned away from the schools they loved. Anne and Lies Goslar were by no means the only Jewish children in their form; there were twenty, and eighty-seven in the school as a whole. They were called in to a special assembly and told that they would not be returning in the new school year. Anne wept when she said goodbye to Mrs Kuperus, who was devastated to see the children leave: 'There were then more Jewish children in Montessori schools than in normal primary schools. The Montessori educational system at that time was seen as "modern" and evidently there are many Jews who have a modern attitude. And the Franks were broad-minded in that respect . . . For a while we saw [Anne] again quite often. But then they were suddenly all wearing the yellow stars, and then we no longer saw them at all . . .'[50]

When the decree was announced, Eva's mother, Fritzi Geiringer, called on the Franks to ask them whether they would like their daughters to join Eva in a small private class with a teacher who had lost his job through the Nazis. Edith and Otto said no, preferring their children to attend 'normal' school instead. In his memoir, Otto recalled how, with the new law, it was very difficult for Anne and Margot 'to keep up their friendships with non-Jewish children, particularly now that it was also forbidden for Christians to visit Jewish families and vice versa . . . When I think back to the time when a lot of laws were introduced in Holland, which made our lives a lot harder, I have to say that my wife and I did everything we could to stop the children noticing the trouble we would go to, to make sure this was still a trouble-free time for them. It was soon over . . .'[51]

Anne and Margot were transferred to the Jewish Lyceum, opposite the much smaller existing Jewish High School, on the Stadstimmertuinen. The Lyceum was in a three-storey building with converted rooms under the roof. There was a long concrete playground in front and one at the back, and an archway under the adjoining houses led through to the Amstel River. Laureen Klein remembers seeing Anne at the tram-stop every morning now that they had changed schools: 'We lived two stops beyond the Franks. Anne and her entourage would get on the street car and I would think, "Isn't she lively?" She definitely was the centre of the circle. Talk, talk, talk.'[52] Anne went into the first form of the Lyceum with Lies Goslar, and Margot went into the fourth with her best friend, Jetteke Frijda.

Anne found a new best friend at the Lyceum, Jacqueline van Maarsen, who lived with her parents and older sister Christiane at 4 Hunzestraat, in the River Quarter. Jacque's father traded in old books and prints, and was Jewish by birth, which meant that the family had to bow to the anti-Semitic decrees. Her mother, a French Catholic who had converted to Judaism, was manager of the Hirsch department store on the Leidseplein. Jacque was born in Amsterdam in January 1929. The family moved to the River Quarter in 1940. According to Jacque, they were not particularly religious: 'We only really went to synagogue for something special. And the Jewish Lyceum wasn't observant as such – I think I went to school on Saturday, for instance. I'm sure there were boys and girls who were religious and so didn't go, but it wasn't enforced.'[53]

Jacque met Anne after their first day at the Lyceum. She was cycling home when someone called out to her, and she turned to see Anne, 'a small wisp of a girl with shiny black hair and sharp facial features', waving at her.[54] Anne pedalled up on her bike and said brightly, 'We can bicycle home together from now on. I live at Merwedeplein.'[55] On the way back she chatted endlessly, telling Jacque all about her friends at her old school. Jacque was more reserved than Anne, and it was Anne's 'assertiveness and the way in which she had initiated our friendship',[56] along with her honesty, that formed the foundation of their relationship. She went home with Anne that day and immediately felt very relaxed with the Frank family, who invited her to stay for dinner. The two girls shared similar interests and liked to read the same books. Jacque remembers, 'We were especially fond of Cissy van Marxveldt and I had a signed copy of one of her books. I think Anne and I had been reading this copy together. Anne bought her other books too and she gave me a book in another series by van Marxveldt. It's a pity that Anne didn't sign it.'[57] More unusually, they were both fascinated by mythology. Jacque's father had bought her *The Myths of Greece and Rome* and she showed it to Anne, who instantly wanted a copy too.

At Anne's house they would often play Monopoly together in the living room, though Jacque has a lasting memory of 'the kitchen where Anne always stood making sandwiches after school at four o'clock and where she fed her cat, Moortje . . . We did our homework, too, in the sitting room of her home.'[58] Anne was no longer having difficulty in concentrating at school; Jacque recalls that whenever they did their homework, 'the diligent Anne excelled'.[59] They swapped film-star photographs which they kept in decorative boxes, along with their postcard collections. Jacque remembers that her postcard collection was better than Anne's, but Anne had a larger collection of film-stars. Shirley Temple was one of Jacque's idols, along with the singing sensation Deanna Durbin. Anne's house became a mini local cinema where she and Jacque organized shows, with Otto manning the projector and Edith providing refreshments. They sent out tickets to friends which read, '— is invited on — with Anne

Frank at Merwedeplein, 37, at 11 o'clock to see a movie. Without this card, no entrance. Please inform in time. Row –, Seat –.'⁶⁰ Jacque explains, 'Together we made little cards to get in – of course, everyone *could* come in – but we wanted to make it real, by having real tickets.'⁶¹

They spent hours on the balcony of the Franks' apartment when the weather was fine, telling each other secrets and gossiping about mutual friends. The spot was a favourite of both Anne and Margot, and there are several photographs of them sitting in deck-chairs on the gravel terrace, books and sun-hats nearby. Jacque remembers how they discussed, as all young girls do, 'sexual behaviour. [Anne] wanted to know what it was all about and I knew much more than she did because my sister told me everything and I just thought, well, I'm not going to tell you, ask your father! . . . At the time, Anne's body was not changing yet, and I think she was curious because she . . . used a bra from Margot with some cotton wool in it, to show a bit of breast and I didn't need that kind of thing.'⁶² Anne was intensely curious about the changes taking place in her body, and later wrote in her diary, 'I remember one night when I slept with Jacque I could not contain myself, I was so curious to see her body, which she always kept hidden from me and which I had never seen. I asked Jacque whether as a proof of our friendship we might feel one another's breasts. Jacque refused. I also had a terrible desire to kiss Jacque and that I did.'⁶³ Jacque was embarrassed about the incident when the diary was published, remembering, '[Anne] didn't like the fact that I wouldn't go along with her proposal, but when I let her give me a kiss on the cheek she was satisfied again'.⁶⁴

When Anne made any discoveries about sex, she took mischievous delight in passing on her new knowledge to others, basking in her advantage over one young boy in particular. Jacque explains: 'This gave her the feeling of being grown-up, which was very important to her.'⁶⁵ Anne's perfectly natural curiosity about her sexuality seems to have troubled her mother who, when Anne tried to broach the subject, replied, 'Anne, let me give you some good advice; never speak about such things to boys and don't reply if they begin about it.'⁶⁶ In her diary, Anne reflected, 'When I had just turned 11, they told me about having a period, but how it really came about or what it meant I didn't find out until much later. When I was 12½ I heard some more, because Jacque was not nearly as stupid as I was. I had sensed myself what a man and a woman do when they are together; at first I thought the whole idea completely crazy, but when Jacque confirmed it for me I was quite proud of my intuition! That it wasn't the stomach that babies came from is something else I learned from Jacque, who said simply: "The finished product comes out where it went in!"'[67] Anne had to be content with what she learned from Jacque and from Otto, who was less inhibited over such matters and understood his daughter's preoccupation with the manifestations of adolescence. He was quite aware of Anne's interest in the opposite sex, which he thought tied in with the move to the Jewish Lyceum: 'This was a big change . . . Through Margot, Anne got to know pupils in the higher classes of the new school. Soon boys started to notice her. She was rather attractive and knew how to use her charms . . . Anne was lively, impulsive and rather vain . . . She wanted to look well, wanted to know, and wanted to do.'[68]

Although Anne sometimes complained about her mother and sister, Jacque thought they were 'always very sweet to Anne and patient with her . . . Margot was very nice to Anne always. She really was the "big sister". I suppose I looked up to her, like my own sister. Margot was very clever, but I don't think I really noticed that then. I never saw any rivalry between them. Margot was always very nice to Anne, and Anne wasn't always nice, but she was never unpleasant with Margot.'[69] Anne never complained about her father, but then the two of them were similar. Jacque remembers: 'Otto was an extrovert, just like his daughter Anne . . . She always had to have someone around to talk to or play with or else she became bored.'[70] Anne had not yet learned to enjoy her own company; that would not come until her confinement in the annexe.

Jacque's mother was very fond of Anne and spoke at length about her to the writer Ernst Schnabel: 'Anne was a little monkey! Very intelligent, very much the girl. She was a great personality. She had grey-green eyes. Like a cat. Only cats have veiled eyes, and Anne's were very candid. That is the difference. She could see things – and how! She saw everything exactly as it was, and sometimes she would make a remark – sharp as a needle. Only it did not hurt, because she always hit exactly to the point . . . My husband was electrified every time she came in at the door – and yet he had two daughters of his own. But the difference was that Anne

78

knew who she was. Our girls didn't. Not even Jacque. The two of them were such good friends . . . But Anne had charm and self-assurance, while Jacque was timid and shy. The plotting and whispering that was always going on between the two of them, and the telephoning all day long, though the Franks lived not three doors away from us . . . And if Anne spent the weekend with Lies – what jealousy! Indescribable. But if she did not go over to see Lies, she came to us, or Jacque went over to the Franks.'[71] Jacque remembers that whenever Anne came to stay with them, she would bring a suitcase and a 'cosmetic case with her curlers, hairbrush and cape'.[72] Jacque's mother confirmed this: 'The suitcase was empty of course, but Anne insisted on it, because only with a suitcase did she feel as if she were really travelling . . . One Sunday, we were just about to sit down to the table, Anne suddenly said good-bye. I said, "Why, Anne, we're going to eat now." But she said no, she had to go home because she had to give Moortje his bath. And I said, "Why, Anne, you're crazy, a cat isn't supposed to be bathed." But Anne said haughtily, "Why not? I've often bathed him and he's never said anything about it!" And she took her suitcase and left.'[73]

Shortly after Jacque and Anne first met, Otto took his daughter out of school to accompany him on a short trip to Arnhem. He sent a postcard to his mother from there on 14 September:

> *Dearest mother, Anne and I have travelled here for a couple of days, the others stopped in Amsterdam. We're not staying long, I just wanted to have a bit more peace and quiet, but didn't want to go off completely on my own. Anne is always good, dear company and she was able to have a few days off school. Everything is well. All our love to everyone, Yours, Otto.*[74]

The front of the card showed their hotel, the Groot Warnsborn, and across it Anne wrote happily, 'We're staying here! In the middle of the forest! Isn't it wonderful?'[75]

When they returned, Anne and the three Klein sisters began to rehearse a play for Hanukkah called 'The Princess with the Long Nose'. The play was eventually performed in the sitting room of the Kleins' home, and although Laureen can no longer remember for certain which role Anne took, she knows that both the actors and the audience thought it was 'great fun'.[76] She observed Anne: 'She was thin, kind of scraggly in that stage. A kid right before puberty. I never thought Anne would settle down . . . she had a kind of charisma, that was clear, but that this would express itself in a diary that would be world-famous, I had no idea.'[77] Laureen, like everyone else, thought Margot was the more promising of the two sisters. Margot had developed a keen interest in classical literature and attended after-school classes given by Anneliese Schutz, who had worked as a journalist in Berlin before emigrating to the Netherlands.

While his daughters still enjoyed the little freedom they had left, Otto was growing increasingly worried about the future of his businesses. In October he received a letter from the head of the Rohstoff Verkehrs A. G. (Rovag) company in Basel informing him that the money Erich Elias had lent him on the company's behalf was now under their control. He asked Otto to confirm the agreement and explain why the licence fee hadn't been paid for so long. Otto replied immediately, explaining that 5,000 guilders of the original debt had been repaid, and the outstanding amount was in the hands of Dunselman. On 12 December, at a meeting of Opekta's shareholders (during which only Otto and Dunselman were present), Dunselman announced that the distribution of Opekta's share capital had to be looked into again. He also said he had spoken to two Pomosin-Werke officials who were in the process of trying to 'Aryanize' Opekta; they were awaiting the approval of the Bureau of Economic Investigation, which they were sure would be granted. The men had made it clear that Pomosin, through the Rovag loan, were the true owners of the Opekta shares, and had suggested to the BEI that Otto's shares should be deposited with a bank dealing with Jewish businesses undergoing Aryanization. Otto informed Dunselman that he was resigning from his position as a company director of Opekta. They both agreed that Kleiman should take over the appointment. These changes were reported to the Amsterdam Chamber of Commerce.

In January 1942 personal matters took precedence in the Franks' household: Edith's mother died, having lost her struggle against cancer. Anne and Margot were devastated by Rosa Hollander's death, and Anne later wrote in her diary, 'No one will ever know how much she is in <u>my</u> thoughts and how much I love her still.'[78] She missed her grandmother's support; Rosa had been able to keep the difficult relationship between Edith and Anne on a relatively even keel. Margot's friend Hilde Jacobsthal was aware of the friction between the two: 'Anne's mother comes off badly in the book [Anne's diary]. Anne paints a picture of a stern, distant, non-understanding mother, whereas the father was very close to Anne . . . actually the woman was a rather saintly, virtuous, handsome woman, very reserved. The conflicts . . . are so utterly understandable and touching, because with this good sister, Margot, it was obvious that the little one would cause turbulence in the family, especially with the mother.'[79]

At the Jewish youth club where Hilde, Margot and Peter van Pels were members, discussions often focused on the measures being imposed upon them in the Netherlands. Hilde remembers the debates well: 'We all had great struggles of faith. Each time we met, we would count heads to see who was there. I felt I had lost my faith because of what was happening. We had the most violent discussions about God and Judaism, whether we should take pride in being a Jew or whether it was a curse to be a Jew. Margot was the serene one. I was the fiery one . . . I remember riding our bicycles home on those Sunday mornings, feeling so with it and alive and thinking there has *got* to be a future for all of us.'[80]

'When we walked together across our little square a few days ago, Daddy began to talk of us going into hiding, he is very worried that it will be very difficult for us to live completely cut off from the world. I asked him why on earth he was beginning to talk of that already . . .'

Anne Frank, *Diary*, 1 July 1942

In the summer of 1941 Heinrich Himmler announced, 'The Führer has given the order for a final solution to the Jewish question, and we, the SS, must carry out that order.'[1] The 'Madagascar Plan', whereby the Nazis contemplated sending four million Jews to an African island to work as slaves under German supervision, had been abandoned as too fantastical. Construction of the Nazi concentration camps – the 'final solution' – had begun in spring 1933 with Dachau, Sachsenhausen and Esterwegen. The most notorious lay close to the small Polish manufacturing village of Oswecim, where the Sola and Vistula rivers entwine in marshy, barren acres of land. The Germans called it Auschwitz. They selected it for its easy rail access; Auschwitz was a main junction taking people to and from all the European capitals. It was isolated and, so the Germans thought, offered great 'physical possibilities'.[2] Thirty convicted German criminals were sent from Sachsenhausen camp to Auschwitz on 30 May 1941 to serve as *kapos* (head prisoners, who acted as guards). Together with 300 Jews from Oswecim town, on 1 June they began to prepare the site. Rudolf Höess, a devout Roman Catholic, became Commandant of Auschwitz on 29 April 1941 and remained there until 1943.

Auschwitz was originally intended as a punishment barracks for Polish political prisoners, but in summer 1941 Karl Eichmann visited the camp to talk to Höess about killing techniques. Amongst those discussed were 'killing with showers of carbon monoxide while bathing' and 'killing people with exhaust gases in trucks'.[3] Experiments had been conducted to find the simplest, most cost-effective method of slaughter; one of the earliest was the 'Euthanasia' project. Special sites were built for the murder of mentally ill, mentally handicapped and physically handicapped people. Some 5,000 children were killed in the scheme. On 3 September 1941 900 Russian prisoners of war and 300 Jews were taken to the cellar of Block 11 in Auschwitz I and gassed using Zyklon B, the trade name of a chemical sold mainly by Tesch & Stabenow, a German company, for pest control. Tiny green-blue crystals emitted a deadly gas upon contact with air. In a further experiment with Zyklon B that year, over 300 Jews were killed in a cottage in the woods near Auschwitz. Their bodies were thrown into shallow graves in a nearby meadow.

At the Wannsee Conference in January 1942, all agencies involved in the Final Solution were given explicit instructions for the co-ordination of the plan. The SS were given control of the entire operation and Eichmann, as head of Section IV B4 in Berlin, gave the directions.

In March 1942 the instructions for enlarging Auschwitz I, Main Camp, were issued. The construction of Birkenau, Auschwitz's killing terminal, started in September. 'Birkenau' is German for birch wood, which is where the terminal was situated, across the railway line from Auschwitz I. It was divided into sub-camps: BI, the women's camp; BII, the men's camp; BIIF, the medical huts; BIIE, the gypsy camp; BIIB, the Czech camp; and later BIII, 'Mexico', begun in summer 1944 and never finished. In addition there were the quarantine camp, a sauna bath-house, 'Kanada' (where prisoners' belongings were collected and dispatched), gas chambers and adjacent undressing rooms, crematoriums, filter plants, where bone mashed to powder was filtered for fertilizer, and immense pits under the shadow of the birches where bodies were burned. Electrified fencing encircled the complex, punctuated by towers where armed guards kept watch. Later came Auschwitz III, the surrounding sub-camps and factories dealing in everything from coal mining to agriculture. Within three years, Auschwitz covered 25 square miles of barracks, factories and killing compounds.

Most 'work-camps' had their own gas chambers by the end of 1942. On the pretext of disinfection or showering, groups of twenty or thirty would be led into the chambers. As the war progressed, more and more were forced in at once, so that people were as likely to die from suffocation as from the effects of the gas. Usually, Jews were sent to the camps under the pretence of having to 'resettle' for 'work in the East'.[4] But in the Warsaw ghetto, where starvation was rife, Jewish families were lured to the death camp of Treblinka with the promise of something as simple as bread and marmalade.

On 20 January 1942 the Frank family applied to the Zentralstelle for a passage to England. The van Pelses had applied for emigration to America in 1939 (Hermann's sisters, Ida and Meta, had escaped to America, and his brother Max was living in Chile). In reply to their requests, both families received long-winded letters from the Zentralstelle that concluded: 'application postponed indefinitely'.[5]

Edith's only contact with her brothers Walter and Julius, who were also living in America, was via her mother-in-law in Switzerland. Alice tried to sound encouraging about the delayed post in a birthday letter to her: 'Hopefully Julius will answer soon so that you get news . . . we're thinking of you with all our hearts . . . I expect your loved ones will make your day as nice as possible . . . If only I could appear on Friday to congratulate you personally and bring a little gift to you . . .' She added that she was looking forward to receiving a photograph of her eldest grand-daughter: 'We are still awaiting Margot's picture. You can imagine how amazed I will be about our big girl.'[6] When the promised photograph arrived, Alice wrote again: 'What great pleasure you gave me with the lovely picture of our big girl. Even if you don't think it's very good, I can see so much love and seriousness in the little photo. I always carry both pictures with me . . . I'm very pleased that little Anne is growing so fast and has a good appetite, but I'm astonished by it, because she never wanted to eat much before. Stephan has an unbelievable appetite, but he's very thin and not looking well, while Berndt momentarily is very handsome, ruddy cheeks, and has great fun on the skating rink. With us, too, the telephone is always busy with girls ringing up. These things never change! Unfortunately, in my youth, the telephone didn't exist.'[7] In April, worried about rationing, Alice sent her son and daughter-in-law a food parcel containing 'one pound of coffee, one of chocolate powder, two cans of sardines . . . I imagine you can use all of it.' She must have heard from Julius Hollander for she writes, 'I received Edith's card from

31 March. I wrote the content of it to Julius, who's longing for news . . . I write him as often as possible, and hope for an answer, but you have to be very patient.'[8]

Like many Jewish families living in occupied territory, the Franks had to contend with unsettling anonymous telephone calls. Sometimes the calls were to the good – through them, Otto successfully avoided several local razzias by staying overnight with friends elsewhere – but it was a known fact that Nazi informants were working in the most unlikely situations. Otto once met a man whose wife worked as an Opekta representative; in reply to the man's confident declaration that the war would be over soon, he replied, 'Do you really think so?' Otto thought no more of it until a week later, when a stranger appeared in his office and gave him a report compiled by the man, which stated that Otto Frank had doubted the German victory and had tried to influence him against the Nazi government. The stranger told Otto he worked as a courier between Dutch Nazis and the Gestapo. He had taken the paper from the file of incoming reports and wanted 20 guilders for it. Otto gave him the money and he left, saying, 'You can keep [the report]. If I was you, I'd tear it up.' After the war, Otto traced his mysterious messenger: 'He was in prison as a political criminal. I went to the commission and said, "That man once saved my life." But they showed me the documents on him and I saw that I was the only person he had saved. He had betrayed a great many others . . . The man did not know me. And if he had come on account of the twenty guilders – he could have extorted far more than that from me. I cannot understand him, but he saved me.'[9]

In April 1942 the Franks and the van Pelses celebrated Passover together. Auguste van Pels's cousin Hermann was invited to the Seder meal at the Franks' apartment. 'It was the last Seder evening I spent with a family,' he remembered. 'I can still see the rooms, the very cultured mother, the charming father, the two sisters. The entire household exuded old Jewish culture. I will never forget Anne's face. The huge, dark, expressive eyes were the most striking thing about her. Obviously none of us had any idea of the genius for writing which was latent in that intelligent and charming child. As the youngest at table, I can still hear her speaking the "Manischtano".'[10]

After the celebrations, Otto's attentions turned to his business again.

Karl Wolters finished his dealings with Pectacon that month, concluding that liquid assets of the business amounted to 17,000 guilders. From this, Kleiman received 5,000 guilders and Dunselman 3,000 guilders in respect of their shares. These were secretly returned to Otto by Kleiman and Dunselman. Of the remaining 9,000 guilders, when charges for liquidation procedures were subtracted, 7,712.83 guilders were left; on 11 May 1943 these were transferred into the Nederlandse Bank, where they remained until 1947. Pectacon continued to function under the Gies & Co. moniker during the war.

Strong friendships had grown up amongst the permanent staff at 263 Prinsengracht. Otto Frank, Johannes Kleiman, Victor Kugler, Hermann van Pels, Miep Gies and Bep Voskuijl worked full-time in the office. Bep's father, Johan Voskuijl, was in charge of the warehouse. Otto allowed his friend, Arthur Lewinsohn, to conduct pharmaceutical experiments and make up ointments every week in the annexe. However, some time in the spring of 1942, Otto told him that the annexe was needed for storage. Lewinsohn moved his equipment out of the damp rear rooms and into the kitchen on the first floor.[11]

In a letter to Yad Vashem many years later, Otto explained, 'I soon realized that the time would come when we would have to go into hiding to escape the danger of deportation. After having discussed the matter thoroughly with Mr van Pels, we came to the conclusion that the best solution would be to hide in the annexe of our office-building. This would only be possible if Mr Kleiman and Mr Kugler would be willing to take full responsibility for everything connected with our hiding, and if the two secretaries of the firm would co-operate. All four immediately agreed though they were fully aware of the dangerous task they would take upon them in doing so. By Nazi law everyone helping Jews was severely punished and risked to be put into prison, to be deported or even shot. During the following months we prepared the hiding place . . . always one of the above named four persons attended to the matter . . .'[12]

After the war, Kugler spoke about his part in the hiding plan: 'To leave Holland was impossible. Only well-known persons could leave. By well-known, I mean they had to be friendly to the system – the German system . . . I didn't think about the dangers it would have for me. Thousands of Dutch people hid others. After the liberation I saw so many people that I knew were Jews who had been hidden by friends . . . Certainly we could have refused. But there was a family atmosphere within the building, and we knew that if we didn't hide them, it would be like committing them to death. So we had very little choice.'[13] Of the moment when Otto asked for her help, Miep has said, 'There is a look between two people once or twice in a lifetime that cannot be described by words. That look passed between us . . . I asked no further questions . . . I felt no curiosity. I had given my word.'[14] A few days after the pact had been made, Hermann van Pels asked Miep to accompany him to a butchers in nearby Rozengracht. She did so on several occasions before she realized that he was making sure that the butcher, who was a friend of his, would recognize and supply her with extra rations when the time came for the two families to go into hiding.

The annexe – that is, the rear attic and the two floors beneath it – was thoroughly cleaned out and made habitable by P. J. Genot, who worked for CIMEX, Kleiman's brother's company.[15] Because Jews were subject to checks when transporting household goods through the streets, items were removed from the homes of both families on the pretext of being cleaned or repaired, then deposited at Kleiman's house in Biesbosch-straat until it was safe to convey them to the annexe. Food (mostly dried and canned products), bedclothes, soap, towels and kitchen utensils were easy to move. Furniture and other large items were picked up in the CIMEX van and taken to the hiding place after office hours. The occupants of the houses opposite the annexe knew it belonged to the offices in front because Miep sometimes left the windows open to get a little air into the musty building. To ensure their suspicions were not aroused, preparatory work in the annexe was only ever done at the weekends and in the evenings and over a prolonged period. Visitors to the office, and Voskuijl's assistants, presented another danger. Blue paper was pasted over the windows of the front house facing the annexe, and opaque paper over the landing windows, under the pretence of blackout regulations. As 1942 wore on, the prospect of going into hiding began to look increasingly likely. A date was pencilled in for July that year.

Otto did not mention the plan to his children, wanting them to enjoy what little remained of their freedom. The fact that the Franks were German Jews who had emigrated from their homeland probably added to their harassment; as the historian Jacob Presser points out, 'It was not exactly a privilege to be a Dutch Jew in those days but it was still vastly better than being a German Jew, whom the Nazis considered natural guinea-pigs and whom they had already plagued in the Fatherland. Anxious for their families, often scattered over the face of the earth, subject to all sorts of humiliating regulations, hounded from pillar to post – one can only admire the way so many managed to carry on at all. To make matters worse, some – though by no means all – Dutch Jews kept their distance from them, much as the German Jews had formerly kept aloof from their Polish brethren. It is a sad fact, but one that is well documented, that many Dutch Jews mistrusted their German co-religionists and even hated them in a way that was almost anti-Semitic.'[16]

The Franks had always regarded themselves as German and still did, despite the Nazis stripping them of their nationality and labelling them 'stateless Jews'. Edith often reminisced to Miep Gies about her childhood in Aachen and life in Frankfurt, and many years after the war Otto spoke with pride about his service in the German Army. Anne, it would appear from her diary, did not suffer the divided loyalties of her parents. She rarely makes the distinction between 'Nazis' and 'Germans' and writes that she has 'no native country'.[17] Most telling of all, perhaps, is her entry for 9 October 1942, which she ends, 'Nice people the Germans and to think that I am really one of them too! But no, Hitler took away our nationality long ago, in fact Germans and Jews are the greatest enemies in the world.'[18]

Eva Schloss explains how a child's experience of the escalating anti-Jewish decrees was different from an adult's: 'It was not so much frightening as disruptive. Children take things more how they come. Things did startle us and frighten us, of course. My brother's friends, who were young men, were arrested. On a hot day, one boy took off his jacket and his star couldn't be seen. A Nazi informer noticed this and had him arrested. He was sent to a camp and never seen again. But we just went out and played. We did talk about it, but more, "Oh, we can't play, we have to be in early," that sort of thing. Not in a life-threatening way.'[19] In her diary, Anne writes, 'Jacque used to say to me: "You're scared to do anything because it may be forbidden."'[20] Jacque reflects, 'I can't remember saying that but I know I felt that way. We talked about the laws as they came in, but not very much. The worst thing was not knowing what was going to happen next. All the time, there were new regulations but you got used to them. But then there were the razzias. I didn't think anyone would be killed, I just thought they would be put to work. I found out that my cousin had died, but I thought it was because of the work they were made to do. I never thought they would kill my cousins! You had no idea, no experience to go on.'[21]

A minor blow came during Easter 1942, when Anne discovered her bicycle had been stolen. Since Jews were banned from using public transport, her only option was to walk everywhere, apart from using the ferry at the Jozef Israelskade, which was still available. Edith had stored her bicycle with some Christian friends and Margot needed hers for her own use. There was no possibility of purchasing another bicycle for Anne, who now had half-an-hour's walk to school each day. The evenings were no longer restful either, as Toosje, Anne's friend and neighbour, remembered: 'Planes were over Amsterdam every night. There was an alarm, and we all stood together under the archway of the wall, at the entrance to the house, we and the Franks and the other people from the house, and searchlights were passing across the sky, and the anti-aircraft guns boomed and flashed, and Anne was standing beside me . . . and we were all frightened. Anne was terribly frightened. But then there was also a man named Dr Beffie from the house next door. He always came over to join us during an alarm, and every time he had a piece of bread in his hand and would eat it. He chewed slowly, so very slowly, and Anne could not help staring at him, no matter how frightened she was. And once, just as the all-clear came, Anne said to me, "Good heavens, if I chewed so slowly I think I'd be hungry all my life!"'[22]

Anne gave her last months of freedom the title 'Do You Remember? Reminiscences of My Schooldays' in her book of short stories written in the confines of the annexe. She mused, 'That one year in the Lyceum was sheer bliss for me; the teachers, all they taught me, the jokes, the prestige, the romances, and the adoring boys.'[23] Even the most mundane events were elevated to the level of 'tremendous' occasions. A letter Anne wrote to her grandmother in 1942 reflects her love of school and the fullness of her young life:

Dear Omi,

I haven't written for so long, but we have so much homework, I never have any time just for me. At Easter we got our grades. In maths I had three points more, but for Dutch, German and French, I had three points less (altogether, of course). How are you? Today we have summer weather for the first time. On Tuesday the holidays will be over. It's going much too quickly.

This letter is addressed to Omi, but is for the whole family. The skating is over again, isn't it, Bernd? I haven't practised lately because the lessons take a long time.

The Lyceum is very nice. We are twelve girls and eighteen boys in the class. At the beginning we went around a lot with boys, but I've finished it and I'm glad because they're too pushy. I'm in the same class as Hanneli again. Her sister is so sweet and she's able to walk all alone now. Sanne isn't in our school, but I see her very often and she's crazy about Moortje, just like me. That's the name of our cat which we've had for six months. She's female and I hope soon for children because she meets a lot of men at the moment.

Everything is all right here. Daddy had some rheumatism in his back, but luckily it's gone now. You must write to me again, I really like to receive letters for myself. Soon we're going to have some photos of ourselves taken, and I think you're going to get one of them. I look very different because I've had my hair cut and I put curls in it, but you'll see it on the photos, if my curls haven't been blown out. Tonight Margot is going out, to a club at school, but she has to come back early, otherwise I'll be all alone.

I have to go now, 'bye to everyone. I hope you'll let me know soon how things are with you.

Anne.[24]

Otto noticed how his daughter was becoming even more gregarious as she grew up: 'She was always on the go, and always brought a whole community of children with her wherever she was. People loved her because she always had ideas, what to play, where to play, some new things to do . . . Anne had one quality that was a bit annoying. She was constantly asking questions, not only when we were alone, but also in the presence of others. When we had visitors, it was very difficult to get rid of her, because everyone and everything was of interest to her.'[25]

On 7 January 1942 the Jewish Council discussed the proposed call-up of 1,402 unemployed Jewish men for work-camps in the eastern Netherlands. The council issued an appeal in *Het Joodsche Weekblad* to all those called up, urging them to comply 'in your own interests . . . what you will be asked to do is ordinary relief work in ordinary Dutch camps under ordinary Dutch instructors.'[26] On 10 January 905 Jews left for Westerbork. Two days later the Jewish Council was instructed to send out call-ups for 1,000 Jews, although no records have been found to show whether the order was met. On 17 January ninety-eight stateless persons were sent to Westerbork, and 270 Jews from Zaandam were taken to Amsterdam, having been instructed to leave behind almost all their belongings; these were appropriated by the German Commissariat for Non-Commercial Associations and Foundations. On 27 January thirteen families from Arnhem arrived under duress in Amsterdam. The city was fast becoming a net in which the Nazis could detain Jews whilst they plotted their next move. Two days later, 137 stateless people from Hilversum were sent to Westerbork, and 240 to Asterdorp, which had been specifically segregated from the rest of Amsterdam in order to house 'asocial elements'.[27]

On 5 March the Jewish Council was instructed to send out call-ups to 3,000 Jews. The council spurned this latest command and the matter passed into the hands of the District Labour Office, who ordered that 600 unemployed men were to be called-up, along with 2,400 others aged between eighteen and fifty-five. The council refused to call up teachers, doctors, technicians and clergymen, but conceded to the deportation of unmarried men between the ages of eighteen and forty. Of the 1,702 Jews named on the list, 863 were sent to the eastern Netherlands. From 20 March Jews were not allowed to drive cars. Three days later the Germans ordered a call-up of between 500 and 1,000 Jews. Since it had become known that married men were largely able to evade the transport lists, marriages amongst Jews had increased tenfold. The Jewish Council claimed it was a coincidence. Their attempts to outwit the Nazis, however, grew less earnest as time drew on. On 25 March a decree outlawed marriages and sexual relationships between Jews and non-Jews. On 8 April thirty Jews who had announced their impending marriages to non-Jews were arrested.

On 29 April, in the Netherlands, France and Belgium, the Jewish badge was enforced, 'a relic of medieval barbarity'.[28] Jews in Germany had been wearing the star since September 1941, and it had also already been introduced in Czechoslovakia. The Dutch decree stated, 'All Jews appearing in public must wear a Jewish star. The Jewish star shall be a black, six-pointed star on yellow material, the size of a palm, and bearing the inscription "Jood". The star shall be clearly visible and affixed to the outer clothing over the left breast; Jews are debarred from wearing orders, decorations and other insignia.'[29] Stars were available from distribution stations for four cents and a stamp from the cloth ration card. If a Jew didn't display his star, he faced imprisonment and a fine of 1,000 guilders. Prison authorities also had to hand out the star to Jewish inmates. Only children under six were exempt. A slogan was coined, 'Wear It with Pride, the Yellow Star!' Some Jews *were* proud of their star, but others were ashamed. When they were first issued, many non-Jews wore them in protest. The Gestapo threatened them with deportation if they carried on in defiance of the law. The decree that came the following day, barring Jews from marrying in town halls, passed almost without notice in the wake of the star.

Miep Gies remembers, 'Mr Frank bowed to necessity. He resigned from the firm when the time came; he wore the star; he said nothing. He never showed his feelings. I can still see him as he came into the office one day, in his raincoat, and when he unbuttoned the raincoat I saw the star on his chest underneath it. I don't think he had one on the coat. We made an effort to talk with him and act with him as we always had in the past and as though it were perfectly natural for him to come to the office now, for we knew that he dreaded pity. It was his way to come to terms with his feelings silently.'[30]

Eva Schloss reflects, 'People always say nowadays, why did you do this and why did you do that, but we were so scared. We thought, "If we do the things that are demanded of us, we'll be all right." You're told to have a "J" on your passport, you go and do it. Especially in a smaller community like Amsterdam where everybody knows who is Jewish and who comes from where. There were a lot of Nazis, and you didn't know who you could trust, who was a spy, who would give you away. We thought, "If we wear the star, if we have the curfew, if we *do* everything, nothing will happen to us." And we really believed that, especially because the Dutch people are very proud and stubborn and saw the Germans as their enemy. Dutch Jews were assimilated very much in Dutch life, they were always called "our Jews", and when the star was worn, a lot of Christians wore the star too, and there had been the strike, so we thought, "Nothing will happen to us because the population is *with us*." '[31] Uppermost was the conviction, common to many, that the war could not last long. 'Nobody dreamt it would take *so* long. Nobody knew how England was unprepared. We thought, "By Christmas, it will be finished." And when we went into hiding, we thought *that* would only be for a few months. If we had known it would take years, we might never have attempted to do anything.'[32]

Yet, in the midst of this nightmare, it was possible for Anne to write that 'life went on in spite of it all'.[33] In a letter to her grandmother in Switzerland, she wrote that her days were very lazy: 'We don't do much in the mornings at school . . . in the afternoons we sit in the garden catching flies and picking flowers.'[34] Although Lies was now 'best friends' with Ilse Wagner, whom she had met at the synagogue, and Anne was 'best friends' with Jacqueline van Maarsen, they were still very attached to each other, and sat together in the classroom. They were frequently in trouble for disrupting lessons with their incessant talking. Lies recalls, 'We copied each other's work, and I remember that we were once given extra work as a punishment for that. One day, a teacher grabbed Anne by the collar and put her in another class because he wanted to keep us apart. We had been talking too much. I don't know how it happened, but half an hour later there I was sitting next to her in the other class, and then the teachers just let us sit together.'[35] Anne's teachers set her essays as a punishment, but in one she shrewdly argued that chatting was a feminine characteristic, inherited from her mother and therefore she had no control over it, so it was pointless trying to stop her. In the end the teachers seemed to concede defeat and Anne talked as much as she always had.

Anne, Lies, Jacque, Sanne and Ilse ('a sweet and sensible girl'[36]) formed a table-tennis club called 'The Little Bear Minus 2'. Jacque recalls, 'We formed the ping-pong club because there was so little we were allowed to do, and also, children were not spoiled with choice like they are now.'[37] The odd name was the result of a misconception. They wanted to name the club after a constellation, and thought that the Little Bear had five stars (like their group). Later they discovered that it in fact had seven, hence the 'minus two'. Mini-tournaments were held in the dining room of Ilse's home with her ping-pong set. Afterwards, being 'very partial to an ice cream',[38] they would visit the Oasis ice-cream parlour on Geleen-straat or the Delphi tea-room on Daniel Willinkplein, both in the River Quarter. Jacque explains, 'We never sat inside Oasis. The Jewish boys and girls from the neighbourhood congregated there, but it was a social encounter played out on the pavement. One bought an ice-cream and went outside to eat it . . . We always ran into people we knew there. Anne loved walking behind boys and fantasizing that they were all her admirers.'[39]

In May 1942 Anne wrote to congratulate Buddy on his seventeenth birthday, and enquired about his romantic affairs:

> *Dear Bernd,*
>
> *Many happy returns on your birthday (birthday letters always start like this!) and many more to come. Hopefully you're all well, as we are. We've had five days' holiday for Whitsun, it was great and I've been busy every day. This evening I won't get home until 10, but I'm usually escorted home by a young man. How's it going with your girlfriend, the one you sent a picture of? Please write more about her, things like that always interest me. Margot also has a boyfriend, but he's even younger than mine. This letter hasn't turned out to be very long, but I haven't any time anyway because I'm going with Father to a film show. Best wishes to everyone. Write back to me,*
>
> *Anne.*[40]

Buddy remembers, 'That letter was the very last one she ever sent me.'[41] He also received congratulations from Edith, Otto and Margot. Otto's letter is full of wonder at the swift passing of time: '. . . we can hardly believe how grown-up you are now. We can see from our own children how the years have gone by and sometimes I even feel as though I'm a grandfather when I think of my own grown-up daughters . . .'[42] Margot muses on the past and the future in her letter: '. . . I said to Mummy yesterday how well I remember seeing you on Omi's birthday when we were ten years old. Hopefully we'll see each other before you're eighteen . . . I don't think it's so nice to have your birthday on a weekday because you have to go to school all day, and now, next year, we will both have finished school. But who knows what will happen then . . .'[43]

On 7 May 1,500 Jews received call-up notices. There were by then already 3,200 Jews in Dutch work-camps. Rumours about the Nazis' long-term plans for them continued to spread. Reports in the illegal press would soon appear about the gassings in Poland, and by the end of 1942 even the Dutch government in London knew that Auschwitz existed, and why. Still, the majority of people appeared to believe that the reports were alarmist hearsay. On 10 May *Het Parool*, one of the illegal newspapers, asserted, 'Even now, many of our people are undisturbed. They hear nothing, know nothing and would prefer to see nothing. They are blind to the criminal acts by which our Jewish compatriots are persecuted, by which a part of the Dutch population in our own, hitherto safe, country, is gradually being forced to live like hunted animals, without any protection from the law, fearing for their lives, without knowing what the morrow may hold for them and what new chicanery the satanic Hun will not think up.'[44] On 11 May the 'satanic Hun' asked the Jewish Council to supply another 3,000 men, and laid out new regulations concerning the star in the Netherlands. It had to be sewn instead of pinned to clothes and displayed in gardens, courtyards and at open doors at all times. On 21 May Jews had to register their bikes and could only purchase groceries at designated Jewish shops and markets.

On 2 June Jews in Hilversum were told they would be moved to Amsterdam from 15 June onward. On 12 June *Het Joodsche Weekblad* announced, 'Every form of outdoor sport, including rowing, canoeing, swimming, tennis, football, fishing etc., must be deemed prohibited to Jews.'[45] Throughout the month, laws were ushered in against Jews so quickly that no one could keep up with them. Jews could not visit or have visitors in their own homes between 6 p.m. and 8 p.m.; after 8 p.m. they were to remain indoors. Jews were permitted on certain trams and trains but had to remain standing on the front platform of trams and could only travel in the smoking carriages of the lowest-class compartments not in use by non-Jews. Jews were forbidden from using all other public transport except ferry boats, carrier bicycles, ambulances and wheelchairs. Jews could only shop in Aryan-owned shops between 3 p.m. and 5 p.m. (other than greengrocers, butchers and fishmongers, from which they were completely barred). Jews could not use public telephones. Rooms, gardens and accommodation belonging to non-Jews were forbidden to Jews, which meant Jews could no longer rent from non-Jews or visit non-Jewish friends. Jews could not receive home deliveries (laundry services excepted). Jews were barred from using the services of non-Jewish hairdressers and doctors. Jews were not allowed to use balconies or gardens opening on to the street, and could not lean out of open windows. Jews standing at open windows had to display the star.

At the end of June Eichmann informed all departments involved in the Final Solution that from the beginning of July 1942 – the very next month – the deportations to the extermination camps in the east would begin.

Friday 12 June was Anne's birthday, her thirteenth, the day on which she received the diary that would bring her a posthumous fame she could scarcely have imagined. She chose the diary – actually a red-and-white checked autograph album of the type local children had been keeping for years – from those on sale in Blankevoorts, one of her favourite shops. Blankevoorts was on the corner of Waalstraat and Zuider Amstellaan, and crammed from ceiling to floor with books and stationery in a pleasant dusty jumble. Her father bought the diary for her. Lies distinctly remembers the morning of Anne's birthday. When she arrived at the Franks' flat to collect Anne for school, she admired the diary briefly before Anne took it through to her bedroom, placing it with her movie-star box and collection of royal-family photographs. In the sitting room all of Anne's other presents were on display, including gifts from the Pfeffers ('a roll of acid drops . . . flowers'), and from Peter van Pels ('a bar of milk chocolate').[46] The room was filled with flowers for Anne's birthday, but Lies remembers the smell came not from them, or from the coffee-grinder as usual, but from the kitchen, where Edith was baking a strawberry tart. Otto was ensconced in his chair, and shared a joke with Lies as he always did. When it was time to leave, Edith handed Anne a basket of sweet biscuits to hand out at school, and Anne added some biscuits she had made. In the afternoon Lies, Jacque, Sanne and Ilse gave Anne their joint gift, a book called *Tales and Legends of the Netherlands*.

At some point on 12 June 1942 Anne wrote in her diary for the first time. She pasted in a school photograph of herself from winter 1941 with the caption, 'Gorgeous photograph isn't it!!!!' On the front endpaper she wrote: 'I hope that I shall be able to confide in you completely, as I have never been able to do in anyone before, and I hope that you will be a great support and comfort to me.'[47] There was enough space left over on the first page for her to add some other comments two months later, when she was in hiding. She wrote then, 'I am, Oh, so glad that I took you along,' and drew up a list of attributes that she believed made a woman beautiful. The list reads:

1. blue eyes, black hair. (no.)
2. dimples in cheeks (yes.)
3. dimple in chin (yes.)
4. widow's peak (no.)
5. white skin (yes.)
6. straight teeth (no.)
7. small mouth (no.)
8. curly eyelashes (no.)
9. straight nose (yes.) {at least so far.}
10. nice clothes (sometimes.) {not nearly enough in my opinion.}
11. nice fingernails (sometimes.)
12. intelligent (sometimes.)[48]

In this original version, as opposed to her own revised text and that of the published diary, the voice of a thirteen-year-old girl comes through as no more than that: a middle-class, indulged, popular, bright child whose main ambition was to buy a dog, name him Rin-Tin-Tin, and keep him with her at school or in the bicycle shed, where she reasoned he would be well looked after by the school caretaker. There are no hints of the future capacity for deft description, the skill for evoking sights and smells with an extraordinary economy of words, or for quick, clever characterization. She gave no reasons for beginning a diary and wrote only a brief family history (although she does write about the situation in the Netherlands in some depth). These came afterwards, when she was rewriting the diary with a view to publication. The original diary is that of an ordinary teenager living in exceptional circumstances, which she largely ignores, preferring to write about boys, school, friends, the ping-pong club, and her birthday party.

All Anne's friends were aware that she had been given a diary. Lies comments, 'I don't know if it was the first or second one that she had, because I remember that Anne was always writing in her diary, shielding it with her hand, even at school during the break. Everybody could see that she was writing. But no one was allowed to see what she had written. And I thought that she was writing entire books. I was always very curious to know what was in the diary, but she never showed it to anyone . . . I have thought that there must have been more than there was in the published diary. Maybe they never found all that she wrote before she went into hiding – she had already been writing for a couple of years . . . Anne already wrote very well then. If she had to do extra homework because she'd been talking again, she did it very well.'[49] Lies raises an interesting question about other diaries Anne may have kept. Unfortunately, if any did exist, they have not yet been found. Jacque echoes Lies's sentiments: 'We were very curious about it . . . We wanted to see what she had written about us.'[50] She also remembers Anne's distinctive method of writing: 'Anne always wrote with her pen between her index finger and her middle finger because she had sprained her thumb at some point. I had always admired her handwriting and tried to imitate it by holding my pen the same way.'[51]

Anne's party was held on the Sunday after her birthday and Jacque's strongest memory of the day is of Anne's happiness at being surrounded by her friends: 'With sparkling eyes she had watched her friends enter and opened her presents expectantly. She had enjoyed being the centre of attention . . .'[52] Lies remembers the gaggle of children in the apartment; Anne's parents handing out slices of strawberry tart on china plates; glasses of cool milk for everyone; Margot and Jetteke Frijda joining in with them all; the shades being pulled down as Otto set up the projector; and then *Rin-Tin-Tin and the Lighthouse Keeper* whirring into life on the blank wall. She also remembers having to leave the party early to help her mother with Gabi, and her feelings of jealousy when she saw Anne and Jacque whispering together. She thought of that moment in the months that followed and always told herself, 'If I'd known what was going to happen, I wouldn't have minded.'[53]

Schoolgirl squabbles were inevitable. In her diary on 19 June 1942 Anne recounts, 'Jacque has suddenly become very taken with Ilse and behaves very childishly and stupidly towards me, the more I know her the less I like her.'[54] Jacque remembers, 'Anne could be a difficult friend. I had to belong to her alone. She was jealous, whereas I didn't mind if she met other girls. But she could be sure of me, because I wasn't attached to anyone else. I only wanted to be free sometimes and she didn't like that much. There is another girl Anne writes about in the diary with whom I was friends. Anne didn't like her at all, and she was quite right because *I* didn't like her either! We had been together at the Montessori school and then we were at the Jewish school again, so I had known her a long time. This girl was also jealous of Anne, but I was too naive at that time to realize what was happening between the two of them, I couldn't see this fight myself. I read about it afterwards in Anne's diary, and then I understood. And when Anne writes, "This afternoon, Jacqueline went to Lies and I was bored stiff" – I remember that day very well. I was sitting with Lies on her bed. Lies wasn't happy with Anne because Anne kept teasing her and being a bit unkind, and I was . . . not exactly angry with Anne, but she always wanted to know everything about me and so on. I talked about this with Lies and I remember it vividly, because afterwards I felt so guilty. I told Anne about it but she didn't put it in her diary. I felt so guilty that we had been talking behind her back.'[55]

By the end of the month Jacque's behaviour was forgotten and Anne was preoccupied with a new boyfriend, Hello Silberberg. Hello was from Gelsenkirchen, where his father had owned a men's outfitters. After Kristallnacht in 1938 the family fled Germany. Hello was placed on a train bound for Amsterdam, where his grandfather had his own business. At the Dutch border, two SS guards ordered him off the train. He sneaked back on when their attention was diverted and arrived in Amsterdam safely, settling in with his grandparents in the River Quarter. Now, living in America, he remembers how he was forced to leave school after the invasion: 'I transferred to a private school and learned furniture design until that was also outlawed. But the director of the school was a very brave man who continued to take in Jewish pupils, teaching them from his own home.'[56] He was a handsome sixteen-year-old when his cousin introduced him to Anne: 'I don't remember the meeting with Anne clearly, but I know we chatted and that I searched her out the next day. I had another girlfriend then, whom my family much preferred to Anne, but that was because Ursula was the same age as me, whereas Anne was much younger.'[57] None the less, it was Anne to whom he was drawn. He reflects, 'The word that always springs to mind when I think about Anne is "articulate". She was *so* articulate for her age, definitely ahead of other girls in that respect. She was very attractive and she liked to laugh and to make people laugh. She was really very entertaining and extremely lively. She did little imitations of people that were very clever. In my memory I always see her sitting in a big club chair, with her hands under her chin and looking directly ahead at whomever she was with. It was a very flirtatious pose that she had, although I don't expect I recognized it as such then . . . I think I was probably in love with her. She seemed to think so too. I was in love with Anne within the context of that moment of being sixteen. We were both middle-class kids. We knew how to conduct ourselves.'[58]

When Hello met Anne's friends, he told her that they were very childish. She added in her diary, rather ungenerously, 'he is right.'[59] She also described taking him home to meet her parents. He muses, 'I don't remember that particular day, although Anne remarks that I brought her home late for the curfew, which probably was my fault because I had a tendency to ignore the curfew. It almost cost me my life on one occasion. I know I visited the Frank family several times. I can't remember her mother well, she was a quiet lady, but her father stood out. He was very talkative and friendly. Margot was about my age and she was very attractive. Her photographs don't do her justice. But it was Anne whom I liked. We had such good conversations, we really did enjoy each other's company. And when I read the diary much later, when I read about her trust in humanity – that didn't surprise me in the slightest because she was like that then. Very bright and optimistic, and the sort of person who always took things in her stride. She got on with things.'[60] Anne knew that her boyfriend's family disapproved of her, but when she questioned him about their future together, he declared winningly, 'Love finds a way.'[61]

At the end of the school year the children received their examination results. Anne noted with grudging admiration that Margot's report was 'brilliant as usual'.[62] Her own was better than she had expected, although she and Lies were told they would have to re-sit the maths exam in September. Lies recalls, 'Anne and I were barely promoted because we weren't so good in math. I remember that we went home together, and after that I didn't see her for a few days.'[63] In that time, Otto told Anne about the hiding plan. Margot already knew, and Anne confided in her diary her impassioned hope that 'the fulfillment of these sombre words remain far distant yet'.[64]

Although she had no way of knowing it then, Anne paid her last visit to Jacque and her family during the first week of July, when she arrived at the flat on the Hunzestraat to show off a new dress. Mrs van Maarsen remembered: 'It looked sweet on her and I told her so. And what do you think Anne said to that? "Why of course," she said, "after all, it's brand new." '[65] Mrs van Maarsen liked Anne very much and had wondered whether she could provide a safe environment for her: 'When it started I told myself: we'll just take Anne to live with us. But my husband was also a Jew, and under supervision, and Jacque also had to wear the star.'[66] Around this time, the young daughter of some friends called at the Franks' apartment. She had been summoned to Westerbork. Otto remembered: 'She told us that she had packed her sketchbook into her rucksack. She was very good at drawing, and she said she wanted to have a few mementos, for later . . .'[67]

Disregarding the curfew on Jews and Christians meeting socially, Victor Kugler and his wife attended a small dinner party the Franks gave shortly before they went into hiding. Having met Anne and Margot on many occasions, Kugler had come to the conclusion that 'Anne was not as intelligent as her sister, or at any rate not as mentally developed, but there was something strange about her, something almost wise.'[68] Anne's 'strangeness' was illustrated at dinner that evening. Kugler recalled, 'To keep my wife from being implicated, I had not told her of the secret annexe plans. But she was a sensitive person, like Anne Frank, and during the dinner a strange event occurred. There was a silence during the dinner and, apropos of nothing, Anne lifted her eyes to those of my wife, who returned her gaze. After a while, in the silence that still prevailed, Anne said, "I have just spoken with Mrs Kugler, and nobody has heard it." Whether this was simply a premonition they both had, or whether some more direct communication passed between them, I will never know, for both are now dead. That the others thought little of this strange statement of Anne's is perhaps more comment on her imaginative nature than I can make.'[69]

On 4 July Otto wrote to his family in Switzerland:

My dears,

We received mother's card dated 22 June. We love to hear every bit of news, especially if it's about you all being in good health. Everything is fine here too, although we all know that day by day, life is getting harder. Please don't be in any way concerned, even if you hear little from us. When I'm not at the office there's still a lot to do and a lot to think about, and one has to come to terms with decisions that are very difficult to take on board.

The children are on holiday now, but they work hard. Anne is trying very hard . . . We haven't forgotten you and know that you're thinking of us continually, but you can't change anything and you know you have to look after yourselves.

Yours,

Otto.[70]

The following day, Sunday 5 July 1942, began inauspiciously. Otto went across to the Joodse Invalide to visit some of the elderly patients there (Goldschmidt, a divorced man in his thirties who rented the Franks' large upstairs room, worked at the Joodse Invalide). The day was uncommonly warm. Hello called round to make arrangements with Anne for an outing later that afternoon. When he had gone, Anne stretched out in the sun on the balcony to read. At three o'clock the doorbell rang and there was a call from the street, 'Miss Margot Frank?' Edith went down and a policeman handed her a registered envelope. Inside was a card ordering Margot to report to the SS the next morning.

The Zentralstelle had sent out thousands of cards that day to German Jews in Amsterdam; 4,000 Jews were to be deported to German work-camps between 14 July and 17 July 1942. There was no indication on the card of what lay ahead: '. . . the clever way the document was phrased; it suggested that the conscripts would be put to work, and gave no hint of what the Germans had in store for them. And the poor victims were, of course, only too willing to swallow the yarn.'[71] Most were boys and girls aged fifteen and sixteen. Eva's brother Heinz and Margot's friend Susi Klein received cards. The envelopes also contained a list of clothing to be packed in a rucksack.

Edith left home immediately to suggest to the van Pelses that they bring the hiding plan forward. Margot told Anne that the SS had sent a call-up for their father; perhaps Edith had told her to say this. When Margot eventually told her the truth, Anne began to cry.

Now that the hammer-blow had fallen, the shock was immense. Neither girl spoke because 'the heat and suspense . . . made us very overawed and silent'.[72] Hello returned at the same time as Edith and Hermann van Pels. Edith told him Anne could not see him just then, and when Jacque telephoned a little later, she was given a similar message. Anne and Margot were sent to their room with instructions to start packing. Anne crammed her diary and old letters into a satchel; 'memories mean more to me than dresses.'[73] She still did not know where their hiding place would be.

Otto returned at five o'clock and when he was given the news, he called Kleiman. 'They telephoned me Sunday afternoon,' Kleiman remembered, 'and that evening I went out to their home on Merwedeplein. A postcard had come ordering Margot to report on Monday to the reception centre for the Westerbork camp. So we said to ourselves, now there is no point in waiting any longer.'[74] Otto did not even consider acquiescing to the call-up: 'We knew that they sent out these cards and many people had obeyed the order. It was said that life in the camps, even in the camps in Poland, was not so bad; that the work was hard but there was food enough, and the persecutions stopped, which was the main thing. I told a great many people what I suspected. I also told them what

I had heard on the British radio, but a good many still thought these were atrocity stories . . .'[75]

Van Pels visited Miep and Jan, who went straight over to the Franks' flat and began taking the family's belongings away to their own apartment for safekeeping until they were in the hiding place. Miep remembers, 'I could feel their urgency, an undercurrent of near panic. But I could see that much needed to be organized and prepared. It was all too terrible. Mrs Frank handed us piles of what felt like children's clothes and shoes. I was in such a state myself that I didn't look. I just took and took as much as I could, hiding the bunches of things the best way I could, under my coat, in my pockets, under Jan's coat, in his pockets.'[76]

Anne wrote of the evening, 'it was still hot and everything was very strange.'[77] Their lodger, Goldschmidt, decided to visit and they found it impossible to get rid of him without being rude. He stayed until ten o'clock and then at eleven Miep and Jan returned. Miep recalls, 'Everyone was making an effort to seem normal, not to run, not to raise voices. More things were handed to us. Mrs Frank bundled and sorted quickly, and gave to us as we again took and took. Her hair was escaping from her tight bun and into her eyes. Anne came in, bringing too many things; Mrs Frank told her to take them back. Anne's eyes were like saucers . . .'[78]

Some time that evening, probably when their friends had gone, Otto wrote to his family in Switzerland, implying as strongly as he dared that they were going into hiding:

> *Dearest Leni,*
>
> *Best wishes today on your birthday, we wanted to be sure that you received our thoughts for you on the right day, as later we'll have no opportunity. We wish you all the best from the bottom of our hearts. We are well and together, that's the main thing. Everything is difficult these days, but you just have to take some things with a pinch of salt. I hope we'll find peace this year already so that we can see each other again. It's a pity that we can no longer correspond with you, but that's how it is. You must understand. As always, I send you all my best wishes,*
>
> *Otto.*[79]

Edith, Margot and Anne added their own greetings. Anne's read, 'I cannot write a letter about the holidays now. Regards and kisses from Anne.'[80] It was half-past eleven when they went to bed. Anne was exhausted and fell asleep as soon as she sank under the sheets.

The weather had broken overnight and rain spattered on the windows as the family ate breakfast in the near darkness at 5.30 a.m. They each wore as much clothing as possible to lessen the amount they had to carry. Margot filled her satchel with schoolbooks and pulled out her bike[81] to wait for Miep, who arrived at 6.00 a.m. on her bicycle. Miep recounts, 'No sooner had I reached the front stoop than the door of the Franks' apartment opened and Margot emerged . . . Mr and Mrs Frank were inside, and Anne, wide-eyed in a night-gown, hung back inside the doorway . . .'[82] Miep and Margot rode off across Merwedeplein with subdued, hasty farewells. Anne was told to put on even more clothes and a headscarf. 'I was nearly stifled before we started, but no one inquired about that.'[83] They left a letter for Goldschmidt, asking him to take Anne's cat, Moortje, to their neighbours. The beds were stripped and the breakfast things left on the table to give the impression they had left under duress. At half-past seven they closed the door of their apartment and set off on foot, in the warm rain. The streets were still dark and cars sped by, their headlights blurred by the downpour. As they walked, Otto told Anne where their hiding place would be. The news that Miep, Bep, Kugler and Kleiman would be taking care of them must have come as a huge relief to her.

Miep and Margot were the first to arrive at the annexe. Fear was taking its toll on Margot. Miep remembers, 'We were soaked through to the skin. I could see that Margot was suddenly on the verge of crumbling . . . I gripped her arm to give her courage. Still we said nothing. She disappeared behind the door and I took my place in the front office. My heart, too, was thumping.'[84] When Otto, Edith and Anne reached the office building later that morning, drenched by the rain and tired by the long walk, they went straight upstairs to the annexe. Margot was waiting for them.

The annexe, decorated throughout with patterned yellow paper and dark paintwork, was in complete disarray, with boxes and sacks piled up everywhere. In Otto and Edith's room were two divans, two small tables, a smoker's table, a small set of bookshelves, a built-in cupboard and 150 cans of food. A window overlooked the scrubby courtyard below and the houses opposite. A door to the right led to Anne and Margot's room. It was about half the size of their parents' room, with a window, two divan beds and three built-in cupboards. Next door was a washroom with a new basin and a small compartment housing the lavatory. A doorway on the right led back into the passageway and to the entrance door.

The floor above would become the van Pelses' apartment. At the top of the stairs a door opened into a large room where double windows offered another view of the courtyard. A sink and cupboard ran along one wall, a sturdy gas stove poked out from the fireplace, and two beds and a table completed the furnishings. A door beside the kitchen worktops led into the damp box-room set aside for Peter van Pels. A small shuttered window faced the front house. The stairs to the attic were in the middle of the room, flanked by a bed and a cupboard.

The Westerkerk could be seen from the tiny, arched side window in the attic. A window above Peter's room faced the front house again, while a third overlooked the courtyard and a magnificent chestnut tree that dwarfed its surroundings.

Visiting the annexe later that day, Miep found Edith and Margot utterly immobile on their beds, but Otto and Anne were busy sorting out belongings and putting things in their place, trying to make as little noise as possible. Miep was distraught herself. 'The situation was so upsetting. I wanted to leave the family alone together. I couldn't begin to imagine what they must be feeling to have walked away from everything they owned in the world – their home, a lifetime of gathered possessions, Anne's little cat, Moortje. Keepsakes from the past. And friends.'[85]

Their neighbours on Merwedeplein already knew that they had gone. Otto had left out a deliberately misleading letter for their lodger to see, which hinted that they were in Switzerland. Anne's friend Toosje remembered, 'On Monday morning, I think it was the sixth . . . at noon, Mr Goldschmidt came to see us and said, "The Franks are gone." And he gave my mother a note he had found on the table in the house and they talked together, and I saw that he had Anne's cat in his arms. I took Moortje from him and he also gave me the plate of meat for the cat, which he had found on the table, and I went to the kitchen and fed Moortje.

After a while my mother came into the kitchen. She watched Moortje eating and said to me, "We'll keep him here." '[86]

Anne's boyfriend, Hello Silberberg, called for her. 'On the Sunday, when I arrived at the Franks' flat in the afternoon, I couldn't see Anne. Margot's call-up had arrived, though no one told me that then. I went home, knowing somehow that I wouldn't see Anne again. These things happened and it didn't come as any great shock to me. I was very disappointed, though. I can't remember now whether I also heard the story about them fleeing to Switzerland, but I was aware that they had family there, so if anyone had suggested it to me, I wouldn't have been surprised.'[87] Margot's friend Jetteke called at the apartment on Monday: 'I went to Margot's home to see what had happened, because I had heard nothing from her. I had already left school by then. We all tried to leave school much earlier because there was a possibility that if you had a job of some sort, you might be spared the call-up. I worked in a children's home. Other people had received these notices from the Germans. When I arrived at Margot's house, the door was open. I went inside and took a book of poetry from her shelves. I still have the book. I believe that someone told me that the family had gone to Switzerland. And that was it. In August 1942 I went into hiding myself.'[88]

Jacque and Lies also knew that Anne had gone. Lies called to ask Mrs Frank for the return of some kitchen scales, and she was stunned when Goldschmidt announced that the family had gone to Switzerland. When she later discovered the truth, Lies knew instinctively why the Franks had asked the van Pelses to share the hiding place instead of her own family. The Goslars had one very young child, Gabi, and another baby on the way. It was almost impossible to go into hiding under those circumstances. The Goslars expected to be treated more leniently than most anyway; they had obtained South American citizenship through a relative in Switzerland and they were on a list of Zionists. None the less, Lies was bewildered by the realization that the Franks had gone. She rushed home to tell her parents, who were as shaken as she was: 'This was a bolt out of the blue . . . My parents got very upset; they couldn't understand what had happened . . . I believe that Anne was the first girlfriend I lost.'[89]

Lies told Jacque that Anne and her family had disappeared. Jacque's mother remembered, 'When we heard that the Franks were gone – to Switzerland, so we were told, a German army officer whom Mr Frank had known in the first war was supposed to have taken them there – we were all glad, everyone I knew.'[90] Goldschmidt let Lies and Jacque into the apartment when they explained that they wanted to find something of Anne's to keep. Jacque muses, 'One particular image from the Frank family's abandoned house has been etched in my memory: Anne's unmade bed and on the floor in front of it, her new shoes, as if they had just been kicked off . . . I saw Variety, the game she had just gotten for her birthday and which we had played like crazy the past few weeks, just lying there . . . I looked around once more to make sure there wasn't a letter for me from Anne lying there somewhere, but I didn't inquire about one. Anne and I had promised to write each other a "farewell letter" if either of us had to leave unexpectedly. I wasn't to receive it until years later.'[91] They found Anne's swimming medals, and took them – a few small reminders of the friend who had vanished.

A Deadly
Sultry
Silence Hangs   Part Three
Everywhere
1942-4

Chapter Five

'Hiding has become quite an everyday word. How many people must
there be in hiding; not many comparatively speaking, of course, but
no doubt we shall still be absolutely amazed later on at how many
good people there are in the Netherlands who have taken in Jews
as well as Christians on the run, with or without money.'

Anne Frank, *Diary*, 2 May 1943

Within days of the Frank family going into hiding, Westerbork discharged
all detainees not classed as 'full' Jews to make room for those who were.
On 14 July 700 Jews were arrested in Amsterdam's Jewish Quarter and
taken to the Gestapo headquarters. They were told that they would remain
in gaol until the original 4,000 summoned for transportation came
forward. The ensuing panic reached its vortex at the Jewish Council offices
where people 'chased after papers, after exemptions, begged for a week's
delay, produced doctor's certificates to the effect that they were dope
addicts, mutilated or invalids. All hell broke loose . . . the door-keepers
had their hands full, endeavouring to keep out a jostling mass of people
all of whom were trying to get in by hook or by crook.'[1] All but forty of
the prisoners at the Gestapo headquarters were released; those still under
arrest were soon deported, and the first transport of the 4,000 left
Amsterdam on 17 July. They were conveyed first to Westerbork and then
to Auschwitz, where 449 of them were gassed.

The Jewish Council's official view on going into hiding was that it
was 'impracticable for very many on financial grounds and quite impossible for the vast majority'.[2] It is hard to judge exactly how many ignored
their advice but estimates put the figure at between 25,000 and 30,000.[3]
Most hid in the countryside, but were at risk there from the organized
hunts by Dutch Nazis, who often raided villages searching for hidden
Jews. Going into hiding was difficult in every sense. Leaving behind all
their belongings and their way of life was only one of the numerous
problems 'divers' faced. They embarked upon an existence unlike any

other, one in which their survival was entirely in the hands of people whom they did not always know or trust. The ordeal could be heightened by a number of factors; for instance, observance of a kosher diet was virtually impossible. Above all, no one knew what to expect, nor what was expected of them. Eva Schloss, who was also in hiding in summer 1942, explains, 'You couldn't imagine what it was like to go into hiding. Not to go out and see people – that's something that, as a child, you can't grasp. But when we actually went into hiding, that's when it started to sink in. I was very lively, I was thirteen, and had so much energy, but I just couldn't do anything. I was very afraid and very upset. I used to have wrestling matches with my mother to get rid of my energy. It was very, very hard.'[4]

Eva's family separated when they hid. She and her mother hid in one place, and her father and brother in another. The Franks chose to hide together, and have been criticized by some for their decision. Bruno Bettelheim suggests that their reluctance to believe in the impending destruction prevented them from taking steps that might have otherwise saved them.[5] However, even those families who did hide singly were also often betrayed or captured (the Geiringers were arrested in May 1944). In all, eight people lived in the Secret Annexe: the Franks, the van Pelses, who arrived during the July razzias, and Fritz Pfeffer, who joined them in November 1942.

Survival depended on a set of components working together. The greatest of these were the actions and support of the hosts, or 'helpers', as Anne called them. Helpers rarely made the offer of rescue.[6] Usually they were approached by a friend in need of assistance and thus the process of protection began. Sometimes people had to rely on hosts found for them by the Resistance, strangers who had no personal loyalty towards them. Some hosts blatantly exploited their charges, while others were indifferent to the plight of Jews and hid them against their 'better' judgement. Presser cites the case of an artist asked to look after a Jewish child: the artist did so, complaining, 'They're a lousy lot, but of course we must help them.'[7] Each had their own reasons for acting as they did. Eva Fogelman outlines several categories of helper in *Conscience and Courage: Rescuers of Jews During the Holocaust*. Miep, Jan, Bep, Kleiman and Kugler were a combination of 'Moral' – 'people who were prompted to rescue Jews by thoughts or feelings of conscience' – and 'Judeophilic' – 'people who felt a special relationship to individual Jews or who felt a closeness to the Jewish people as a whole'.[8] Moral rescuers had values that were 'self-sustaining, not dependent on the approval of others . . . The bystanders who ultimately became rescuers knew that unless they took action, people would die . . . Ideological morality was based on rescuers' ethical beliefs and notions of justice. A congruence between moral beliefs and actions had always been a part of their lives. They stood up for their beliefs.'[9] Kugler's strong religious convictions (he was Lutheran) may also have influenced his decision to help. Moral rescuers were most likely to act as a result of being asked and were inclined to help more than just one person. Miep and Jan Gies hid a young Jewish man previously unknown to them in their own home, and Jan was in the Resistance, a secret he shared only with Kleiman initially, and then later with Miep; their friends in hiding were never told. After the war Judeophilic rescuers tended to continue their relationships with the people they had helped, often very closely. This was the case with Otto Frank and his helpers, particularly with Miep and Jan.

Rescuers had to feel that they would ultimately be successful; 'they needed to have faith in their capacity to outsmart the Nazis . . . There were scores of unknowns. No one knew how long the war would last, or, until the end, who would win . . . To shelter a Jew was an illegal act. An offer to help immediately pitted the bystander against his or her law-abiding family, friends, and neighbours. It ruined any chance of a normal life. Moreover, it meant being totally responsible for the survival of another person.'[10] It was important that rescuers' families who were told the secret would support their actions. Miep and Jan formed one protective unit; Bep and her father formed another, and Kleiman and his wife formed a third. Kugler chose not to tell his wife.[11] Their reward was not financial: their confidence and courage came from seeing how their conduct helped those in need, the high esteem in which they were held, and from the belief that their actions were justifiable even when the law dictated otherwise. Anne's helpers were under tremendous pressure to make things as easy as possible for their friends in the annexe, but they did so willingly. Miep declares, 'I never felt the desire to be free of the Frank family. It was my fate, my burden and my duty . . . but when I came in, in the middle at the table, all the people were standing in a line. No one said anything, but waited for me to begin. It was always an awful moment for me. I so felt the dependence of these people – except Anne. Anne was in front and she'd ask, "Hey, hello, Miep! What's the news?!" '[12] When asked whether she herself was ever afraid, Miep replied, 'No, especially not in the beginning . . . caring for those people was the main thing. Sometimes I lay awake at night and thought, "Oh, those poor people hidden up there, how awful. How would I feel?" . . . We, the helpers, were aware that occasionally there were difficult moments for each one of us, but we didn't talk about it. Everything had to take its course, and if you were to talk about it you'd begin to feel a certain pressure. You'd spend the day thinking about the people in hiding, and that couldn't happen. We had to appear as relaxed as possible to the rest of the world, otherwise people would become suspicious.'[13] Although they had each other for company, the annexe inhabitants still craved their helpers' visits. Presser explains, 'For the lonely Jewish exile and fugitive, the host or hostess was, like the sun, the only source of human warmth and comfort.'[14] Whenever one of the helpers was absent, a small cloud of gloom descended on those in hiding.

In return for their friends' help, the annexe dwellers helped out with the office work, which ranged from checking accounts to stoning cherries for preservation, from filling gravy packets to writing up invoices. When Bep left briefly to care for her sick relatives in autumn 1943, Anne and Margot relieved Miep of some of the extra work that fell to her. In her diary Anne writes of how industriously they applied themselves to their duties: 'Bep gives Margot and me a lot of office work; it makes us both feel quite important and is a great help to her. Anyone can file away correspondence and write in the sales book, but we take special pains.'[15] Such repayment was quite common amongst rescuers and their charges. 'Jews were aware that they lived only through the good graces of their rescuers, and most did everything possible to hold up their end . . . Even under the most extreme conditions, Jews tried to make themselves as useful as possible to their rescuers.'[16]

Anne frequently wrote about the relationship between the two sets of individuals. Her entry for 28 January 1944 focuses on all rescuers: 'it is amazing how much noble, unselfish work these people are doing risking their own lives to help and save others. Our helpers are a very good example. They have pulled us through up till now and we hope they will bring us safely to dry land . . . Never have we heard *one* word of the burden which we certainly must be to them, never has one of them complained of all the trouble we give. They all come upstairs every day, talk to the men about business and politics, to the women about food and wartime difficulties, and about newspapers and books with the children. They put on the brightest possible faces, bring flowers and presents for birthdays and bank holidays, are always ready to help and do all they can. That is something we must never forget; although others may show their heroism in the war or against the Germans, our helpers display heroism in their cheerfulness and affection.'[17] Otto's helpers also ensured that he had a livelihood to which he could return when the war was over. The business even showed a decent profit during the period 1942–5.

In hiding, security was obviously one of the main concerns. The idea of concealing the annexe entrance came to Kugler and Johan Voskuijl in mid-summer 1942, when houses were regularly being searched for hidden bicycles. Voskuijl, a gifted carpenter, constructed a special bookcase that could be moved by those who knew where to look for its hidden hinges. The high step in front of the annexe door was removed and the bookcase, its shelves stacked with old files, was fitted into place, screening the entrance completely. The inhabitants of the hiding place were careful not to jeopardize their safety, pinning strips of material across the windows and strengthening the blackout boards for the evening. They added small touches to give their prison the feel of a home; Anne's pictures and postcards on the walls of her room are amongst the few surviving indications of how hard they tried to sustain normality. Various 'house rules' had to be upheld at all times. Keeping 'as quiet as baby mice'[18] during office hours, never moving the curtains aside, and only using facilities during certain hours were among the regulations enforced. The simplest of matters required special precautions. For instance, in September 1942 there were problems with the office toilet and the workmen who came to change the pipes asked if they could check the plumbing in the annexe. Kleiman bluffed that he had mislaid the key and the workmen said they would call back the next day. Fortunately the problem sorted itself out, but then Lewinsohn the chemist appeared to work in the kitchen directly beneath the annexe. For an entire day, the fugitives could not move at all. Kugler kept surreptitious watch on Lewinsohn. In her diary Anne refers to the plumber, Lewinsohn, and the charlady as 'the three black perils'.[19]

According to Presser, 'There is, in fact, not a single Jewish survivor who went into hiding and did not have a narrow escape . . .'[20] The annexe stowaways seem to have had more cause than most to worry about discovery. Several burglaries occurred at the offices during the war, with the worst of these, on 8 April 1944, culminating in the thieves rattling the bookcase while the eight in hiding listened in horror. Anne writes about the terrifying incident at length in her diary, after the danger had passed. She also mentions how, in spring 1943, they learned that the owner of the building had sold it to a Mr F. J. Piron without informing Kleiman or Kugler. Piron had turned up unexpectedly at the offices, accompanied by an architect, and announced his intention to buy the house. Kleiman showed them around, again using the mislaid keys ruse. Piron did not seem very curious about the annexe and asked no awkward questions. He bought the building on 22 April 1943. The helpers and their charges considered finding an alternative hiding place, but after much deliberation decided that their best option was to stay where they were and hope for the best. The pressure this additional danger put on them all was immense, especially since there was also a new face in the warehouse, Willem Gerard van Maaren. He replaced Bep's father, who had cancer. At first, the people in hiding were untroubled by van Maaren, but as time wore on and his behaviour became what can at best be described as inquisitive, and at worst sinister, there was every reason to suspect him of being a potentially treacherous presence.[21]

The biggest headache aside from the fear of being discovered was food. Every morning, Miep and Bep gave the families their rations, which they collected on their behalf. Bread was purchased from a friend of Kleiman who ran a well-known chain of bakeries in Amsterdam. A fixed amount of bread was delivered to the office twice weekly, ostensibly for the staff. Part of the cost was paid on delivery, but the outstanding sum was charged to an account due for settlement when the war ended. Meat was supplied by van Pels's butcher friend, Scholte. Miep gave him notes from van Pels to let him know what was required on either coupons or the black market. She regularly visited the grocery store on the Leliegracht run by Mr van Hoeven, a huge, friendly man in his early thirties who was involved with a Resistance group. He and his wife hid two Jewish men in their West Amsterdam apartment until they were betrayed in 1944. He delivered the heavy sacks of potatoes to the offices himself every lunchtime, depositing them in a small cupboard in the kitchen. Peter van Pels collected them at night and took them up to the attic where 270 lbs of dried peas and vegetables were also stacked, along with scores of tins. Milk was Bep's responsibility. She smuggled several bottles a day from the office to the annexe. She also provided them with fruit when the prices were low. The expense of going into hiding was phenomenal. Much of the food was bought on the black market. Anne commented in her diary, 'Ration cards have also been bought illegally. Their price is going up all the time; it has now gone up from twenty-seven florins to thirty-three. And all that for a little slip of printed paper!'[22] These cards and others were obtained by Jan Gies through the National Relief Fund, the Resistance organization in which he was involved. In her diary Anne sometimes grumbles about the lengthy food 'cycles' they had to endure, weeks where only one or two options were available. Anne reckoned the wane in reserves was attributable to the van Pelses – 'real greedy pigs on the top floor'[23] – but she kept this observation to herself, knowing that on the subject of food, Mr van Pels could 'spit like a cat'.[24]

As the war dragged on, Miep often spent hours queuing for groceries, only to be told at the counter that there was nothing left. Butter and fat rationing was repeatedly cut and the food was often rotten. At one point, the menu in the annexe consisted of dry bread and ersatz coffee for breakfast, followed by lettuce or spinach with potatoes for dinner. Many rows erupted over the poor food and its distribution. Anne was furious at the van Pelses' and Pfeffer's apparent lack of consideration: 'At table, when Pfeffer takes ¼ of a half-full gravy boat while all the rest are still waiting for the gravy, then I lose my appetite and feel like leaping to my feet and chasing him off his chair and out the door . . . The van Pels motto is: "If we have got enough, then the rest may have some too, but we get the best, we get it first, we get the most." '[25] By 1944 they were using their last reserves and the men who provided them with ration cards had been caught by the NSB. Jan supplied five new cards, but they quickly ran out of butter, fat and margarine. They had to eat porridge for breakfast instead of fried potatoes and kale hash for supper, to Anne's disgust: 'The smell is a mixture of W.C., bad plums, preservatives + 10 rotten eggs. Ugh! the mere thought of eating that muck makes me feel sick!'[26] The situation deteriorated further when their grocer was arrested. Although the annexe inhabitants were profoundly sorry for him, their thoughts turned to what this could mean for them: might he break under torture and give the game away about them? They were disturbingly short of food. Miep visited a different grocer on the Rozengracht, but it took time and patience to inveigle the elderly owner into giving her extra rations. The eight in hiding had to skip breakfast and make do with porridge for lunch and bread, potatoes, spinach and lettuce for dinner. It was a miserable spread, to say the least, but Anne summed up their attitude: 'We're going to be hungry, but nothing is worse than being discovered.'[27]

Everyone was afraid of their rations running out. Soap, for example, was difficult to obtain. They drew on their soap-hoard initially, but later they had to share whatever Miep or Bep could spare. The contrast in their circumstances before and during the war was painfully obvious. Anne writes in 1942, 'At home I would never have believed that one day I'd be taking a bath in a W.C.'[28] Each person took their baths in a different place, using a tin washtub which could be set down anywhere. Anne and Margot occasionally used the front office after hours: 'The curtains there are drawn on Saturday afternoons, so we wash ourselves in semi-darkness while the one awaiting her turn peers out of the window through a chink in the curtain and gazes in wonder at all the funny people outside.'[29] Electricity had to be used sparingly, and when they exhausted their allowance, candles replaced electric light and coats were piled high on the beds to ward off the cold. In the darkness, they amused themselves and kept warm by exercising and dancing. Their helpers worked hard to provide them with more rations, blankets and thick clothing.

In his memoir Otto writes, 'Nobody can imagine what it meant for us that my four employees proved to be sacrificial helpers and genuine friends in a time when bad forces had the upper hand. They demonstrated a true example of humane co-operation, whilst taking a huge personal risk, in looking after us. As time went by, this became more and more difficult. Their daily visits gave us an enormous lift. Anne, particularly, waited impatiently every day for someone to come and explain what was going on outside. She missed nothing. She was most intimate with Bep, the youngest typist, and the two of them often stood whispering in the corner.'[30] He discusses the helpers' individual duties in his letter to Yad Vashem: 'Miep and Bep had the extremely difficult task to provide food. To nourish eight people while most of the food-stuff was rationed, was a hard job . . . Mr Gies and Mr Kleiman bought ration cards on the black market for us, and when we became short of money, they sold some of our jewellery. Mr Kugler also sold spices without booking sales to help finance our needs. All these activities were risky and they always had to be careful not to be trapped by collaborators or *agents provocateurs*. Apart from food, there were lots of other items which we needed during our 25 months in hiding, such as toilet-articles, medicine, clothes for the growing children, etc., as well as books and other materials to keep us busy . . . Their moral support was very important for us. They gave us an optimistic view on the situation if possible and tried to conceal bad news. There was much tension in their lives during these two years and Mr Kleiman, who had a very delicate health, had several attacks from ulcers, due to all the excitements. In spite of all precautions and the devotion of our friends we were betrayed . . .'[31]

If their betrayer had kept silent, the annexe occupants would have been confronted by the 'Hunger Winter' which claimed so many lives in the Netherlands, and one wonders how they would have survived the last long months before the liberation. Their poor diet had already taken its toll upon their health, and illness was particularly feared because normal treatment was unavailable to them. In winter 1943 Anne suffered a high fever caused by influenza, and all manner of potions and theories were employed to cure it, none of which worked. When she recovered both health and humour, she wrote that the greatest misfortune of being ill was not a sore throat, aching limbs or pounding headaches, but rather when 'Mr Pfeffer thought he'd play doctor, and came and lay on my naked chest with his greasy head, in order to listen to the sounds within. Not only did his hair tickle unbearably, but I was embarrassed although thirty years ago, he once studied medicine and has the title of Doctor. Why should this fellow come and lie on my heart? He's not my lover after all! For that matter he wouldn't hear whether it's healthy or unhealthy inside me anyway; his ears need syringing first, as he's becoming alarmingly hard of hearing.'[32]

Pfeffer was invariably the target for Anne's wicked sense of fun and her outbursts of anger. Two people less alike would have been hard to find, and being forced to share a tiny room for so long (Margot moved in with her parents) only intensified their irritation with each other. Pfeffer was an intelligent, serious man who had enjoyed a busy sporting life before the German occupation, and the enforced inactivity was intolerable for him. Unlike his companions, he had no family members in the annexe, and his sole communication with his wife was via Miep. She met Lotte every week and passed letters and small gifts back and forth. Lotte had no idea where her husband was living and was unaware of the extent of Miep's involvement. On the day before he went into hiding, Pfeffer wrote his wife a farewell letter. It reveals a very different 'Dr Dussel' from the character portrayed in Anne's diary, and in subsequent stage and screen adaptations:

> *15/XI 1942, S. Amsterdam. Dearest beloved, my one and only,*
>
> *I'm sending you a kiss this morning. I find writing to you so difficult now, compared with when we were able to discuss everything every day. My love for you, however, impels me to write as I'm so proud of you, my darling. I have long admired your brave serenity, your greatness of soul, and the nobility with which you have coped with these indescribably difficult times. My pride lies in my total devotion to you and in all my endeavours, actions and sacrifices to show myself worthy of your love. What is the meaning of this hopefully extremely brief break in our eternally unbreakable bonds? Don't lose your magnificent courage and your trust in God. Your love will strengthen both our spirits. Hugs and kisses, with love,*
> *Your Fritz.*
> *P.S. Of the cigarettes I've kept for you so long I'm smoking only one a day.*[33]

The view we have of Pfeffer in Anne's diary is an invariably biased one. At first, she had been magnanimous about sharing her room with him, but exasperation and resentment soon set in. In her diary she grumbled, 'He gets more tiresome and selfish by the day, I didn't see a single one of the generously promised biscuits after the first week. He makes me furious . . .'[34] The tension between them never lessened. There was a constant battle for the use of the small table in their bedroom, and Otto frequently had to intercede in their arguments. Interviewed for Jon Blair's documentary, *Anne Frank Remembered*, Werner Peter Pfeffer contemplated the stormy relationship between his father and Anne: 'Here we're talking about a little girl under very difficult circumstances who first of all decided that my father was not a nice man. Therefore she named him "Dr Dussel", which in English is "idiot". As for my point of view, retrospectively to the age of eleven and below, that's a very large inaccuracy. First of all, my father was a very strict man, but a very kind man. What other people didn't recognize was his love of life, his love of freedom . . . He loved to row, he loved to ride horses, he liked to climb mountains. So if you take a man who's been active all his life and then in flight, he ends up here, it's like caging a bird.'[35]

Being cramped in a few rooms with no opportunity to escape affected them all. Squabbles broke out over insignificant matters and relations grew extremely strained. Most arguments were about food, but other things also caused dissension. In her diary Anne reports how Mrs van Pels removed her sheets from the linen cupboard to prevent them from being used by non-family members. When Edith discovered, to her astonishment, what Mrs van Pels had done, she promptly took theirs out as well. That same morning, the Franks witnessed their first battle between the hot-tempered van Pelses, whose quarrels were usually about money. Mr van Pels felt the only solution to their impoverishment was to start selling their clothes. Mrs van Pels was loathe to part with her rabbit fur, which, her husband insisted, would raise more money on the black market than the rest of their clothing put together. In the end she capitulated with bad grace, and Kleiman gave the fur to a friend to sell. When they received the money, there were more rows. Mrs van Pels wanted to save the cash to buy herself new clothes after the war. It took her husband an entire week of shouting, coaxing and threats to change her mind.

The pettiest affairs were used to give vent to their feelings – for example, whether they should eat tinned vegetables. The Franks generally won the arguments. Edith could be as vociferous as her youngest daughter, particularly where her children were concerned. When van Pels teased Margot about her poor appetite, saying, 'I suppose you do it to keep slim,' Edith glared at him and said loudly, 'I can't bear your stupid chatter any longer!' Van Pels, always a coward when faced with Edith's wrath, sat speechless, while his wife turned scarlet with embarrassment.[36] Mrs van Pels and Anne had numerous rows, and Anne's despair of the older woman is evident in her diary, but Otto recalled that 'when I later spoke to the sister of Mrs van Pels, when she read the diary, she told me that Anne had described her sister exactly as she was'.[37] Mrs van Pels's flirtatious nature infuriated Anne, particularly when Otto was the subject of her attentions. He ignored her, but Anne, in her fearless way, told her, 'Mummy doesn't behave like that with Mr van Pels.'[38]

Anne's high spirits sometimes failed her and she took valerian pills every day to combat depression. Her mother was also despondent, privately confiding her pessimism to Miep, who explains, 'She was suffering under a great weight of despair . . . she was deeply ashamed of the fact that she felt the end would never come . . . She'd complain that Mrs van Pels was always impatient with her girls, especially Anne . . . This criticizing of Anne and Margot upset Mrs Frank very much. In a dark voice, she would express the fear-laden thoughts she was secretly harbouring. "Miep, I see no end coming," she would say. Once she said, "Miep, remember this: Germany will not come out of the war the same way it went into it." I would listen with a sympathetic ear to whatever Mrs Frank needed to say . . . But I would leave her sitting in that room, wearing a look of gloom and depression . . .'[39]

The blackest chapter came at the end of 1943. Miep tells us, 'I suspected that one and a half years of forced idleness and isolation were taking their toll on everyone's nerves. I saw Margot and Peter fading more and more into remoteness. I could feel the sparks of unfinished conflicts left sizzling in the air when I would enter and everyone would put on a welcoming face. Anne was more often off by herself, writing in her diary, or up in the attic, alone and sullen.'[40] Anne was sensitive to the mood around her, noticing how even her normally placid father was suffering: 'Daddy goes about with his lips tightly pursed, when anyone speaks to him, he looks up, startled, as though he is afraid that he will have to patch up some tricky relationship again.'[41] Otto was indeed the arbitrator of the group in hiding, and was aware of his role: 'We had thought that communal life hiding with the family of my partner would make life less monotonous. We had not foreseen how many difficulties would arise through the difference in personalities and views . . . There were differences of opinion between different people in our small community. My main task was to ensure as happy a communal life as possible, and when I compromised, Anne reproached me for being too yielding.'[42]

Despite all the discord, Anne's diary bears witness to the many humorous moments in hiding. An entry for 1942 reads, 'In the evening we laughed ourselves silly at table because I put Mrs Drehrer's[43] fur collar round Daddy's head which made him look so divine you could have died laughing, Mr van Pels tried it on too and he looked even sillier, particularly when he put Margot's spectacles on his nose as well. He looked just like a little old German lady, and no one would have been able to recognize Mr van Pels inside.'[44] Anne's love of theatre was unexpectedly shared by Peter van Pels: 'He appeared in one of Mrs van Pels's very narrow dresses and I in his suit, we topped it all off with a hat and a cap. The grownups were doubled up with laughter and we enjoyed ourselves as much as they did.'[45] Peter's father wrote the comical 'Prospectus and Guide to the Secret Annexe', billing the hiding place as a 'Special institution as temporary residence for Jews and suchlike'.[46] Anne copied down van Pels's jokes in her diary, and her descriptions of events exhibit a deft irony and innate good humour. Her rendition of Pfeffer trying out his dental skills on Mrs van Pels, who had two painful teeth, is as entertaining as any staged comedy sketch: 'Pfeffer began to scrape away at one of the holes, but, no fear – it was out of the question – the patient flung her arms and legs around wildly in all directions until at a given moment Pfeffer let go of the scraper – which remained stuck in Mrs van Pels's tooth. Then the fat was really in the fire! She cried (as far as it was possible, with such an instrument in one's mouth), tried to pull the thing out of her mouth, and only succeeded in pushing it further in. Mr Pfeffer stood with his hands against his sides calmly watching the little comedy. The rest of the audience lost all control and roared with laughter; it was rotten of us, because I for one am quite sure that I should have screamed even louder.'[47]

When Otto looked back upon this period, he tried to view it in a positive light: 'I have to say that in a certain way it was a happy time. I think of all the good that we experienced, whilst all discomfort, longing, conflicts and fears disappear. How fine it was to live in such close contact with the ones I loved, to speak to my wife about the children and about future plans, to help the girls with their studies, to read the Classics with them and to speak about all kinds of problems and views about life. I also found time to read. All this would not have been possible in a normal life, when all day long one is at work. I remember very well that I once said, "When the Allies win, and we survive, we'll look back later with gratitude on the time that we have spent here together . . ." '[48]

Any cause for celebration was welcomed in the annexe. Birthdays, Hanukkah, Christmas and New Year were greeted with more pleasure and festivity than ever before. The helpers joined in, and threw a surprise party in the annexe to mark the approach of 1943. Such occasions alleviated the monotony of two years spent in isolation. The fugitives tried to keep themselves as busy as possible. Miep recalls, 'They looked like living cameos, a head lowered intently over a book, hands poised over a pile of potato peelings, a dreamy look on a face whose hands were mindlessly knitting, a tender hand poised over Mouschi's[49] silky back, stroking and touching, a pen scratching across a blank page, pausing to chew over a thought, and then scratching again. All of them silent. And when my face would appear above the landing, all eyes would light on me. A flash of enthusiasm would widen all eyes.'[50] Anne asked Miep and Jan to stay overnight, and their acceptance caused great excitement, even amongst the adults. Edith and Margot cooked the dinner, which Miep and Jan enjoyed far more than their actual night in the annexe. The wind in the trees, the creaking beams in the attic and the thunder of car wheels in the dark streets stirred them from their slumber. Miep remembers, 'All through the night I heard each ringing of the Westertoren clock. I never slept, I couldn't close my eyes . . . The quietness of the place was overwhelming. The fright of these people who were locked up here was so thick I could feel it pressing down on me. It was like a thread of terror pulled taut. It was so terrible it never let me close my eyes.'[51] Bep experienced the same sense of horror when she stayed overnight in the annexe. The usual occupants of the hiding place were always brighter the following morning than any of their guests. They had learned to live with their fear.

During office hours, the only activities that took place in the annexe were those which could be accomplished quietly: reading, writing, studying, playing board games, and talking softly. The fugitives were voracious readers who liked to discuss the books Kleiman lent them and the ones Jan borrowed from his friend's lending library in the River Quarter. They were an intellectual group, delighting in biographies of artists and musicians, listening to 'The Immortal Music of the German Masters' on the radio, quoting and writing poetry, learning Spanish, English, French and Latin, and conversing about politics past and present. To her annoyance, Anne was not always allowed access to the books Margot and Peter read, but she devoured biographies, tales of mythology, romances and family epics, and recorded in her diary how she had enjoyed John Galsworthy's *Forsyte Saga*, because Jon reminded her of Peter and Fleur of herself. A different kind of literature was offered by her father in the evenings. Otto put aside his own preference for Dickens and read aloud to his family from Goethe, Schiller and Körner. Anne kept a notebook in which she wrote down new words, foreign phrases and lines that appealed to her. She compiled royal family trees and studied shorthand with Margot and Peter. Otto tutored the three teenagers in a variety of subjects including languages, algebra, geometry, geography and history. The attic became a peaceful spot for study on an individual basis. Anne also used it as a writing room, and Peter had fashioned a small workshop for himself against one wall. At night Anne sometimes borrowed her father's binoculars and zoomed in on the houses opposite the courtyard. Past the black skeleton of the chestnut tree, she could see a dentist's surgery where the patient one evening was an elderly woman who was 'awfully scared'.[52]

With the resilience of youth and her own bold spirit, Anne regarded life in hiding as a great adventure and declared on paper that although she did not feel 'at home' in the annexe, she did not hate it either, but thought of it 'more like being on vacation in a very peculiar boardinghouse . . . The "Secret Annexe" is an ideal hiding place, although it leans to one side and is damp, you'd never find such a comfortable hiding place anywhere in Amsterdam, no perhaps not even in the whole of Holland.'[53] Fear descended at night: 'It is the silence that frightens me so.'[54] The minutes crawled by and each sound became a portent, every car passing below a possible Gestapo truck, and every creak a conceivable boot on the stair. Planes flew past, firing at the enemy in the dark, and Anne was sure that the annexe would ultimately be hit by a bomb. Otto remembered, 'Anne came to me in bed then, scared to death, a small bundle of nerves, looking for protection. I took her in my arms, comforted her whilst telling her stories. I was so happy when I succeeded in distracting her and when she fell asleep at the end of the air-raid siren.'[55]

Night-time terrors aside, she repeatedly writes about her relief in finding such a hiding place: 'How fortunate we are here, so well cared for and undisturbed. We wouldn't have to worry about all this misery were it not that we are so anxious about all those dear to us whom we can no longer help';[56] '. . . we are luckier than millions of people . . .';[57] 'If I just think how we live here, I usually come to the conclusion that it is a paradise compared with how other Jews who are not in hiding must be living.'[58] At first, her idealism only truly deserted her when she thought of her friends and her cat, Moortje, whom she missed terribly. She composed a farewell letter to Jacqueline van Maarsen, imploring, 'I hope that we'll always stay "<u>best</u>" friends until we meet again.'[59] Her old anger and jealousy were forgotten, she only wanted to 'apologize and to explain things'.[60] She knew that Jacque would never receive the letter, but it seems she wanted to protect herself from the thought that she might never see her friends again, and she even drafted a reply to Jacque's imaginary answer. When Jacque later learned about these letters, she understood how hard it must have been for Anne to contemplate months in hiding with an uncertain end: 'She must have been so lonely without any friends. I think she wrote the letters *because* she was lonely, and because we had agreed to write letters if one of us had to go. I'm so glad that she wrote them and kept them in the diary. Otherwise I would never know, and for me it's proof that her anger with me was just a passing thing and everything was OK again. That was a comfort to me.'[61]

Anne's active imagination often provided her with a respite from the misery of being cooped up in the annexe. One of the many daydreams she had about 'after the war' involved her cousin Buddy. Anne fantasized that they would become skating partners: 'we make a lovely pair and everyone is mad about us . . . There will be a film later for Holland and Switzerland, my girl friends in both Holland and Switzerland think it's great.'[62] When Buddy read the diary years later, he was deeply moved by

Anne's flight of fancy: 'It must have been a painful thought to her . . . we over here in Switzerland were free . . . all her dreams were caged in and we, the boys, her cousins, could fulfil everything she was dreaming of. It must have been a very, very hard thing for her.'[63] On learning that Anne had even designed herself a special dress to wear for the skating film, he was 'overwhelmed. It made me cry, to be very honest. Especially then, I knew she was not alive when I saw it. I would have loved to go skating with her.'[64]

The false trail Otto had left implying that they had escaped to Switzerland with the aid of an army captain he had known fooled almost everyone. Anne was tickled by 'the way people can let their imagination run away with them. One family from Merwedeplein had seen all four of us pass on bicycles very early in the morning and another lady knew quite definitely that we were fetched by a military car in the middle of the night.'[65] Obviously, the Eliases knew that the Franks were not in Switzerland, but they had no idea where they actually were until Kleiman began writing to Erich, dropping subtle hints. Buddy remembers, 'We had no more word. Actually, that's not strictly true because my father corresponded with Kleiman on business, and in his letters, Kleiman would write something, some little thing, that we knew referred to the Franks, and so we knew that they were safe.'[66] Even in neutral Switzerland, the Eliases had their own misfortunes: 'We weren't without fear. My mother was brave, very brave. My father, being Jewish, was thrown out of his German firm during the war and we didn't have any money. We really were lost.'[67] Leni panicked badly at one point and fled with her youngest son to another part of the country. When she returned home, however, she seemed to have found new strength. Buddy recalls, 'My mother had never had to work in her life, but she started selling old shoes and old clothes that she got from refugees who came to Switzerland and went on their way. This was early on in the war. Then she bought furniture from them. From time to time, she got a chair, then a table, and slowly – very slowly – this developed into the most beautiful antiques store. She really, really pulled us through.'[68]

In occupied Amsterdam, thinking about her cousins and friends who were still able to live relatively normal lives sent Anne spiralling into depression. She knew Kleiman's daughter was free to come and go as she pleased, while she and everyone else in the annexe were 'stuck here as if we're outcasts . . . When someone comes in from outside, with the wind in their clothes and the cold on their faces, then I could bury my head in the blankets to stop myself thinking: When will we be granted the privilege of smelling fresh air . . . Believe me, if you have been shut up for 1½ years, it can get too much for you some days . . . Cycling, dancing, whistling, looking out at the world, feeling young, to know that I'm free – that's what I long for . . .'[69] Just as there are many entries in Anne's diary that illustrate her thankfulness at evading capture, so there are those which deal with her pessimism and desperation: 'I simply can't build my hopes on a foundation consisting of confusion, misery, and death, I see the world gradually being turned into a wilderness, I hear the ever approaching thunder, which will destroy us too, I can feel the sufferings of millions . . .';[70] 'Again and again I ask myself, would it not have been better for us all if we had not gone into hiding, and if we were dead now and not going through all this misery . . . let the end come, even if it is hard.'[71] When their greengrocer was arrested, Anne could not stop herself from thinking that this might be her own fate: 'The police forced the door there, so they could do it to us too! If one day we too should . . . no, I mustn't write it down, but I can't put the question out of my mind today. On the contrary all the fear I've already been through seems to face me again in all its frightfulness.'[72]

She tried to quell her apprehensions and sorrow by reading, writing, chatting to someone, or going up to the attic to gaze at the sky and the tower of the Westerkerk. Staring at the chestnut tree 'on whose branches little raindrops shone, at the seagulls and other birds that looked like silver in the sun'[73] brought her peace because she believed that 'nature sets all fear at rest'.[74] Very often, when the last employee or visitor had gone, Anne would slip downstairs to the front office, eager to see what was happening beyond the confines of the hiding place. Bep was there on one occasion, catching up on her work after a sleepless night in the annexe. In *The Footsteps of Anne Frank*, Ernst Schnabel reconstructs the scene: 'Suddenly the door opened and Anne's face appeared in the crack. She whispered, "Has everyone left?" Anne was in fine fettle, as she had been since the morning. She had slept perfectly well – she was accustomed to the grinding gears of the night. "Have they left, Bep?" "Yes, long ago,"

Bep said. Then Anne tiptoed across the big office, stooping so that no one could see her from the street. She posted herself behind the curtain and peered through a tiny opening in order to catch a glimpse, a prisoner's perspective, of the world.'[75]

The helpers were unable to keep their friends in ignorance of the deportations and persecutions taking place. Kleiman remembered, 'When we had our plate of soup upstairs with them at noon, we tried to say nothing about what was happening outside. But it could not be concealed. The air was charged with it. It penetrated through the walls.'[76] When the van Pelses and Pfeffer first arrived in the annexe, they brought news about friends and neighbours. Anne refers to these people and their probable fates on a surprising number of occasions in her diary: 'Bep told us that Betty Bloemendal from my class has been packed off to Poland, too, it's horrible isn't it, and we are so well off here;'[77] 'Rosel and Wronker have been sent to Poland;'[78] 'Miep told us about a man who escaped from Westerbork, things are terrible there, and if it's so bad there what can it be like in Poland?';[79] 'Aunt R. must really be feeling low, she's now got a daughter and a son-in-law in Poland, her son and daughter-in-law have been picked up and L. is dead. Only P. is left.'[80] When writing about her former boyfriend, Peter Schiff, she adds, 'I just wish he would come and hide with us here too. Perhaps the poor boy is already dead in Poland.'[81] They listened to the radio regularly, and Otto recalled how important it was to them, 'so that we could feel connected with the outside world. We regularly heard the broadcasts from London.'[82] The BBC Home Service news carried reports of Jews being 'regularly killed by machinegun fire, hand grenades – and even poisoned by gas'.[83] The German broadcasts were punctuated by ranting Nazis; on 4 October 1942 Anne wrote, 'This morning I put on the radio for a bit. Göring was cursing the Jews something awful!!!!'[84]

Miep remembers the dilemma over how much information to impart: 'Jan, my husband, said, "Miep, you don't always have to tell them everything. You have to keep in mind that these people are locked up. They can't go outside. Bad news depresses them more than it does us. Limit yourself to sort of half and half." So I did. But Anne was dissatisfied. She thought that I knew more. And when I had said all I was going to say and was about to leave, she would take me aside, pretending to want to chat. And she'd say, "Miep, what's going on . . ." She'd ask me so much! Finally I couldn't hold out any more, and I'd tell her everything. That was Anne . . . She always had questions for everybody. When I came downstairs, Kleiman would ask, "Did she smother you with questions too?" And then I'd defend her again. I'd say, "Yes, so many I could barely breathe. But let's be happy that she asks so many. Just imagine Anne saying, I can't take it any more . . . How would we handle that?" "Yes," said Kleiman, "you're right." '[85] Attempts to protect their friends from the truth were hopeless. Kugler remembered, 'I went upstairs every day except Sunday, when everything was closed. We talked about the news, about what happened. They read the papers also.'[86] Bep, too, recalled that little escaped them: 'They knew everything . . . Anne herself once saw two Jews passing by in the street, when she was in the office with me, peeping through the crack in the curtain. And there was not a Jew walking in the street whose look did not tell the whole story.'[87]

After the war, Otto revealed how they had kept up their spirits: 'I remember to have once read a sentence: "If the end of the world would be imminent, I still would plant a tree today." When we lived in the secret annexe we had the device "fac et spera", which means "Work and Hope" . . . Only with a certain time allocation laid down from the start and with each one having his own duties, could we have hoped to live through the situation. Above all the children had to have enough books to read and to learn. None of us wanted to think how long this voluntary imprisonment would last.'[88] In her diary Anne discusses how they overcame the constant battery of appalling news: '. . . we shall still have our jokes and tease each other when these horrors have faded a bit in our minds; it won't do us any good or help those outside to go on being as gloomy as we are at the moment and what would be the object of making our "Secret Annexe" a "Secret Annexe of Gloom"? Must I keep thinking about those other people whatever I am doing and if I want to laugh about something, should I stop myself quickly and feel ashamed that I am cheerful? Ought I then to cry the whole day long? No, that I can't do and, besides, in time this gloom will wear off.'[89]

Otto later claimed that the persecutions had 'made the Jews take a new look at their Jewish identity'.[90] Of the eight in hiding, Pfeffer was the most religious. Anne mentions his observance of rituals and prayers in her diary, and in a post-war letter Lotte Pfeffer declares him to have been a master of the Hebrew language, whose 'religion meant everything to him'.[91] After the war Otto expounded on the varying degrees of religious awareness of Pfeffer, himself, and his family. According to Otto, Pfeffer 'had a rather orthodox education whereas my wife was progressive and had a deep religious feeling'; Margot 'followed more or less my wife'; he himself 'was not educated in a religious sphere' but his marriage and the Nazi persecutions had made him re-evaluate his religion; while Anne, he felt, was yet 'more inscrutable. Religious forms and ceremonies did not seem to impress her very much, but she did stand next to me while the candles were lighted and joined in singing the Maoz Tzur, the well-known Hanukkah song . . . she didn't show any feeling for religion. Margot showed an interest, but Anne never did. She never had a real Jewish education . . . Anne had never shown much interest when we went to Jewish celebrations or when Pfeffer gave the Friday evening prayers. She merely stood there quietly. I believe the religious forms of Judaism meant little to her, rather its ethical teachings.'[92]

Otto said nothing about the van Pelses, but Anne considers their seeming ambivalence in her diary. Mrs van Pels would remark, 'I'll have myself baptized later', but then state, 'I always wanted to go to Jerusalem, because I only feel at home among Jews!'[93] Peter seems to have been as confused as his mother. Anne writes, 'he talked about the Jews. He would have found it much easier if he'd been a Christian and if he could be one after the war. I asked if he wanted to be baptized, but that wasn't the case either. He couldn't possibly feel like a Christian, he said, but who was to know whether he was a Jew after the war was over and what his name was! . . . Peter also said "The Jews have always been the chosen people and will always be so!" I replied: "I keep hoping that for once they've been chosen for the good!" '[94]

Religious observance was a weekly habit in the annexe, whatever the mixed emotions of those involved. When candles were still obtainable, they were lit every Friday in the hiding place to mark the Sabbath, with Pfeffer leading the prayers. They all enjoyed traditional Jewish food and celebrated the religious calendar, albeit in a rather subdued manner. The Christmas festivities were an excuse to bring a little joy into their lives rather than a form of worship, and when Otto offered to give Anne a copy of the New Testament as a Hanukkah present, Margot voiced her disapproval.

Anne's interest in her religion increased as she moved towards adulthood. In retrospect, she claimed that 1943 was the year when she 'came to know God'.[95] Her references to God, and to Jews, become more frequent throughout 1943 and 1944; even in 1942 her guilt at having apparently escaped her co-religionists' fate was profound: 'I feel wicked sleeping in a warm bed, while my dearest friends have been knocked down or have fallen into a gutter somewhere out in the cold night. I get frightened when I think of close friends who have now been delivered into the hands of the cruellest brutes the world has ever seen. And all because they are Jews.'[96] She is sceptical when she hears a bishop addressing his congregation and urging them to keep up their morale, and demands, 'Will it help? It won't help the people of our religion.'[97] Her understandable but illogical guilt manifested itself in nightmares; she saw Lies dressed in rags, starving and crying for help. For Anne, Lies became a symbol of Jews whose lives hung in the balance. She questioned their fates in her diary: 'why should I be chosen to live and she probably to die? What was the difference between us? Why are we so far from each other now?'[98] A month later, Anne could not shake off the distressing image of her friend and prayed that God would protect her: 'Hanneli, I see in you all the time what my lot might have been, I keep seeing myself in your place . . . I am selfish and cowardly. Why do I always dream and think of the most terrible things – my fear makes me want to scream out loud sometimes.'[99]

Although Anne had spoken of cowardice then, as she matured she found solace and strength in her religion. In March 1944 she was able to write, 'What I have to bear is so hard but then I am strong . . . I know I am not safe, I am afraid of prison cells and concentration camps, but I feel I've grown more courageous and that I am in God's hands!'[100]

The following month, after the last in a series of burglaries in the building, their helpers' vehement warnings to be more careful about how they conducted themselves whilst in hiding stirred up feelings of resentment amongst the fugitives. Evidently angry about the admonitions and their plight, Anne wrote one of the most emotionally charged passages in her diary: 'We have been pointedly reminded that we are in hiding, that we are Jews in chains, chained to one spot, without any rights, but with a thousand duties . . . Who has made us Jews different from all other people? Who has allowed us to suffer so terribly up till now? It is God that has made us as we are, but it will be God, too, who will raise us up again. If we bear all this suffering and if there are still Jews left, when it is over, then Jews, instead of being doomed, will be held up as an example . . . God has never deserted our people; right through the ages there have been Jews, through all the ages they have had to suffer, but it has made them strong too, the weak are picked off and the strong will remain and never go under!'[101]

The diary is not only a sequential account of events and a sounding board for Anne's frustration with the war and their situation; much of its power lies in the writer's ability to combine all of these with an interior monologue on her transition from girlhood to womanhood. This progress is so finely woven into the other aspects of Anne's existence that it appears seamless, but it is the unfolding of her character, and the way in which she deals with all the usual trials and tribulations of a teenager while in the midst of such catastrophic circumstances, that has given the published diary its longevity. Anne was thirteen when she went into hiding, and almost immediately we see her trying, as all adolescents must, to establish her independence from her parents. This often caused explosive arguments, particularly between Anne and her mother. Otto's second wife, Fritzi, explains, 'Otto often told me how difficult it was for a lively child like Anne, who had been surrounded by so many friends her own age, to live in hiding, keeping quiet for hours on end. Therefore there was often friction between Anne and her mother and with other people in the attic, which was certainly not only their fault, but Anne's too.'[102]

A few days after they arrived in the annexe, their lives for ever changed, Anne wrote of her family, 'I don't fit in with them and that's something I've been feeling very much, especially lately. They get so soppy with each other that I would rather be on my own.'[103] Gradually, Anne began to understand her mother a little better, but her new knowledge did not make her more tolerant: 'I can't really love Mummy in a dependent, childlike way.'[104] One thing did change, however: Anne found herself wanting to protect her mother from her hostility instead of confronting her with it as she had in the past.

Otto was deeply unhappy at the lack of harmony between his wife and daughter: 'I was concerned that there was no particularly good understanding between my wife and Anne, and I believe my wife suffered more from this than Anne. In reality she was an excellent mother, who went to any lengths for her children. She often complained that Anne was against everything that she did but it was a consolation for her to know that Anne trusted me. It was often hard for me to mediate between Anne and her mother. On one hand, I didn't want to hurt my wife, but it was often difficult for me to point Anne in the right direction when she was cheeky and naughty to her mother. Usually I would wait until after such a scene, then I'd take Anne aside and speak to her as if she were an adult. I explained to her, that in the situation we were in, each one of us had to control himself, even when there were grounds to complain. That often helped for a while.'[105]

Anne was convinced that neither Margot nor Peter, who were both only three years her senior, felt and thought as she did. She initially condemned them as 'staid and quiet',[106] Peter as a 'rather soft, shy, gawky youth',[107] and Margot as 'a little wretch who gets on my nerves horribly day and night . . . I keep teasing her all the time about being a model child which she can't stand, perhaps she'll give it up, it's high time.'[108] Anne saw things with a child's uncompromising eye and an adult's awareness, and the two made for an uneasy alliance. Her outspokenness irritated the van Pelses and Pfeffer. They told the Franks that Anne was badly brought up, causing enraged outbursts from Edith, who despite frequently being the object of Anne's derision, would defend her to the end. On one occasion van Pels asked Kleiman if he would find him some cigarettes, and Anne, who was sitting nearby, admonished him: 'These people are doing so much for us as it is. Do forget about the smoking, Mr van Pels. Otherwise Mr Kleiman will have to go trotting through half the town on your account.'[109] Van Pels left the room, patently embarrassed and irate. Anne often despaired of herself: 'If I talk, everyone thinks I am showing off; when I'm silent they think I'm ridiculous; rude if I answer, sly if I get a good idea, lazy if I'm tired, selfish if I eat a mouthful more than I should, stupid, cowardly, crafty, etc., etc. The whole day long I hear nothing else but that I'm an insufferable baby, and although I laugh about it and pretend not to take any notice, I *do* mind. I would like to ask God to give me a different nature, so that I didn't put everyone's back up. But that can't be done.'[110]

Being in hiding did not lessen Anne's care and pride in her appearance. She began to bleach the dark hairs that grew like soft down on her upper lip with hydrogen peroxide. She pin-curled her hair in the same style as Margot, and made a combing-shawl out of rose-patterned material, which tied under her chin to catch stray hairs when she brushed out her curls. Her dream of going to stay with her cousins in Switzerland led to the compilation of a long, expensive list of all the cosmetics and clothes she would have to buy if her goal were ever realized. She studied her face in the mirror and asked Margot if she thought she was attractive. Margot replied that she had 'nice eyes'.[111] The helpers were sympathetic to Anne's needs and desire for attention. Kleiman reflected, 'Of course, we tried to keep in mind how hard it was for the child. She was hungering for the world outside, for life with other children, and when my wife came up, Anne would greet her with an almost unpleasant curiosity. She would ask about Corrie, our daughter. She wanted to know what Corrie was doing, what boyfriends she had, what was happening at the hockey club,[112] whether Corrie had fallen in love. And as she asked she would stand there, thin, in her washed out clothes, her face snow-white, for they all had not been out of doors for so long. My wife would always bring her something, a pair of sandals or a piece of cloth; but coupons were so scarce and we did not have enough money to buy on the black market. It would have been nice if we could have brought her a letter from Corrie occasionally, but Corrie was not allowed to know that the Franks weren't abroad, as everyone thought, but were still in Amsterdam. We did not want to burden her with this almost unendurable secret.'[113]

Everyone tried to make a fuss of Anne, to compensate for the life she should have been living. Kugler brought her the magazine *Cinema en Theater* every week, amongst other treats. 'They were probably the only publications in Holland at that time not containing some sort of Nazi propaganda,' he recalled. 'When we bought magazines we made sure that the vendors were good, that we could trust them.'[114] Sometimes Anne asked him for a newspaper, and although he knew her parents had forbidden them, occasionally he sneaked one in for her to read. 'You have no idea of the immense expression of which Anne's eyes were capable,' he wrote after the war; 'sometimes it seemed as if she were looking to see whether she had been correctly understood at all. But then again, suddenly and without transition, she could be quite childish . . .'[115]

Anne accepted the move to the annexe in her easily adaptable way, but there were times when the enforced inactivity was particularly hard. Her father thought she suffered more than any of them: 'From the start it was clear to us that a life in total seclusion would be much harder for the lively Anne to put up with than for us. We knew that she would miss greatly her many friends and school. Margot, who was more mature, would come to terms with our situation.'[116]

Anne's ability to put into words the most complicated aspects of her development reveals her literary talent more clearly, perhaps, than anything else. She was as curious about herself as she had ever been, and wrote candidly about the changes taking place both in her mind and in her body: 'I get the feeling lately of being embarrassed in front of Margot, Mummy and Daddy . . . I think what is happening to me is so wonderful, and not only what can be seen on my body, but all that is taking place inside . . . After I came here, when I was scarcely 13, I began to think about myself rather early on and to know that I am a person. Sometimes, when I lie in bed at night, I have a terrible desire to feel my breasts and to listen to the quiet rhythmic beat of my heart.'[117] She appreciated her periods despite the discomfort, feeling as though she had 'a sweet secret'[118] within. The process of self-discovery was accelerated by her confinement and being unable to mix with contemporaries of both sexes with whom she could have discussed such things. In her desperation to share her thoughts, she sought out Peter van Pels.

Originally she had thought him a fool and a softy. Now he became 'beloved and good',[119] a combination in Anne's imagination of himself and her first love, Peter Schiff. She made a clear decision to pursue his friendship in ways that were so subtle that at first she did not realize she was falling in love with him. A conversation they had about Mouschi's sexuality made her realize that there were 'young people . . . who can discuss these things quite naturally without making fun of them'.[120] Anne had no one else with whom she could talk about sex; at that time very few parents were willing to talk about sexual matters with their offspring. When she broached the subject with her father, he told her that she 'couldn't possibly understand the longing yet'.[121] This was no use to Anne, who wrote that she 'always knew that I did understand it and now I understand it fully'.[122] She tried to find words to describe the new emotions taking their hold of her: 'The sun is shining, the sky is deep blue, there is a lovely breeze and I'm longing – so longing – for everything . . . I believe that it's spring within me, I feel that spring is awakening, I feel it in my whole body and soul . . . I feel completely confused, I don't know what to read, what to write, what to do, I only know that I am longing.'[123] Two days later, her desires were quenched by the joyful suspicion that Peter had begun to take notice of her, which gave her 'a lovely feeling inside'.[124] Soon he was confiding in her, which was exactly what she wanted. When he complimented her, she felt 'a tender glow'.[125] She wondered if Margot was in love with Peter, but when asked, Margot replied that she was not, nor had she ever been. Anne felt free to pursue him, and they spent hours in the attic together, sitting by the window and looking out at the Westerkerk or across the courtyard and watching winter turn to spring on the chestnut tree.

In March 1944 Anne wrote a long, perceptive passage in her diary about how she had changed since her birthday in 1942. She now felt that she was a young woman, one who wanted something different from the lives led by other women she knew, something more than a husband and family (though she wanted those too): 'Although I'm only fourteen, I know quite well what I want, I know who is right and who is wrong, I have my opinions, my own ideas and principles, and although it may sound pretty mad from an adolescent, I feel more of a person than a child, I feel quite independent of anyone . . .'[126] A few days later, she received her first 'proper' kiss from Peter, and wrote an exuberant diary entry about it, but she was quickly assailed by a sense of guilt. Was it right, she wondered? Margot would never dream of doing such a thing and her friends at school would be scandalized. She decided to tell her father about the relationship. He warned her to be careful, that 'It is the man who is always the active one in these things; the woman can hold him back'.[127] Otto spoke privately to Peter, suggesting that he and Anne spent less time alone together. Anne was afraid that Peter would see that as a betrayal of trust and carried on as before, annoying and worrying her father in the process. She wrote Otto a long letter in which she tried to explain her behaviour, saying that no one had helped her and that she had rid herself of unhappiness through her own efforts. She told him to have faith in her, because 'I am independent both in mind and body.'[128] After reading the letter, Otto sat down with her and an emotional discussion ended with them both in tears. Anne was very ashamed of having upset her father and promised to behave better in future: 'I will take Daddy as my example and I *will* improve.'[129] Gradually and inevitably, the intense feelings Anne had for Peter began to fade; he could not satisfy her need to talk about 'deeper' subjects, and he was not her intellectual equal. When Otto looked back upon the episode, he viewed it as having been a comfort to his daughter: 'At the start, there was very little contact between him and my children. He was lazy and uninterested. But then he was disturbed by the eagerness of my children to learn and was embarrassed to be left behind. There was a kind of camaraderie between them and later, when Anne was more mature, they discovered their feelings for one another. This brought a few problems, but because I had trust in both Anne and Peter, I could speak openly with the two of them. I understood that this friendship would make life easier for Anne in the annexe.'[130]

Anne knew the reason for her quick maturity was, in part at least, due to her exceptional circumstances. 'Am I only fourteen? Am I really still a silly little schoolgirl? Am I really so inexperienced about everything? I have more experience than most; I have been through things that hardly anyone of my age has undergone.'[131] She spurned self-pity, declaring that, 'I have often been downcast, but never in despair; I regard our hiding as a dangerous adventure, romantic and interesting at the same time. In my diary I treat all the privations as amusing . . . My start has been so very full of interest, and that is the sole reason why I have to laugh at the comical side of the most dangerous moments. I am young and I possess many buried qualities; I am young and strong and am living a great adventure . . . Every day I feel that I am developing inwardly, that the liberation is drawing nearer and how beautiful nature is, how good the people about me, how interesting and amusing this adventure! Why, then, should I be in despair?'[132] She sometimes had to struggle to retain that level of optimism: 'It's twice as hard for us young ones to hold our ground, and maintain our opinions, in a time when all ideals are being shattered and destroyed, when people are showing their worst side, and do not

Anne's paternal grandparents,
Alice and Michael Frank, shortly after
their wedding, 1885.

Anne's maternal grandparents,
Abraham and Rosa Hollander, with
Margot, 1926.

Otto Frank with two unidentified women, *c.*1917 (*above left*).

Edith Hollander as a young woman, Aachen, date unknown (*above right*).

Otto and Edith on honeymoon in San Remo, 1925 (*right*).

The Frank and Elias family, c.1928. Left to right, back row:
Erich Elias, Robert Frank, Herbert Frank, Otto Frank;
middle row: Leni Frank Elias, Lottie Frank (Robert's wife),
Alice Frank, unknown woman (possibly Herbert's wife),
Edith Hollander Frank; front row: Berndt (Buddy) Elias,
Margot Frank, Stephan Elias (*top*).

Margot, Anne, Stephan Elias and Edith, 1931 (*above left*).

Margot and Anne, 1933 (*above right*).

Anne in Laren, 2 September 1939, the day before France and Britain declared war on Germany (*left*).

Anne's tenth birthday party, 1939. Anne, Sanne and Lies are respectively second, third and fourth from the left; Kitty Egyedi is fourth from the right (*bottom left*).

Anne enjoying the sun at Sils-Maria, 1935 (*bottom right*).

Anne peeping from behind a newspaper at the swimming baths in Amsterdam, 1941 (*below left*).

Anne and Margot at Zandvoort, 1940. Anne pasted the picture in her diary (*below right*).

Margot, Hermann Whilp and Anne in Merwedeplein, 1941 (*bottom left*).

Anne in the outfit she chose for Miep's wedding in July 1941. She captioned this, 'Anne tries on her brand-new coat' (*bottom right*).

Mrs van Pels, Mr van Pels and Victor Kugler on their way back from Miep's wedding (*below*).

Peter van Pels, date unknown (*bottom left*).

Charlotta (Lotte) Kaletta and Fritz Pfeffer in 1939 (*bottom right*).

The offices at Prinsengracht, 1941. Front: Victor Kugler, Bep Voskuijl, Miep Gies; the two women in the background are temporary office workers (*top right*).

Johannes Kleiman next to the swinging bookcase that covered the entrance to the annexe, date unknown (*middle right*).

The Secret Annexe (top two floors and attic of central house) (*bottom left*).

Otto Frank, his second wife, Fritzi, and Audrey Hepburn, 1957. Hepburn later became a patron of the Anne Frank Educational Trust (copyright: Eva Schloss) (*bottom right*).

The last known photograph of Anne, 1942.

know whether to believe in truth and right and in God . . . It's really a wonder I haven't dropped all my ideals, because they seem so absurd and impossible to carry out. Yet I keep them, because in spite of everything I still believe that people are really good at heart.'[133]

Anne's longing to have someone – an identifiable entity – to write to when she was in hiding resulted in the entries taking the form of letters to different people. The 'recipients' were in fact characters from Cissy van Marxveldt's four-volume series *Joop ter Heul*, which was hugely popular with young girls in Holland at the time. The books revolved around Joop, her friends and their club, and followed them through their lives from school to motherhood. Anne wrote to each character in turn, but eventually settled on one, Kitty Francken, to become her correspondent. Presumably Kitty was her favourite character, but it may also have been because the surname was similar to her own, or even because she had known and admired a girl called Kitty Egyedi at Merwedeplein. Otto explained, 'I remember that Anne had a real friend with this name. Once Anne showed me a drawing from her friend. She was greatly impressed and said, "Look how well Kitty can draw!" Today Kitty lives in Utrecht. I visited her recently, but we cannot say for sure if she served as a model for the diary.'[134] Kitty Egyedi herself did not believe that the diary was named after her: 'I like the fact that, out of all her friends, she used my name. But only Anne could say to what extent she had me in mind when she did so. It may well be that she had me in mind in the beginning, when she started writing to Kitty. But Kitty became so idealized and started to lead her own life in the diary, that it soon ceases to matter who is meant by "Kitty". The name in her diary is not meant to be me, truly it isn't.'[135]

Anne usually wrote in her diary in her parents' room, her own room, or at the desk by the window in the attic. Everyone was aware that Anne had a diary. Otto remembered, 'She often said, "Papa, I am writing. Please see that no one disturbs me. I want to write my diary!"'[136] Anne sometimes read aloud from the diary, although she never let anyone else read it independently. Otto's second wife, Fritzi, recounts, 'Anne always kept the people in the attic entertained by reading her stories or funny accounts of the episodes that happened in the secret annexe. So everybody knew, of course, that Anne was writing and that she had a certain gift for it. But nobody imagined that she was really as gifted as she was.'[137] Kugler remembers how Anne would watch everyone, in order to better record them in her diary. 'Little things I did when I came upstairs . . . she was a keen observer . . . between the pages of the cardboard-covered notebook she set down a sensitive registry of the tensions and despair, the small joys and the moments of terror experienced by the eight locked-up human beings.'[138]

When Anne misbehaved, the diary became a useful bargaining point. Otto would threaten to confiscate it, much to Anne's dismay: 'oh insuperable horror! I'm going to have to hide it in future.'[139] Miep remembers, 'Anne continued to be very secretive about her writing and always put her papers in her father's worn-out leather briefcase . . . As the Franks believed in respecting the privacy of everyone, including children, and there was so little privacy in the hiding-place in other ways, Anne's privacy was always taken seriously and respected. No one would dare to touch her papers or to read her words without her permission.'[140] Anne worried that she would run out of paper. 'Perhaps I'll ask Bep if she can go and see sometime if Perrij's still sell diaries, or else I'll have to use an exercise book, because my diary is getting full, what a pity! Luckily I can stretch it a bit by sticking in pages.'[141] The helpers kept her supplied with blank accounting books and materials. Bep recalled, 'she asked me again and again to get her a book with a lock, adding expressly that she needed it for keeping a diary. Unfortunately I was unable to grant her wish. But I frequently gave her copy paper from the office that came in various colours, for instance red, yellow, blue and white.'[142]

In summer 1943 Anne discovered a new passion: short-story writing. On 7 August she told Kitty, 'A few weeks ago I started to write a story, something that was completely made up and that gave me such pleasure that my pen-children are now piling up. Because I promised to give you a faithful and unadorned account of all my experiences, I'll let you judge whether small children may perhaps take pleasure in my tales . . .'[143] The story 'Kitty' follows. Some of Anne's tales, such as 'The Battle of the Potatoes' and 'Villains!' are straightforward objective pieces, drawing directly on her experiences in the annexe. Others, such as 'Kitty', 'The Porter's Family' and 'Eva's Dream' are stories with an unusual, ethereal quality to them. Anne kept a record of all her non-diary work in an oblong office cash-book, providing an index and details of when they were written.

Sometimes she read aloud from this book to her companions and to the helpers. She often wrote about the daily routine in the annexe and these 'Tales' are her best and most animated compositions. The story she entitled 'Villains!' was about the persistent flea problem, though the villains of the piece were not the fleas but the van Pelses, who had ignored the advice they had been given about how to get rid of them, leaving the annexe under siege to 'the critters'. 'Villains!' ends: 'They're to blame for bringing the fleas here. We get the stink, the itch and the bother. Mrs Van Pels can't stand the smell at night. Mr Van Pels pretends to spray, but he brings back the chairs, the blankets etc., again unsprayed. Just let the Franks stifle in their fleas.'[144]

At the start of 1944 Anne was already considering the importance of her diary after the war: 'the world will still keep on turning without me; what is going to happen, will happen, and anyway it's no good trying to resist. I trust to luck, but should I be saved, and spared from destruction, then it would be terrible if my diaries and my tales were lost.'[145] Her writing, she felt, was 'the finest thing I have . . . [I] have nothing for myself alone, except my diary.'[146] She knew now what her purpose would be after the war: 'I want to write later on, and even if I don't become a writer I won't neglect my writing while doing some other job. Oh yes, I don't want to have lived for nothing like most people . . . I want to go on living even after my death! And therefore I am grateful to God for giving me this gift, this possibility of developing myself and of writing, of expressing all that is in me!'[147] The worst thing of all would be 'to lead the same sort of life as Mummy and Mrs van Pels and all the women who do their work and are then forgotten, I must have something besides a husband and children, something that I can devote myself to!'[148] On several occasions she mentions this determination to 'lead a different life from other girls and, later on, from ordinary housewives'.[149]

The lot of 'other' women was something she considered in depth in an entry dated 13 June 1944. Her musings were sparked by something she had read in Paul de Kruif's book *Strijders voor het leven* (*The Fight for Life*). Anne was struck by the notion that 'women suffer more pain, more illness and more misery than any war hero just from giving birth to children'.[150] With some foresight, she wrote that women were only just beginning to come into their own, and that soon there would be another fight for their rights. She disregarded the theory that women were no more than child-bearers whose obligation it was to look after their husband, children and home: 'Women are much braver, much more courageous soldiers, struggling and enduring pain for the continuance of mankind, than all the freedom-fighting heroes with their big mouths! . . . I believe that the idea that a woman's duty is simply to bear children will change over the centuries to come and will make way for respect and admiration for one who without complaint and a lot of talk shoulders these burdens!'[151] Education was the way forward, Anne wrote, and she herself condemned 'all the men, and the whole system, that refuse ever to acknowledge what an important, arduous, and in the long run beautiful part, women play in society'.[152]

A *Radio Oranje* broadcast put everything into perspective for her. On 28 March 1944 Gerrit Bolkestein, the Minister of Education, Art and Science in the Dutch government in London, made a speech which Anne felt was aimed directly at her. Bolkestein told his listeners: 'History cannot be written on the basis of official decisions and documents alone. If our descendants are to understand fully what we as a nation have had to endure and overcome during these years, then what we really need are ordinary documents – a diary, letters from a worker in Germany, a collection of sermons given by a parson or a priest. Not until we succeed in bringing together vast quantities of this simple, everyday material will the picture of our struggle for freedom be painted in its full depth and glory.'[153] To this end, he suggested, a centre should be set up when the conflict was over to deal with personal documents from the Second World War. The other occupants of the annexe immediately turned to Anne and began talking excitedly about her diary. A seed had been planted in Anne's fertile mind: 'Just imagine how interesting it would be if I were to publish a romance of the "Secret Annexe", the title alone would be enough to make people think it was a detective story.'[154]

At the beginning of April, she took a long, hard look at the task that lay before her. 'I must work . . . to get on to become a journalist, because that's what I want! I know that I *can* write, a couple of my stories are good, my descriptions of the "Secret Annexe" are humorous, there's a lot in my diary that speaks, but – whether I have real talent remains to be seen . . . I am the best and sharpest critic of my own work, I know myself what is and what is not well written. Anyone who doesn't write doesn't know how wonderful it is; I used to bemoan the fact that I couldn't draw at all, but now I am more than happy that I can at least write. And if I haven't any talent for writing books or newspaper articles, well, then I can always write for myself . . . I can shake off everything if I write; my sorrows disappear, my courage is reborn! But, and that is the great question, will I ever be able to write anything great, will I ever become a journalist or a writer? I hope so, oh, I hope so very much, for I can recapture everything when I write, my thoughts, my ideals and my fantasies.'[155] A few days later, she was disheartened. ' "The unbosomings of an ugly duckling," will be the title of all this nonsense; my diary really won't be much use to Messrs. Bolkesteyn or Gerbrandi.'[156] The downbeat mood did not last and a week later she wrote, 'I want to send in to "the Prince" to see if they will take one of my stories, under a pseudonym, of course, but because all my stories so far have been too long, I don't think I have much of a chance.'[157]

On 11 May she felt ready to start work on 'Het Achterhuis' (literally, 'The House Behind'): 'you've known for a long time that my greatest wish is to become a journalist someday and later on a famous writer. Whether these leanings towards greatness (insanity!) will ever materialize remains to be seen, but I certainly have the subjects in my mind. In any case, I want to publish a book entitled *het Achterhuis* after the war, whether I shall succeed or not, I cannot say, but my diary will be a great help.'[158] Then the actual business of writing began. 'At long last after a great deal of reflection I have started my "Achterhuis," in my head it is as good as finished, although it won't go as quickly as that really, if it ever comes off at all.'[159] Her new version was written on sheets of coloured carbon paper. Anne altered parts of the original text, deleted some details, added others, and combined a number of entries. She possessed four diaries. The first was dated 12 June 1942–5 December 1942 (the original checked diary); the second 5 December 1942–22 December 1943; the third 22 December 1943–17 April 1944; the last covered the period from 17 April 1944 to 1 August 1944, and was another exercise book, on the first page of which she had written: 'The owner's maxim: Zest is what man needs!'[160] The second diary in its original state has never been found, but Anne must have had it with her then to work from it. She compiled a list of name changes for everyone she had mentioned, in the event of the diary being published, calling herself 'Anne Robin'.[161] The last date of the revised diary is 29 March 1944. Anne turned fifteen on 12 June 1944. Miep and Bep gave her a collection of unused office ledgers to write in. She asked Bep about the possibility of sending her stories off to magazines under an assumed name. When Bep asked her if she really wanted to be a writer, she answered, 'Yes . . . no . . . yes . . .' then decided with a brilliant smile, 'No, I want to marry early and have lots of children!'[162]

An incident that occurred in the summer of 1944 disturbed Miep and left her wondering whether the diary had not come to mean too much to Anne. After finishing her work early in the office, she went upstairs to pay a surprise visit. Entering the annexe, she noticed Anne sitting beside the window in her parents' room, writing in her diary. As Miep came up behind her, Anne turned, and presented a very different face from the smiling one with which Miep was so familiar: 'It was a look of dark concentration, as if she had a throbbing headache. This look pierced me, and I was speechless. She was suddenly another person there writing at the table. I couldn't say a word. My eyes were locked with Anne's brooding eyes.' At that moment Edith came into the room and tried to diffuse the situation by saying lightly, 'Yes, we have a daughter who writes.' Miep recounts, 'At this Anne stood up. She shut the book she was writing in and, with that look still on her face, she said with a dark voice that I'd also never heard before, "Yes, and I write about you too."' For a moment Miep was dumbfounded, then answered sarcastically, 'That will be very nice,' before returning to her office, very distressed. She could find no explanation for the sudden switch in Anne's attitude. 'I was upset by Anne's dark mood. I knew that more and more her diary had become her life. It was as if I had interrupted an intimate moment in a very, very private friendship . . . it wasn't Anne up there . . . it was another person.'[163]

The following month, on 1 August, Anne wrote her last letter to Kitty. She ended it: 'A voice sobs within me: "There you are, that's what's become of you, you're uncharitable, you look supercilious and peevish, people you meet dislike you and all just because you won't listen to the advice given you by your own better half." Oh, I would like to listen, but it doesn't work, if I'm quiet and serious they all think that it's a new comedy and then I have to get out of it by turning it into a joke, not to mention my own family, who are sure to think I'm ill, make me swallow pills for headaches and sedatives, feel my neck and my head to see whether I'm running a temperature, ask if I'm constipated and criticize me for being in a bad mood, I can't keep that up, if I'm watched to that extent I start by getting snappy, then unhappy, and finally I twist my heart round again, so that the bad is on the outside and the good is on the inside and keep on trying to find a way of becoming what I would so like to be and what I could be, if . . . there weren't any other people living in the world. *yours, Anne M. Frank*.'[164] Inside the back cover of her diary she had scribbled, 'Soit gentil et tiens courage!'[165]

Three days later, on 4 August 1944, the intimate friendship between writer and diary was broken. On that date, Kugler entered the secret annexe and stated helplessly, 'The Gestapo is here.'

Chapter Six

'I am afraid of prison cells and concentration camps . . .'

Anne Frank, *Diary*, 12 March 1944

Whilst the Frank family were in hiding, the expulsion of the Netherlands' Jewish population gathered pace.

On 6 August 1942 ('Black Thursday') 2,000 Jews in Amsterdam were arrested, beaten, and sent to Westerbork to await the trains for Auschwitz. The following day various parts of Amsterdam were raided and 600 Jews driven to Westerbork. Two days later, in another massive razzia, hundreds of Jews were seized in Amsterdam-Zuid. On 5 September 714 Dutch Jews arrived in Auschwitz; 651 were gassed. October 1942 saw the start of three weeks of violent raids in which almost 5,000 Jews were captured. The Hollandse Schouwburg, a theatre in Amsterdam's Plantage region, replaced the Zentralstelle as the main departure point for the camps. Below its ornate ceiling, hostages lay slumped on the floor for days, dying of thirst and hunger. There was no fresh air and only dull, artificial light. Dr Jacob Presser recounts, 'There were screaming children everywhere, in the corridors, in the halls, the foyers, the balconies, the pit, the staircases, the stalls. Then there were those who could not lie still and kept walking about the building. On top of it all there was the gnawing agony of uncertainty.'[1]

As rumours of what was happening in the camps began to spread, Jews throughout the Netherlands descended on the Jewish Council offices, pleading in vain for the coveted 'Bolle' exemption stamps which enabled them to remain at home a little longer. Lists of Jews eligible for the stamps were drawn up with great care, but only half of those listed actually received them.

Despite the increase in activity and membership of Jewish and non-Jewish Resistance groups,[2] the enforced exile continued. On 18 October 1942 1,594 Dutch Jews from a transport of 1,710 entered the gas-chambers of Auschwitz. Jewish rest homes in the Netherlands were targeted in raids in early November, and 450 people were taken to Westerbork, from where 1,610 people were shipped to the east a few days later.

At the beginning of 1943 there were further attacks on Jewish rest homes, Jewish hospitals and Jewish orphanages. Apeldoorn's Jewish Mental Hospital was emptied on 21 January, along with many houses in the town centre. The transports that arrived in Auschwitz from Apeldoorn were gassed, and the nurses who had insisted on travelling with their charges were thrown into a pit and burned alive. On 8 February 1,000 Jews from Westerbork, including every child in the camp hospital, were deported to Auschwitz. The children, most of whom had scarlet fever or diphtheria, were gassed, together with over 500 others. On 10 February all Jews still living in the provinces were ordered into Amsterdam. A new decree passed that month instructed Germans to consider displaced children as Jewish and to 'treat them accordingly'. Amsterdam's Joodse Invalide Hospital was emptied on 1 March. The Jewish Council had warned staff there would be a raid and most officials had fled, leaving only a handful of nurses to calm the patients. When the council was assured that the raid had been called off, they informed the hospital and all the staff returned. Nazis promptly turned up and arrested everyone, apart from a few employees who managed to hide under a makeshift stage; 355 staff and 416 patients were gassed in Auschwitz.

The raids and deportations continued throughout March 1943. On 22 March Hans Rauter told an SS meeting that Jews were to be completely expelled from the Netherlands, province by province. By this point, two trains were leaving each week, carrying approximately 12,000 Jews a month to their deaths. *Vrij Nederland*, an underground newspaper, described life in the shadow of the transports: 'At the stroke of eight, as darkness falls, the dread ordeal of waiting begins once again for our Jewish fellow citizens. Each footstep is a threat, each car an approaching doom, each bell a sentence. The squad cars are out, the boys in green and the Dutch Jew-baiters ready for their deadly night's work. Each evening the doors are flung open, and women, children, old people, the sickly and the rest, are dragged out like so many fish from a pond, defenceless, without appeal, hope or help. Night after night, by the hundred, dragged away, always to one and the same destination: death. When the morning comes, those left behind do the rounds of their friends and relations to see who is left. Next come the removal vans, taking away what furniture is left, and in the evening, it starts all over again . . .'[3]

On 21 May the commander of the German Security Police, Aus der Fünten, announced that 7,000 members of Amsterdam's Jewish Council were to report for deportation. The council's presidents drew up a list of names, but it fell far short of the quota. Random raids were stepped up in retaliation. On 26 May during an air-raid, 3,000 Jews were arrested, leaving the former Jewish quarter of Amsterdam empty, apart from the Jewish Council and those in hiding. On 20 June dawn raids in the east and south of the city picked up 5,500 people. The only Jews now permitted to remain in Amsterdam were those with a certain serial number on their identity card, sterilized Jews, some married to non-Jews, and the 'Calmeyer Jews', so called because they tried to prove that they were not Jewish and submitted petitions to this effect to the German judiciary led by Hans Calmeyer.

On 23 July 1943 Aus der Fünten ordered another raid on Amsterdam, this time directed at the Jewish Council. The staff who remained after the raid believed a new stamp would guarantee their exemption from future deportations. But on 29 September 1943 approximately 5,000 Jews, almost all those who had managed to evade the deportations, were seized in one last immense raid. At this point the Jewish Council ceased to exist. The debate about how useful its members had been in saving lives remains controversial. The council stands accused of lulling Jews into a false sense of security by telling them to go 'on transport' instead of going into hiding, and while thousands of Jewish families perished in the camps, the relatives of the Council's presidents were spared. Asscher and Cohen were arrested after the war, but charges against them were dropped. Presser expresses the view that, 'If the war had come to an end in 1942, the Jewish community would have built a monument to Asscher and Cohen as the brave and resourceful leaders by whose hands Dutch Jewry was saved.'[4] But Dutch Jewry was not saved, and the Jewish Court of Honour advised that both men should be prohibited from Jewish organizations for the rest of their lives. The Netherlands' wartime prime minister, Professor P. S. Gerbrandy, said: 'We believe that the Jewish Council let itself be used for the liquidation of Dutch Jewry. They collaborated with the Germans . . .'[5]

After the last raid, the only Jews still living in Amsterdam were those with false ID cards, and those who were in hiding. In 'Tramhalte Beethovenstraat', Grete Weil describes the oppressive silence in the city that tore at the nerves of every hidden individual after the deportations ended: 'In the Beethovenstraat the nights were still. Now and then a car passed by, sometimes they heard footsteps and pricked up their ears. If this was the sound of jackboots, they crouched, motionless. Often there was an air-raid warning, the crack of anti-aircraft guns, the bombers on their way to Germany droning high overhead. Then again the sirens and the silence. The silence drove away sleep, just the silence . . .'[6]

On 4 August 1944 the nightmare of being in hiding ended for the Frank family, and another began. It extended not only to those friends who had been arrested with them, but also to those who had been left behind.

Immediately after the raid, Miep found herself alone in the offices. The warehousemen were still there, but she did not see or hear them. Kleiman had given her the keys to the building, but at some point that afternoon, the senior warehouseman, van Maaren, took possession of them.[7] This did not strike Miep as strange: 'One of the SD [Security Service] men saw the name Gies on my identity card and remembered that the name of Gies was also connected to the business . . . in the view of the Germans at the time, I was an accomplice, after all . . . From what van Maaren told me, I gathered that he was really to be considered the "Verwalter" (administrator). At the time it was usual to appoint an administrator for every Jewish business. Since I did not then harbour any suspicions against van Maaren, I preferred to see him appointed administrator rather than anyone else . . . van Maaren boasted to me that he was on good terms with the SD and I need not fear they would arrest me. He would go to the SD himself.'[8]

At about five o'clock Jan returned and shortly afterwards Bep also reappeared. Jan had already visited Lotte Pfeffer. 'She suspected nothing, had not even known that her husband had been in Amsterdam all those two years, and so I told her. Now everyone concerned knew about it. At least they *knew*.'[9] Bep had wandered aimlessly about the city until she returned to the Prinsengracht. The three of them were joined by van Maaren, who locked the outside doors behind his younger assistant, Hartog. Jan suggested that they go up to the annexe to inspect the damage. With van Maaren still carrying the keys, they went up the short twisting staircase to the link corridor. The bookcase was still in place and the hidden door had been locked by the SD. Miep produced a duplicate key and opened it. They went in.

In the Franks' room the cupboard where the valuables were kept was empty, drawers had been wrenched open, and the floor was lost under mounds of books and papers. Miep recalls, 'Everything was in utter confusion . . . I came across Anne Frank's diary on the floor . . . together with an account book with notes by Anne and a number of loose sheets of copy paper, which were also covered with Anne's handwriting.'[10] She pointed out the diary to Bep, who picked it up. Jan watched them searchings amongst the mess: 'The officials from the Gestapo had obviously rummaged through everything. I know my wife picked up from the floor a book with a checked pattern on it. It is possible that she said at the time that this book was Anne's diary.'[11] Miep and Bep were able to salvage the diary, a photograph album, papers, schoolbooks, reading books, a shoe-bag embroidered with the initials 'A F' and a little book of quotations compiled by Anne. Jan extracted the library books that needed to be returned, and Pfeffer's Spanish textbooks and leaflets. Van Maaren held on to a bundle of Hermann van Pels's belongings.[12] They left the annexe when they could carry no more, but as Miep passed through the bathroom, she glimpsed Anne's combing shawl hanging from a rack. 'Even though my arms were filled with papers, I reached out and grabbed the shawl with my fingers. I still don't know why.'[13]

In the office Miep opened one of her desk drawers and shuffled in the diary, the loose papers, the accounting books, and the photograph album. Bep told her she would go along with whatever she decided. Miep motioned for Anne's papers. 'I will keep everything,' she said, adding them to the pile in the drawer, 'I'll keep everything safely for Anne until she comes back.'[14]

*

On that same afternoon, 4 August 1944, the police van carrying the Franks, the van Pelses, Pfeffer, Kugler and Kleiman, pulled up outside the Gestapo headquarters on Euterpestraat in the south of the city. In the courtyard a black flag emblazoned with the SS insignia flew from a tall white pole. The offices were in a massive, red-brick requisitioned school with a high clock tower at one end. The much-hated Zentralstelle stood directly opposite. Affairs at the Gestapo headquarters are still shrouded in secrecy because the relevant archives have never been found, but what *is* certain is that 'a large number of prisoners underwent interrogation here, as the SD tried to break the Resistance and preserve order in the occupied territory. During these interrogations many people were tortured, and the cellars, particularly, now used for garaging bicycles, have a sinister and evil history.'[15]

The ten prisoners were led into the building and locked in a room where a number of others already sat on long benches. They waited. Pfeffer seemed numbed, while Margot, Peter and Anne occasionally whispered to each other. Otto turned to Kleiman and said in a low voice, 'You can't imagine how I feel, Kleiman. To think that you are sitting here among us, that we are to blame . . .' Kleiman cut in, 'Don't give it another thought. It was up to me and I wouldn't have done it any differently.'[16] Eventually, Kugler and Kleiman were escorted to another cell. The Franks and their friends were taken for questioning. Kugler remembered his last glimpse of them: 'At a distance, in the corridor outside Silberbauer's office, we saw the Franks, the van Pelses and Pfeffer. All eight looked serious and troubled, not knowing what the future would bring. We waved to each other and that was goodbye.'[17]

The interview with the former occupants of the secret annexe was brief. A woman typed up their statements. Silberbauer asked Otto if he knew the whereabouts of any other Jews still hiding in Amsterdam. Otto replied that he did not, that having been in hiding himself for two years he had lost touch with everyone. Silberbauer appeared to believe him and did not pursue the matter. The prisoners returned to their cells.

'*Mitgefangen, mitgehangen*' – 'Caught with them, you will be hanged with them.'[18] With these words Silberbauer greeted Kleiman and Kugler as they were escorted into his office. He leaned back in his chair, lit a cigarette and began questioning them. On the desk were several objects belonging to Otto, Pfeffer's dental equipment and a small amount of money. Peter's bicycle, which he had hardly used before going into hiding, was also in the room. Kugler recalled, 'I felt a great pang when I looked at these inanimate objects which had belonged to my friends. These objects were mute witness to the tragic fate which had overtaken all of us. The interrogation began. "Where were you born?" Silberbauer asked me. I answered proudly, "Austria," and followed it up by saying, "I served in the Austrian Navy in the First World War." I particularly emphasized that, because from his dialect, I noticed that he himself was an Austrian. Maybe the shock was too great for him. First, Mr Frank – a Jew – an officer in the German Army, and then, somebody from the Austrian Navy. He leaned forward, put out his cigarette, and stopped further interrogation . . . "That's enough for today."[19]

Kugler and Kleiman were escorted to the cells in the basement but that evening they were transferred to the prison on Amstelveensweg in Amsterdam. During their month-long incarceration, one of the other prisoners, an old man who had been caught listening to the radio, was taken for questioning. When he returned he was distraught and incoherent. Kugler remembered, 'We, the prisoners, finally managed to calm him and learned that he had witnessed the torture of Jews (as well as Gentiles accused of hiding Jews). He had seen a professional boxer hitting those unfortunate prisoners. And he had heard their anguished cries as they were subjected to the terrible thumbscrew torture.'[20] Shortly after this incident, Kugler was told to report to Silberbauer again. 'Silberbauer tried to get out of me that [the businesses on the Prinsengracht] were actually owned by a Jew (Mr Frank),' he recalled. 'However, I insisted that Mr Kleiman and I owned the firms. Finally Silberbauer grew weary and said, "Enough." The interrogation was over.'[21] Kugler and Kleiman were placed in adjoining cells, each containing six people, although they were intended for one. They left their cells once a day for exercise in the prison yard, and took advantage of this to slip each other messages and words of support. They had no idea whether they were going to live or be executed.

The eight Jewish prisoners were kept overnight at the Euterpestraat. Eva Schloss understands something of their fear and desperation, for her family were also detained at the Gestapo headquarters after their betrayal. 'The old school building was completely overtaken by the Nazis, crawling with them. There were soldiers everywhere, and offices, rooms for documentation, and cells, too. They wanted us to give them information on who had protected us. But my mother secured the freedom of those people by offering the Germans her jewellery. And the Germans kept their side of the bargain, isn't that something? But we couldn't believe we'd ended up there.'[22]

The Franks and their friends were transferred the following day to the Huis van Bewaring on the Weteringschans. It was a large, ugly, dark building with two wings stretching out from a centre block, overlooking a filthy stretch of canal. Metal bars obscured the windows. Eva and her family were sent to the same place. 'It was a proper, regular prison for real criminals. Everyone ended up in these huge rooms where there were rows of bunks. Hundreds of people and no toilets, just buckets in a corner. The noise through the night of people crying and shouting, babies wailing – after being in hiding – it was like a madhouse. Terrible, terrible.'[23] The Franks, the van Pelses and Pfeffer remained there for the next two days.

Miep had taken charge of business at the Prinsengracht. The sales representatives and the warehousemen all knew now about the arrest. One of the reps, Daatselaar, told Miep to try bribing the Gestapo for her friends' release. Daatselaar was a member of the NSB, but Otto had always thought him trustworthy. 'The SD has a really soft spot for money,' he told Miep, adding that the Germans were 'doing badly on all fronts and so would probably be ready to co-operate if the ransom was high enough'. He said he could raise the funds if necessary. Miep telephoned Silberbauer, who told her, 'Come early on Monday morning.'

On Monday 7 August Miep visited the Gestapo headquarters. Silberbauer was in his office, surrounded by busy typists. Miep stood in front of him and gestured with her thumb and forefinger: money. He shook his head. 'I can't do anything for you today. Come back tomorrow.' She did so, but Silberbauer said, 'I'm sorry, I can't do anything for you. I'm not senior enough.' Miep, in despair, called him a liar. He shrugged his shoulders. 'Go upstairs then, to my boss.' Miep climbed the stairs and entered a room where a group of high-ranking Nazis sat around a table, listening to the forbidden British broadcast from London. One of them approached her, screaming, '*Schweinehund!*' Miep rushed downstairs.

Silberbauer was waiting for her. 'You see?' he said. She knew she could do no more.[24]

In a statement given after the war, Miep claims that when she returned from the Gestapo 'in a mood of dejection', van Maaren told her, 'I know people who can make enquiries for you'. She asserts, 'He did not tell me who or what these people were or if they had any connection with the SD, but he gave me the clear impression that in one way or another he had some influence with the Germans.'[25] Van Maaren denies the charge in his statement: 'It is absolutely untrue that I told Mrs Gies that I was on good terms with the SD and that she need not worry about being arrested. On the contrary, I was known among my friends as a good anti-German.'[26]

Miep's efforts on her friends' behalf were all in vain. Although she did not know it then, when she had entered the Gestapo headquarters on Euterpestraat for the second time, the Franks, the van Pelses and Pfeffer were, at that very moment, passengers on the train to Westerbork.

In his memoir Otto mentions the transportation of 8 August only fleetingly: 'After a few days in the Amsterdam jail we were all transferred to a Dutch concentration camp. We had heavy hearts because two of our helpers, Kleiman and Kugler, had been arrested as well, and we didn't know what fate lay in front of them.'[27] When the train arrived, it was a standard passenger train with compartments on both sides, but as soon as the passengers climbed aboard, the doors were locked and bolted behind them. This did not trouble the Frank family unduly. Otto recalled, 'We were together again, and had been given a little food for the journey. We knew where we were bound, but in spite of that it was almost as if we were once more going travelling, or having an outing, and we were actually cheerful. Cheerful, at least, when I compare this journey with our next . . . The war was so far advanced that we could begin to place a little hope in luck. As we rode toward Westerbork we were hoping that our luck would hold.'[28] The Franks had had their spirits raised by D-Day on 6 June, and still felt that they would come through to see the end of the war. Anne stayed resolutely by the window, mesmerized by the countryside. Otto later explained, 'It was summer. Meadows, stubble fields and villages flew by. The telephone wires along the right of way curvetted up and down along the windows. It was like freedom.'[29] By late afternoon, the train had reached its destination.

Kamp Westerbork was in the province of Drenthe, approximately eighty miles north of Amsterdam, a site 'about as inhospitable as could be. Far from the civilized world, in the isolation of the Drenthe moorland. Difficult to reach, with unpaved roads where even the slightest shower would turn the sand to mud.'[30] It was originally a refugee camp for German Jews, set up at the instigation of the Dutch government, and known as 'the Jerusalem of the Netherlands'.[31] When war broke out, 750 refugees were in the camp. They were evacuated while the Germans re-designed the area for its new purpose as a departure point for the camps in the east. Most returned when work was completed.

A high, barbed-wire fence ran around the perimeter of the camp, interspersed with watch-towers. The 107 wooden barracks, containing rows of three-tier bunks, were designed to hold 300 people each. There were electric lights in the barracks, but few actually worked. Men and women were segregated at night, but there were no restrictions on their movements during the day. The main street running through the camp was nicknamed 'Boulevard des Misères' or 'Tsores [*Trouble*] Avenue'.

Westerbork was a town within itself. It contained a laundry and wash-house, a well-equipped hospital with maternity wards, workshops, an old people's home, a huge modern kitchen, a school for children between the ages of six and fourteen, an orphanage and a religious service; there was a stocking repair shop, a tailor, furniture maker, locksmith, decorator, book-binder, bricklayer, carpenter, vets, optician, a gardening section, building section, an electro-technical division, a garage and boiler room, a sewage works, a phone exchange, an industrial department, a punishment block and a prison barracks. Just beyond the barbed wire there was a farm, tended by the agricultural section of the camp. Services within the hospital included dental clinics, hairdressers, photographers and a postal system. Sports were available, with boxing, tug-of-war and gymnastics on offer. There was a cabaret, a choir, and a ballet troupe which was rumoured to have the best performances and most expensive costumes in the country.[32] In a café, two crooners from Amsterdam, 'Johnny and Jones', sang regularly to the accompaniment of a string band. Toiletries, toys and plants could be purchased from the camp warehouse.

Westerbork's administration section registered all newcomers and the central registry kept details of everyone who passed through the camp gates. The registry was responsible for compiling the weekly lists of deportees. The Antragstelle tried to obtain exemptions for the inmates. The most despised section was the OD, the Special Service Corps, who bullied people around and patrolled the punishment barracks. Westerbork was spared the daily jurisdiction of the German SS because it was under Jewish leadership, but the leaders were answerable to the camp commandant, Albert Gemmeker, who lived in a house on the edge of the camp and ran a small chicken farm. He was an enigma to the inmates. He rarely raised his voice or dealt out punishments and was said to be incorruptible. He took an interest in the staged entertainments in the camp, and joked with the Jewish performers afterwards. Flowers in the greenhouse were cultivated especially for him by Jewish gardeners and he was treated by Jewish hairdressers, dentists and doctors. Yet every Tuesday he stood quietly watching the trains depart to the east.

The railway line into the camp was completed in November 1942. Trains came right into the middle of the compound. To keep their names off the transport lists people would do anything – 'sacrifice their last hoarded halfpenny, their jewels, their clothes, their food, or in the case of young girls, their bodies'.[33] The days of the week were determined by the transportation routine. Trains left every Tuesday morning and 'by Tuesday evening everything was smoothed over; sociability and peace reigned once more. Wednesday and Thursday were days of calm optimism and euphoria. On Friday, fears again began to stir . . . On Saturday everyone was edgy. On Sunday they were agitated. On Monday the panic spread and everyone would run around in circles, looking up relatives, trying to get information, keeping an ear to the ground. And on Tuesday – the next transport.'[34]

When the Franks, the van Pelses and Pfeffer disembarked at Westerbork on the afternoon of 8 August, they went through the usual routine for new arrivals. They were met by the OD, ushered down from the train and across to the registration desks in the main square. Ration cards were surrendered, then personal details entered on forms and cards. The process was repeated at the classification desk and in the office of the accommodation bureau. The Franks were questioned by Vera Cohn, who remembered them well: 'A small group, Mr Frank, his wife and his two daughters, another couple with a son, and a dentist – all had hid together in Amsterdam. Mr Frank was a pleasant-looking man, courteous and cultured. He stood before me tall and erect. He answered my routine questions quietly. Anne was by his side. Her face, by certain standards, was not a pretty one, but her eyes – bright, young, eager eyes – made you look at her again. She was fifteen then . . . None of the Franks showed any signs of despair over their plight . . . Their composure, as they grouped around my typing desk in the receiving room, was one of quiet dignity.'[35] Vera's husband worked in Westerbork's Antragstelle, where newcomers found out whether they might qualify for exemption from the transportations. Vera's husband discussed the Franks' case with her. 'When the Franks were led into the office (he told me later), he knew they were to get red patches on their shoulders; he was painfully aware of the futility of their petition. But hope, no matter how slender its thread, is one of the most powerful forces in a concentration camp. These formalities over, the Frank family was shut up in their special barracks. We never saw them again.'[36]

Before being led to their barracks, arrivals were taken to the quarantine block, where a representative of Lippmann, Rosenthal & Co. asked them if they had any valuables. New inmates were subjected to a body search. They had to strip and kneel down, and were screamed at and often punched. Then they were assigned to their block. Because they had been in hiding, the Franks and their friends were labelled 'convict Jews'. They were placed in the punishment compound, Barrack 67. In all, about 10,000 Jews entered the disciplinary block. Their freedom was curtailed even by camp standards, and instead of keeping their own clothes, they were given blue overalls with red shoulder patches, and wooden clogs. Men had their heads shaved and women had their hair cropped. They were not allowed soap and they received less food than other prisoners, although their work was harder, including heavy duties outside the camp when necessary, and a punishing drill system inside.

Friendships and family were the lifeblood of survival in the camps. On their first day in Westerbork, the Franks met Rosa and Manuel de Winter and their daughter Judy, who was the same age as Anne. The de Winters had been in hiding for a year when a spy betrayed them to the

Gestapo. Sal and Rose de Liema, a young couple who had been arrested whilst in hiding, became acquainted with the Franks whilst working in the battery factory in Westerbork. Another couple, Lenie de Jong-van Naarden and her husband, whose circumstances were similar to the de Liemas', met the Franks in the camp. Lenie recalled, 'My husband had quickly made contact with Otto Frank and got along with him very well. They had profound conversations and we had a very good relationship with Mrs Frank, whom I always addressed as Mrs Frank. I never called her by her first name; she was really a very special woman. I had less difficulty saying "Otto". She worried a lot about her children. She was always busy with those girls . . . Anne, especially, was a nice child . . . those children expected so much from life.'[37] Ronnie Goldstein-van Cleef also knew the family: 'The Franks were pretty depressed. They had had the feeling that nothing could happen to them. They were very close to each other. They always walked together.'[38]

Every day followed a pattern. Roll-calls and then work began at 5 o'clock in the morning. Children were sent to the cable workshop and adults to the industrial department, where they spent the day dismantling old aeroplane batteries at long trestle tables. Conversation was permitted, but guards stood over them as they laboured, shouting at them to speed up. For sustenance, workers received a piece of stale bread and a few ladles of watery soup. Janny and Lientje Brilleslijper, who were also in the punishment section, worked alongside the Frank family. Lientje remembered, 'On the way to and from work I spoke very much with Edith Frank . . . She was a friendly, intelligent person of warm feelings . . . Her open character and her goodness attracted me very much.'[39] Anne's antagonism towards her mother whilst they had been in hiding was now forgotten. All that mattered was staying together. Lientje recalled, 'The two girls were very attached to their mother. Anne wrote in the diary that her mother didn't understand her, but I think that was just an adolescent mood. She clung to her mother in the camp.'[40]

Rachel van Amerongen-Frankfoorder was another young woman who had been interned in the punishment compound for her involvement with the Resistance. She worked for the camp's internal service, and Otto approached her to ask if she could find some small job for Anne. Rachel remembered, 'Anne was very nice and also asked me if she could help me.

She said, "I can do everything; I am very handy" . . . Unfortunately, I had no say in the matter. I sent her to the people in charge of the barracks . . . Cleaning batteries wasn't so pleasant, nor was cleaning toilets, but people preferred doing the latter. I think Otto Frank was eager to arrange that for Anne. That's the reason he came to me with Anne – not with his wife and not with Margot. I think that Anne was the apple of his eye.'[41]

People who remember the Franks from Westerbork recall that Anne seemed happy there. Rosa de Winter recalled, 'I saw Anne Frank and Peter van Pels every day in Westerbork. They were always together . . . Anne was so lovely, so radiant . . . her movements, her looks, had such a lilt to them that I often asked myself, Can she possibly be happy? She was happy in Westerbork, though that seems almost incredible.'[42] The mood in the camp was hopeful in summer 1944. Eva Schloss, who was also in Westerbork at the time, reflects, 'We hadn't been especially afraid of going to Westerbork. It wasn't a concentration camp and we thought we might stay there until the liberation. I was very happy to be with my father and brother again. Their hiding place had given them no opportunity to go outside (my mother and I could, occasionally), so they viewed Westerbork as a kind of freedom. We had begun to be really hopeful again. We never thought that we wouldn't survive.'[43]

Rosa de Winter was impressed by Otto's inner strength. 'Anne's father was quiet . . . but it was a reassuring quietness that helped Anne and helped the rest of us too. He lived in the men's barracks, but once when Anne was sick, he came over to visit her every evening and would stand beside her bed for hours, telling her stories. Anne was so like him that when she recovered and David fell ill, a twelve-year-old boy who lived in the women's barracks, she acted in just the same way, stood by his bed and talked to him. David came from an orthodox family, and he and Anne always talked about God.'[44] Otto's memoir reveals that his confidence was not all that it seemed: 'At the camp, we had to work, although we had the evenings off and we could be together. It was a particular relief for the children to no longer be locked away and to be able to talk with other people. We, the old ones, however, feared the danger of being transported to the rumoured death camps of Poland . . .'[45]

At the beginning of September, Westerbork's commandant, Gemmeker, summoned the section leaders and instructed them to compile a list of about 1,000 persons for another deportation to the east. Bedlam broke out in the camp. The train's expected time of departure from Westerbork was announced at the enquiries department in Groningen; it would leave on the morning of 3 September 1944.

The night before, one of the OD, accompanied by a German official, entered the punishment barracks and read out the names on the list. Amongst them were Hermann, Auguste and Peter van Pels; Fritz Pfeffer; Otto, Edith, Margot and Anne Frank.

In Amsterdam Miep and Jan listened to the radio every night. On 28 August the British RAF began dropping arms for the Resistance, in preparation for the Allied invasion of the Netherlands. In one place alone, sixty-five tons of weapons and sabotage equipment were landed. The Germans announced a stricter curfew, afraid that the Netherlands would become a theatre of operations, and cut food rations again. Coal, electricity, gas and transport were also further restricted. People living in the south of the country were evacuated to the north, away from the Allied advance.

A week or two after the raid on the Prinsengracht, the annexe was cleared of its remaining furniture and objects by German agents, who shipped their spoils to Germany. Miep, who was in the office at the time, could not bear to watch them, but she asked van Maaren to go up to the annexe and bring back any papers he could see with Anne's writing on them. He found some, and handed them to Miep, who placed them in her desk drawer. The company representatives sometimes asked to see Anne's diary, knowing it had been found on the floor of the annexe. Miep always refused: 'No, it's not right. Even though it's the writings of a child, it's hers and it's her secret. I'll only return it back into her hands, and her hands alone.'[46] After the final plundering of the annexe, Peter's cat Mouschi suddenly emerged from wherever he had been hiding since 4 August. Scooping him up with emotion, Miep took him into the kitchen for some milk. She took care of him at the offices from then on, knowing how much Peter and Anne had loved him.

Miep had been authorized by the bank to sign cheques for bills and to pay the staff whilst Kleiman and Kugler were absent. There was enough work to keep the business afloat. Silberbauer turned up at the office occasionally to check up on Miep, but no conversation passed between them. Van Maaren, in his new capacity as 'administrator', dismissed Hartog, his assistant, and ran the warehouse by himself, acting 'at times as if he were the head of the business'.[47] Kleiman later claimed that 'when van Maaren had the keys and was put in charge by the SD, he thought of himself as the administrator and acted as such. He borrowed money from people connected with the business and forgot to repay it. During arguments with the office staff he once claimed that he could do anything he liked and that he would not balk at anything, not even at walking over dead bodies.'[48] These unpleasant boasts and traits aside, Miep and Bep seem to have paid him little attention in the months following the arrest. Their thoughts were elsewhere. Bep had taken time off to be with her family, and Miep was working harder than ever, arriving home in the evenings tired and depressed. Jan had resigned from his work in the Resistance, and Karel, their clandestine lodger, had found a new address.

On 3 September the news came across the radio airwaves that Lyons had fallen to the Allies. A day later, with the help of Belgian Resistance fighters, the British succeeded in capturing Antwerp.

In Amsterdam, Miep wept on hearing the news: 'We knew we were next.'[49]

Rosa de Winter remembered, 'On 2 September we were told that a thousand persons would leave in the morning . . . During the night we packed up the few things we had been allowed to keep. Someone had a little ink, and with that we marked our names on the blankets we were to take with us and we made the children repeat again and again the addresses where we were to meet after the war, in case we were separated. I again gave Judy the address of her aunt in Zutphen and the Franks had agreed on an address in Switzerland.'[50]

Eva Schloss, who together with her family had been deported from Westerbork only a short time before, recalls, 'When we heard that we were on the list, we tried everything we could to change things, but it was no good. The people who compiled the list were mainly Jews, I think, and they did what they could to protect their friends and relatives. But for the rest, well, we just had to go. Everyone packed what they had, though later they took it all from us. But at that time you still thought that if you had a little suitcase, or some belongings, you would be able to keep them with you. We really had no idea how brutal the treatment in Auschwitz would be. Or how immediate that brutality would be.'[51]

There were 1,019 persons (498 women, 442 men and 79 children) listed on the ninety-third transport from Westerbork. It was the very last train to leave the Netherlands for the extermination camps. As the sun rose on 3 September 1944, the Boulevard des Misères was being cordoned off. The train had already arrived: 'A long chain of trucks had rolled in during the night, right into the middle of the camp. Now it was waiting, motionless, like a masked executioner concealing his bared axe.'[52] On the platform Gemmeker stood with his dog at his side. Guards strolled about, relaxed and smiling. At 7 a.m. men, women and children began filing out of the barracks. 'Their names were called, their camp papers collected . . . they were all lined up; a deadly hush fell on the camp.'[53] Each passenger carried a haversack over one shoulder and a rolled-up blanket attached to the other with string. They were instructed to walk forward in groups of three. The sick and the disabled were guided through on stretchers and carts. It was a high step from platform to train and a long wait until the carriages were filled. An observer of one transport noted, 'The freight cars had been completely sealed, but a plank had been left out here and there, and people put their hands through the gaps and waved as if they were drowning. The sky is full of birds, the purple lupins stand up so regally and peacefully, two little old women have sat down on the box for a chat, the sun is shining . . . and right before our eyes, mass murder.'[54]

At 11 o'clock the whistle blew. The guards still standing on the platform could read the inscription on the rear of the train as it pulled away: 'Westerbork–Auschwitz: Auschwitz–Westerbork. Do not uncouple the carriages, the entire train must return to Westerbork intact.'

Straw lay on the floor of the crowded, rocking carriages. In each a small bucket was filled with water for drinking. A larger bucket served as a toilet and next to it lay a sandbag to soak up the spillage. Some trucks were draughty, while in others the only ventilation came from holes spiked through the roof. A tiny square window and a suspended lantern gave poor illumination. Seventy-five persons were packed tightly against each other in the darkness. The trucks stank from the start and later the stench became unbearable when the dysentery cases became worse and the weak began to die.

In one carriage the Franks, the van Pelses, Pfeffer, the de Winters, Ronnie Goldstein-van Cleef, Lenie de Jong-van Naarden, and Lientje and Janny Brilleslijper sat together on their rucksacks, pressing themselves against the walls. They shared their carriage with the desperately sick in a space that was cramped and cold. No one knew for certain where they were going, but the rumour was that they were bound for Auschwitz.[55]

Hours passed and they knew they were in Germany. Whenever the train stopped, a guard would open the door and throw in a bucket of beet marmalade and a few pieces of bread. They sometimes stopped for hours, and the guards outside would shout for them to surrender their valuables. A few handed over coins and jewellery that they had sewn into their clothes. The toilet pail was yanked out, emptied, and flung back in.

Anne, Margot, Peter and Judy sat together, talking quietly and occasionally climbing up on the bars to peep out of the window. A young man who was keeping watch stepped aside for them; he had been trying to determine where they were. 'Anne was riding through the country of her birth,' Rosa recalled, 'but it might as well have been Brazil or Asia, for even when they were able to read the name of a station as it flitted by outside, the name meant nothing to us; the place was only a small village. All we did know was that we were headed east . . . we adults were silent. At most we would ask the children once again whether they still remembered the addresses, nothing more.'[56]

At night it was impossible to sleep. The jarring of the cattle-trucks, the stench and the fear kept them awake. Tempers frayed and people argued, shouted and sobbed. Lenie de Jong-van Naarden remembers how Edith tried to occupy herself: 'Mrs Frank had smuggled out a pair of overalls and she sat by the light of the candle, ripping off the red patch. She must have thought that without that red patch, they wouldn't be able to see that we were convict prisoners . . . for her it was important and she got some satisfaction from doing it. Many people, among them the Frank girls, leaned against their father or mother, everyone was dead tired.'[57] In his memoir, Otto recalled the journey in just two sentences: 'The awful transportation – three days locked in a cattle truck – was the last time I saw my family. Each of us tried to be as courageous as possible and not to let our heads drop.'[58]

The night of the third day, the train started to slow down. The passengers got to their feet, steeling themselves. A murmur of prayer filled the cattle cars. The train turned sharply in the direction of a long, low building with an arched entrance and a high pointed roof. Searchlight beams swept across marshland. The train stopped.

Rifle butts pounded on the doors: '*Juden, raus, schnell, RAUS!*'

Who Has Inflicted This Upon Us? 1944–5

Part Four

Chapter Seven

'My fear makes me want to scream out loud . . . I have not enough
faith in God . . .'

Anne Frank, *Diary*, 29 December 1943

The doors of the train were wrenched apart. 'The first we saw of Auschwitz were the glaring searchlights fixed on the train, and outside on the platform men were running back and forth as though they were crazy to show how hard they were working,' Rosa de Winter remembered.[1] The men were *kapos* (head prisoners), who reached in and pulled those nearest to them down to the uneven ground. Behind the *kapos*, SS officers greeted the guards who had accompanied the train.

The *kapos* yelled at the newcomers to hurry. There were shouts and screams of anguish as relatives disappeared from view. The *kapos* rushed through, dragging luggage from the train and stacking it at the rear of the platform. The corpses of those who had died on the last part of the journey were slung beside the suitcases. Above the hissing steam of the cooling train, a loudspeaker bellowed: 'Women to the left! Men to the right!' Otto Frank, Hermann van Pels, Peter van Pels, Frits Pfeffer and all the other men from the train were herded away as SS guards stepped forward, shoving the women into columns of five, then again into two rows.

Eva Schloss recalls the procedure: 'Those first few minutes when the doors of the train were thrown open were wonderful in a way because of the fresh air and sudden freedom of movement. But then we saw Mengele.' Dr Josef Mengele was known in the camp as the 'Angel of Death'. He had a particular interest in twins and the physically deformed. His experiments on twins included killing one to judge the effect it had on the other. Since his arrival in Auschwitz in May 1943, over 1,500 twins had been brought to him for experimentation. 'He was good-looking really,' Eva admits, 'very clean, with these highly polished boots. Tall, too. Normally you would have said that he was a nice-looking man. But he decided who lived and who died . . . We said good-bye to our menfolk – there was time enough in all that to say our farewells. I said goodbye to my father and I had no idea if I would ever see him again. When the men had gone to their side, the next command was "Get into rows of five". Always rows of five, one behind the other, rows of five, rows of five. My mother gave me an extra hat and a coat, which saved me from the gas chamber because it was impossible then for Mengele, who never bothered to look at anyone closely, to tell my age.'[2]

The selection that took place on the platform decided who would be admitted to the camp. Two columns were formed. Mengele's silver hair gleamed in the light, his veiled eyes flickered over the newcomers dispassionately, and an almost imperceptible movement of his white-gloved hand sent people to the left or to the right.

The loudspeaker roared again: 'It's an hour's march to the women's camp. For children and the sick we've provided lorries at the far end of the platform.' The trucks were painted with red crosses and people ran towards them, hanging on desperately as the motors started up. Within minutes, they had disappeared. Eva recalls, 'The Germans were so crafty, calling for the old and the sick or the very young to climb into those lorries. It was a sort of natural selection. Those lorries went straight to the gas chamber.'[3]

The women were forced to march quickly. They came to a gateway where black iron letters formed an arch overhead: ARBEIT MACHT FREI – 'Work Brings Freedom'. They passed through the gate, beneath the blue gleam of the electrified fences that ran the length of the entire area. Silhouetted figures stood motionless in the watchtowers. This was the entrance to Birkenau, the killing terminal of Auschwitz, 'the greatest death-factory of all'.[4] There was no longer any doubt about where they were. Janny Brilleslijper recalled, 'It was so insane – that moment of realization, "Yes, this is an extermination camp." It was dreadful . . . The horrible effect of that very bright, dirty-looking neon light, a bluish light, and that grey sky above, more or less lit up by the neon lamps . . . it was a kind of nightmare, an inferno.'[5]

The women were led into a narrow building euphemistically called the sauna. Each new arrival had to strip and stand under the showers while her clothes were confiscated for 'decontamination'. She was then led to the 'hairdressing section' where her hair was shaved from her underarms and pubic area. Heads were either shaved or the hair cut very short. The prisoner received 'new' clothes – shoes and a grey sack-like dress, often with a large cross on the back marking her out as a newcomer. Wearing her sack, she went across to a row of desks where she gave her personal details and had her forearm tattooed. Eva remarks, 'At first, this process, hard as it was, gave us new hope, because we thought, surely they're not going to kill us after going to so much trouble! That would not have made any sense! But it was the *kapos* who did this, and they were even more cruel than the Germans, who only patrolled the camp. It was the *kapos*, then, who asked us while this process was taking place, "Did you say goodbye to your mother, brother, father? They have gone to the gas chamber now. You won't see them again. You see that chimney and the smoke coming from it? That's probably them already." '6

All newcomers were then assigned to their barracks. Anne Frank, Margot, Edith, Rosa and Judy de Winter were placed in Block 29. The buildings were identical. 'A barrack typically consisted of a large hut called a Block, measuring 44.20 metres by 8.50 metres. There would be a primitive washroom and a privy. There would be a private room for the *blockälteste* (block-leader). Bunks (*koje*) were in tiers of three, with not enough space between them for a person to sit up. They were made of coarse wood . . . covered by straw mattresses or loose straw. In each berth there were generally two blankets. Blankets and straw mattresses were filthy . . . In addition, faeces and urine often dripped from one storey to another from prisoners suffering from hunger, diarrhoea and polyuria . . . Those who could not get a place on a bunk would be forced to sleep under them – and the earth floor would be a mire of excrement.'7

Of the 1,019 passengers from the Westerbork transport, 212 women and 258 men were admitted to Auschwitz. Otto Frank, Fritz Pfeffer and Peter van Pels were among them, but before they entered the camp compound, they saw what happened to the men, women and children who had been sent to the other column. Otto reflected, 'I'll never forget the time in Auschwitz when seventeen-year-old Peter van Pels and I saw a group of selected men. Among those men was Peter's father. The men marched away. Two hours later, a lorry came by loaded with their clothing.'[8]

Hermann van Pels was amongst more than 500 people from Westerbork who had been detained on the illuminated platform. Every child under the age of fifteen was there. As suitcases, rucksacks, toys and other items from the train were wheeled away, the selected group were taken from the platform and down a flight of steps into a windowless, rectangular building. *Kapos* told them to undress and offered assistance in folding clothes, keeping shoes in pairs, locating towels and soothing embarrassment as men, women and children sat naked on the cold benches. The prisoners were ushered into a large, empty room. Rows of shower fitments bulged through the low ceiling. As 549 people were crammed in together, the doors slammed behind them.

On the roof of the building an SS man climbed up a ladder, sliding a drawstring bag after him. Crouching down, he took out a mask and gloves, then a hammer. He pulled on the protective clothing and, using the hammer, bore down on the lid of the canister he had carried in his bag, exposing its contents – green crystals – to the air. He reached into one of two ducts in the roof and lifted up a tin can on a length of wire. The green crystals flowed into the can and the lid was sealed before being lowered through the enclosed steel pipes and protective wire mesh. He shoved his mask and gloves into the bag and climbed back down the ladder.

Far below, screams pierced the darkness as the lights in the chamber dimmed. The first fume of gas burned the lungs. The weakest fell to the floor quickly, but the stronger ones clamoured towards the door, reaching out their arms. As the gas grew more powerful, the fumes became visible. After fifteen minutes, there was no more screaming.

The doors of the chamber were opened by the *Sonderkommando*. The pyramid of bodies stood caked with excrement, menstrual blood, sweat, vomit and urine. The *Sonderkommando* dragged them apart. Iron hooks opened mouths, pliers explored crevices and extracted gold teeth, wedding rings were pulled from fingers, and long hair was hacked away. In the crematorium, sixty pounds of coal were heaped into each oven;

new corpses burned easily. The larger crematoria had a burning capacity of 6,500 per twenty-four hours. The bodies were loaded on to shelves. Small windows in the doors allowed the observer to gauge the swiftness of the procedure. Cadavers engorged and exploded inside the iron cages, turning to ash within a quarter of an hour.

The gassing of the ninety-third Westerbork transport was among the last to occur in Auschwitz-Birkenau. The summer of 1944 had seen 'an orgy of killing . . . The furnaces in the crematoria became so hot that firebricks cracked, and additional burning pits had to be dug. Once started, the flames were fuelled with the fat that had run off the burning bodies. The hot fat was channelled into concrete gutters which ran along the bottoms of the pits, at the sides, into vats, from which prisoners on this particular *Kommando* scooped it up with long-handled ladles, to pour over the bodies burning in the pits. The pits were designed by the 29-year-old SS Hauptscharführer, Otto Moll. As at this period it was not considered worth gassing babies and small children, Moll would throw them live into the gutters of boiling human fat . . .'⁹ However, towards the end of 1944, as German defeat loomed, Himmler ordered the end of the gassings.

His command was too late to save Hermann van Pels, who died in Auschwitz on 6 September 1944.

In the Netherlands 5 September 1944 became known as 'Dolle Dinsdag' (Mad Tuesday). After the liberation of Brussels and Antwerp, in a case of collective mistaken euphoria, the Dutch convinced themselves that the liberation was about to happen. People hung flags from their windows, waited excitedly to cheer in their champions, and sang in the streets. Dutch collaborators jammed the railway stations, hoping to escape before the Allies arrived. But as the day drew to a close without any sign of liberators, a mood of despondency settled on the Netherlands.

Two days after Mad Tuesday, Kugler and Kleiman were transferred from their prison on the Amstelveenseweg. Kugler recalled, 'It was 7 September 1944, past 8 p.m., the curfew hour for the citizens of Amsterdam. In the stilled city, frightened eyes peered furtively from behind closed windows. Fingers were pointing at the strange scene taking place on the street outside. Streetcars were passing by, transporting prisoners from the Amstelveensweg prison. German soldiers with automatic rifles on their laps were riding in automobiles, alongside the streetcars. Kleiman and I were among these prisoners.'[10]

They were taken to the prison on the Weteringschans, where their friends from the annexe had been interned the previous month. They were separated upon their arrival, and Kugler was astonished to find himself in a private cell: '. . . the luxury astonished me. The walls were painted and the cell contained a bed. On the bed was a pillow, clean sheets and blankets. There was even a bright electric light in the ceiling. This was certainly different from the one I had recently left. I sat down on the bed in order to get better acquainted with my new surroundings. Soon I discovered some pitiful messages scratched on the walls: "I too will be shot, pray for me"; "I die for the Queen and our Fatherland, God is with me." It became clear to me that I was in a cell reserved for those who had been sentenced to death for actions against the enemy. I broke into a cold sweat, for I was sure that my last hours had come.'[11] Fortunately they had not. Kugler had been placed in the cell by mistake. A guard took him to another cell where he was reunited with Kleiman.

The following day Kugler was picked out from a roll call for work beyond the prison walls. For one week he was taken every day to a plant on Valckeniersstraat to dismantle machines for shipment to Germany. On 11 September, together with Kleiman, he was sent to Amersfoort transit camp. At the administration block, they handed over their wedding rings and watches, and were asked why they were there. 'I answered *Judenbegünstigung* [helping Jewish people],' Kugler recalls. 'This won for me some dirty looks.'[12] Kugler and Kleiman were placed in a small hut together and slept side by side on a narrow bunk. They were not in the same work group, but their treatment was identical: exacting, tiresome work punctuated by roll-calls, beatings and clubbings. Kleiman's health swiftly deteriorated and a gastric haemorrhage prevented him from further work.

On 17 September in tandem with the first Allied incursions into the Netherlands, Queen Wilhelmina, speaking from London, urged Dutch railway workers to strike so that German military trains could not reach their destinations. The ensuing strike, expected to last two weeks, did not end until May 1945. The German government responded by withholding all supplies of food, electricity, gas and coal. The Dutch 'Hunger Winter' was under way.

Kugler had been awaiting transportation to Germany on 17 September, when American planes began bombing the main railway station in Amersfoot. The transfer was cancelled, but angry guards retaliated by severely beating the prisoners. Kleiman was released the following day, due to ill health. He returned to Amsterdam, where he spent almost two months recuperating. His reappearance at the Prinsengracht offices provoked an ecstatic welcome from Miep and Bep. Miep recalls, 'All three of us were laughing and crying at the same time . . . the good feeling of his return swept over me like a soft wave of relief. His safe and healthy return gave me great hope for all the others.'[13]

Kugler was now alone in Amersfoort, and at the end of September he was amongst 1,100 men taken from Amersfoort to Zwolle to dig anti-tank trenches and perform other tasks under German armed guard. Back at the office on the Prinsengracht, Miep, Bep and Kleiman (who had taken charge of the business upon his return) sat at their desks and tried to keep optimistic. Miep remembers, 'We continued to wait for our liberators to come. The days passed slowly as we waited . . . the weather became foul. Nothing had changed for us, the Germans had not budged. In fact, they were meaner and more vengeful than ever. Slowly, so slowly, our hope that the end had come began to fade . . .'[14]

At Auschwitz-Birkenau whistles blew at 3.30 a.m. every day to call out the inmates. There was always a mad rush to the latrine huts at the back of the camp where a long bench with hundreds of holes in it served as the lavatory. Breakfast was a brown liquid slopped into one's bowl. Bowls could not be replaced if they were lost, other than through 'organizing' – camp slang for bartering or stealing. Anne had acquired a pair of men's long-johns from another woman by 'organizing' them. Rosa recalled, 'We had no clothing apart from a grey sack, and under that we were naked. But when the weather turned cold, Anne came into the barracks one day wearing a suit of men's long underwear. She looked screamingly funny with those long white legs, but somehow still charming.'[15]

During roll-call women had to stand in rows of five in the mustering square while block-leaders counted them. The dead were included in the count to make the numbers tally. Roll-call in the morning usually lasted forty-five minutes. Evening roll-call could last from an hour to five hours. They were forced to stand in sun, rain, hail and snow for as long as the roll-call leader desired and while punishments were carried out. Ronnie Goldstein-van Cleef, who had been on the Westerbork transport, stood beside Anne Frank many times during roll-call. They always shared a mug of 'coffee': 'We used the same little cup and passed it to each other . . . Margot was close by, next to [Anne] or in front of her, depending on how it worked out, because you stood in rows of five. Anne was very calm and quiet and somewhat withdrawn. The fact that they had ended up there had affected her profoundly – that was obvious.'[16] At the end of roll-call, the dead were thrown into meat wagons and driven away.

The march to work took half an hour from Anne's block. The work itself consisted of digging an area of grass which they threw on top of a heap of sod. It was completely pointless, but the *kapos* would run amongst them constantly, screaming, 'Faster! Faster!' and beat those who disobeyed. At 12.30 p.m. huge vats of soup were carried into the field. Each woman held out her bowl and received one ladle's worth of green fluid. For half an hour they sat in groups of five, drinking from their bowls, and then returned to another six hours of work. At 6 p.m. they marched back to the camp.

Their evening meal was a slice of bread and a tiny piece of margarine. The block-leader's assistants distributed the bread. Anne was one of the assistants. Rosa remembered, 'Anne was the youngest in her group, but nevertheless she was the leader of it. She also distributed the bread in the barracks, and she did it so well and so fairly that there was none of the usual grumbling.'[17] At 9 p.m. the whistles blew and they were allowed into the barracks. For the next six and a half hours, they tried to sleep.

Most of the inmates formed their own support groups. Edith, Margot, Anne, Rosa and Judy regularly met with three women they had known in Westerbork: Bloem Evers-Emden, Lenie de Jong-van Naarden and Ronnie Goldstein-van Cleef. Bloem recalls, 'They were always together, mother and daughters. Whatever discord you might infer from the diary was now swept away by existential need. They were always together. It is certain that they gave each other a great deal of support. All the things that a teenager might think of her mother were no longer of any significance.'[18] Edith's only thought was for her daughters. Ronnie remembers, 'Mrs Frank was always near her children and saw to it that they had something to eat.'[19] Lenie confirms, 'Mrs Frank tried very hard to keep her children alive, to keep them with her, to protect them. Naturally, we spoke to each other. But you could do absolutely nothing, only give advice like, "If they go to the latrine, go with them." '[20]

On 27 October there was another selection from Anne's block for a work detail. The youngest and strongest would leave Auschwitz to work in a Czechoslovakian munitions factory. Everyone desperately wanted to be chosen, knowing that they would have a far greater chance of surviving elsewhere. Judy de Winter and Bloem Evers-Emden were amongst those taken. Anne, Margot and Edith remained in Auschwitz. They were rejected at the selection because Anne had scabies and her mother and Margot would not consider leaving her alone in the camp. Bloem recalls, 'I spoke to Mrs Frank who was with Margot. Anne was somewhere else, she had scabies . . . she had to be isolated. As a result, Anne couldn't go out with our group. Mrs Frank, echoed by Margot, said, "We are, of course, staying with her." I remember that I nodded, that I understood that. That was the last time I saw them.'[21]

Scabies is caused by lice burrowing under the flesh, causing the skin to erupt in a welter of agonizing red and black sores that itch unbearably. Anne was put in the Krätzeblock (the Scabies Barrack) and Margot joined her there voluntarily. Lenie remembers Edith being 'in total despair. She didn't even eat the piece of bread that she got. Together with her, I dug up a hole beneath the wooden wall of the barracks where the children were. The ground was rather soft and so you could dig a hole if you had strength and I did. Mrs Frank stood next to me and just asked, "Is it working?" "Yes," I answered. I dug in close under the wood and through the hole we could speak with the girls. Margot took that piece of bread that I pushed underneath and they shared that.'[22] Inevitably, Margot also contracted scabies. Ronnie Goldstein-van Cleef, who was in the barracks with them and another girl named Frieda Brommet, remembered how

Frieda's mother and Edith Frank searched the entire camp for scraps of food to give to the sick girls.

On one occasion Ronnie found a platinum watch inside her mattress where a previous prisoner had hidden it. She slipped it through the hole underneath the barracks to Edith and Mrs Brommet, who exchanged it for a whole loaf of bread, a piece of cheese and a piece of sausage. Margot and Anne needed every scrap of sustenance that could be found because their health was failing rapidly. Ronnie remembers, 'The Frank girls kept very much to themselves. They no longer paid any attention to the others. When food arrived, they became a little more animated, and they shared the food and spoke a little. During that time, somewhat intuitively – since I thought, it will keep their spirits up a little – I sang a lot for them . . . The Frank girls looked terrible. Their hands and bodies were covered with spots and sores from the scabies. They applied some salve, but there was not much that they could do. They were in a very bad way; pitiful – that's how I thought of them. There wasn't any clothing. They had taken everything from us.'[23] Lying naked on their hard, cold bunks, the prisoners in the Krätzeblock could see corpses piled up alongside the barrack wall. Every day the mound grew higher.

Otto, Peter van Pels and Fritz Pfeffer were managing to survive in the men's camp. Their group included Rose de Liema's husband, Sal. He remembers Otto Frank saying, ' "We should try and get away from these people because if you talk all the time about food and stuff, your brain is going to go, we should try to survive mentally" . . . The biggest problem was to save your brain. Don't think about every day. We talked about Beethoven and Schubert and opera. We would even sing, but we would not talk about food.'[24] Otto and Sal became very close and their relationship helped Otto at least as much as it helped Sal, who remembers, 'He said, "You know, why don't you call me Papa Frank, because I need to have something in my life that I can be a Papa to." I didn't know what he was talking about. I said, "What do you mean? I have a father hidden in Holland – you don't have to do it for me." "I know," he said. "But do it for me. I'm the type of man who needs this, I need somebody to be a Papa for." So I told him, "If it helps you, I will." '[25]

On 29 October a selection took place in their barracks. Otto, Sal and Peter van Pels stayed in Auschwitz, but Pfeffer was put on a transport to the camp at Sachsenhausen. From there, he was sent to Neuengamme concentration camp, in Germany. All that is known about the remainder of Fritz Pfeffer's life is that he died in Neuengamme on 20 December 1944.[26]

On 30 October there was a selection in the women's camp at Auschwitz-Birkenau. Only sixty miles away, the Russians were advancing. The cry of 'Block closed!' went up at evening roll-call. Lientje Brilleslijper remembered, 'We were hunted and beaten out of the huts, but not to go to work. We were driven to the big parade ground and forced to strip. For one day, one night and another day, we stood there. Standing, standing, then a few steps and then standing again, with only a small piece of hard bread for nourishment. Then we were whipped into a big hall where it was at least warm. Here the selection took place.'[27]

Josef Mengele stood impatiently beside the blue gleam of the spotlights. Lientje recalled, 'He made us step on a scale and then waved his hand right or left to indicate life or death. Just a casual wave – to the gas chamber.'[28] Rosa de Winter was together with Edith, Margot and Anne Frank in the queue. 'It took a long time,' she remembered. 'We saw that he picked out a great many who were not too old or sick and then we knew that they would escape and that the old and the sick would be gassed.'[29] To save themselves, the women took several years off their actual age and lied about their health. Rosa called out, 'I am twenty-nine, and I have never had dysentery yet.' Mengele jerked his thumb, 'and sent me to join the old and the sick. Then came Mrs Frank – and she, too, was sent to join our group at once.'[30]

'Next!' he shouted.

Anne and Margot walked forward. They were still in a pitiful condition from the scabies, but they were both young. Rosa and Edith waited in terror to see whether they would join them or if they would be sent to the left and to an unknown fate. Rosa remembered watching the two girls: 'Fifteen and eighteen years old, thin, naked but proud, approaching the selection table with the SS men . . . Anne encouraged

Margot, and Margot walked erect into the light. There they stood for a moment, naked and shaven-headed, and Anne looked over at us with her unclouded face, looked straight and stood straight . . .'[31]

'To the left!' Mengele shouted, and Anne and Margot walked on.

Edith Frank's anguished scream spiralled upwards: 'The children! O God, the children . . . !'[32]

Chapter Eight

'Let the end come, even if it is hard . . .'

Anne Frank, *Diary*, 26 May 1944

The women selected to remain behind in Auschwitz moved towards the open door of the empty scabies block. Searchlights in the watchtowers picked out corpses on the electrified fencing. Inside the unlit barracks Rosa and Edith clutched each other's hands. 'We were lying strewn about on top of each other,' Rosa recalled. 'Lots of women were crying. I sat up straight and looked around me. My mother taught me always to make good use of my eyes and ears. Suddenly the barrack door opened. A woman entered with a torch. She let the light play over us. She picked me and twenty-five others who also looked worth rescuing out of the heap. "Run, run," she said, "after roll-call run to another block." This was a Greek block-leader. From a distance, later on, we saw lorries stopping in front of the scabies block in order to load up the others for the crematorium.'[1] Although they had escaped this fate, Edith became ill and was eventually taken to the camp hospital, where she grew weaker and weaker.

Anne and Margot Frank were amongst 634 women selected for the transport.[2] They were each given old clothing, mismatching shoes, a blanket, a quarter of a loaf of bread, five ounces of sausage, and a piece of margarine. Then they were herded out to the train. No one knew where they were going, but the journey was appalling. It was bitterly cold and cramped in the wagons and they received no more food, or water. After four days the train stopped and the SS guards unbolted the doors. The exhausted women climbed out on to the platform at Celle station. A few miles away was the concentration camp of Bergen-Belsen.[3]

In its earliest days Belsen had provided accommodation for the

German Army and served as a prisoner-of-war camp for 600 French and Belgian soldiers. They were joined in the summer of 1941 by 20,000 Russian prisoners of war. Overcrowding led to an outbreak of typhus in the camp and thousands of prisoners died. In April 1943 Himmler proposed holding 10,000 Jews who could be exchanged for German hostages. Belsen was requisitioned by the SS, but found to be 'in the worst condition conceivable. The barracks were dilapidated, and sanitary installations and kitchens non-existent.'[4] Labourers from concentration camps were brought in to repair and reconstruct the barracks. Between January and September 1944 approximately 4,000 'exchange Jews', with their families, arrived in Belsen. Most were Dutch Jews from Westerbork who had exemption stamps or were on an autonomy list. Few were released under the terms of exchange.

The decision to bring in sick prisoners from other camps – and thus potentially infect the existing camp population – marked a turning point in Belsen's history. The first transport of invalids, mostly suffering from tuberculosis, reached Belsen at the end of March 1944. There were no medicines, sanitation, care or food supplies with which to nurse them back to health. Only fifty-seven people from that first transport of 1,000 ailing individuals survived to witness the camp's liberation a year later.

Belsen's twelve square miles of land were divided into several sub-camps. Construction of the last of these, the 'tents camp' began on 7 August 1944, in anticipation of the arrival of thousands of Hungarian and Polish Jewish women from ghettos and labour camps. Ten or twelve tents were standing when the first transport reached the camp on 11 August. By mid-August approximately 4,000 women were living in the tents, but most of them were there only a short time before being sent away to work. On 5 September 1944 inmates were forced to assemble huts intended for 3,000 women who would be transported from Auschwitz-Birkenau in late October and early November. When the newcomers arrived, the barracks were still uninhabitable. Amongst these 'ill but potentially curable women'[5] were Margot and Anne Frank.

Lientje and Janny Brilleslijper were also on the transport from Auschwitz. As they wandered about the camp, they met Margot and Anne again. Lientje recalled, 'We had had a look round, and heard that there was a tap on a little hill, we hurried there to wash. And as the two of us went up the hill, two thin figures approached, and we fell about one another's necks. The two spoke Dutch. We were four shaven-headed figures, thin and shaking. Anne and Margot had many questions, and we, too, had many questions. We asked about their mother, for we knew that in Auschwitz the men had been separated from the women. Anne began to cry bitterly and Margot said quite softly, "Selected." '6 The four girls sat together on the hill, watching the line of stragglers from Celle station approach. Lientje observed Anne and Margot as they huddled beneath their blankets: 'The two were inseparable, like my sister and I. They looked like two frozen birds, it was painful to look at them. After we had washed, naked in the open air, we were speedily dressed, for we had nothing except a dress and a thin blanket, a blanket which one treasured like a costly possession. Then we crept together in one of the tents. We were thin and we had four blankets and we warmed each other . . .'7

Anne and Margot argued at first over whether to enter the tents, but decided it would be better than remaining outside. Janny Brilleslijper recalled, 'We waited until the last moment and then had to go into the top of the tent. It was not pleasant because it had become burning hot in the tents, how that is possible I don't know, it was probably from so many people. It was filthily hot and stank, like the lion's cage at the Artis zoo . . . we were sitting at the top with the rain dashing and pelting on the tent. Water broke holes in it.'8 They slept on sparse layers of straw, cramped together with two hundred others. There was no lighting and no toilets. One occupant recalled, 'When we wanted to go to the open latrine in front of the tent, there was no way one could squeeze through the mass of people to the exit.'9 Another prisoner, Anita Lasker-Wallfisch, reflected, 'For some days we lived like this. In a great big heap, on the bare ground in a flapping tent, cold and wretched.'10

On the evening of 7 November a wild storm broke out over the heath. The wind picked up strength, coming in ferocious gusts, ripping the tents from their moorings and blasting them across the ground. Women screamed and cowered as the poles crashed down around them. 'It was pitch dark and there we were, with the tent flattened, and everybody struggling to get free,' Anita recalled. 'Somehow we managed to untangle ourselves. When we finally achieved this, we just stood there in the open in the pouring rain, the wind howling, for the rest of the night.'[11] Eventually a group of SS guards arrived and drove them into the kitchen tent, beating them as they ran. The following day, still shivering with the cold, they were moved on again. 'We were quartered in an old barn filled with rags and old shoes,' Lientje remembered. 'Anne asked, "Why do they want us to become animals?" and one of us replied, "Because they are themselves beasts of prey." And then we talked about how things would be when it was all over; for we believed that the time only seemed so long to us in our misery, but that the misery could not last much longer. We did not know that the worst was still to come.'[12]

The hospital, the old people's home, and two huts in another part of the camp were evacuated to house the freezing women. Lientje and Janny lost sight of Anne and Margot for a few days whilst the accommodation was sorted out. In time they ended up in the same barracks, sleeping on wooden berths in a stone hut, where several thousand people had only one washroom between them. Before long the compound was said to resemble 'one single latrine, especially since many of the weakened and dying prisoners suffered from diarrhoea. People could not drag themselves to the latrines but relieved themselves wherever they were; sometimes dirty laundry from diarrhoea patients was kept on the beds for weeks . . . Hygienic conditions reached their horrifying low when the corpses of thousands of victims were simply left lying in the compound.'[13] Approximately half the prisoners in Belsen were transferred to the women's camp on 2 December 1944. More transports were arriving from concentration camps and outposts close to the front lines. Belsen became dangerously overcrowded, with many of the new arrivals succumbing to the diseases and illnesses rapidly taking hold.

Anne and Margot had the bunk below Lientje and Janny in their barracks. Their spirits had not yet been broken by the misery surrounding them. 'Anne used to tell stories after we lay down,' Lientje remembered. 'So did Margot. Silly stories and jokes. We all took turns telling them. Mostly they were about food. Once we talked about going to the American Hotel in Amsterdam for dinner and Anne suddenly burst into tears at the thought that we would never get back . . . we compiled a menu, masses of wonderful things to eat. And Anne said she still had a lot to learn.'[14] They should have been sent to work outside the camp but their poor health meant they were put to work every day in the shoe-shed, a former stables where old shoes from Germany lay in huge piles. The shoes had to be unstitched by hand, the leather soles ripped away, and the usable pieces put to one side. The work was difficult and painful, made worse by the constant beatings they received from the SS. Lientje and Anne found the task impossible: 'Our hands began to fester. Several people died of blood poisoning. Anne and I were the first who had to stop working. Margot and my sister stood it for rather longer, but they shared their food with us . . . we got for this a little more watery soup and a piece of bread . . . Anne and I began to "organize" things, to steal from the kitchen or to beg. If you were caught, this meant a beating, but we were not caught . . . we did better than those who were working. But we never stole from another prisoner; we stole from the Nazis.'[15]

At the end of November Auguste van Pels arrived in Belsen from Auschwitz. Anne and Margot had not seen her since the journey from Westerbork two months before. She joined their small group, which included the Brilleslijper sisters, Deetje and Hannelore Daniels, and a young girl named Sonya ('a gay, gifted child'[16]), all from the Netherlands. Everyone took care of each other. Lientje remembered, 'One of us constantly stood watch for when the food came. You had to jump for it, or it would disappear immediately. Auschwitz was organized hell, but the part of Belsen we were in was an unorganized hell.'[17] Anita Lasker-Wallfisch was also in a group. 'We watched each other like hawks for any signs of giving up. It was tempting not to strip and wash every day in the freezing cold of winter. The water supply was outside. We saw ourselves getting thinner and thinner, and shared whatever food we could get hold of . . . There was nothing to do. We merely existed.'[18]

On 2 December 1944 Josef Kramer was appointed commandant of Belsen. Kramer had been drafted in from Auschwitz and brought with him his most sadistic staff. He introduced *kapos* into Belsen, rid the camp of its remaining vestiges of Jewish self-administration, deprived prisoners of food for several days at a time, organized work commandos for all and stripped exchange Jews of their last privileges. Although food had been the 'main topic of conversation' since mid-1944, it became an obsession as rations were reduced to 'a daily bowl of so-called "soup", turnips cooked in water without meat or fat, and a daily slice of bread about one and a half inches thick'.[19] Lientje noted, 'We grew ever thinner. Anne seemed to consist only of her eyes . . . eyes with a greenish glint.'[20]

In the midst of this crisis the inmates tried their best to celebrate Christmas and Hanukkah. Lientje recalled: 'We saved scraps from our scanty bread ration and received a special ration of one quarter of a Harz cheese. Anne had found a small piece of garlic somewhere. I had sung some songs in another block and been rewarded with a little sauerkraut. The Daniels sisters, with whom we were together, had organized a beetroot and a carrot. With our six blankets we improvised a table and with these ingredients we made a Christmas feast. We had saved a little ersatz coffee from breakfast and warmed it secretly on a stove and we had roasted some potato peels. That was our Christmas feast. Anne said, "And we are celebrating Hanukkah at the same time." '[21] Crouched together under the sloping roof of the barracks, the women sang their favourite songs. 'Jewish songs,' Lientje remembered, 'and wept. Anne's eyes glittered. She told us stories. We thought they must be old stories which we did not happen to know. But now I know that they were stories that Anne had made up herself. Margot started to tell a story too, but she could not go on and Anne completed it for her. She said that her father knew much better stories and Margot began to cry, asking whether he was still alive. Anne was confident, "Of course he is alive." '[22]

The Netherlands were desolate. Gas and electricity supplies had been cut off. The terrible winter weather added to the misery caused by no light, no heating and hardly any food. City dwellers walked miles to reach the countryside, where the situation was only slightly better, and begged for food and fuel from farmers. Rations were cut and cut again, until each person was allowed no more than 500 calories a day. Typhoid fever and diphtheria swept across the country. The Germans took anything and everything, from cattle to clothes, and despatched them all to Germany. Just when it seemed impossible to imagine anything worse, the Germans blew up the sluices at Ijmuiden. Canals rose, the sewage system broke down and a plague of rats infested Amsterdam. The Hunger Winter claimed 22,000 victims.

On 30 December 1944 Victor Kugler was transported to the village of Wageningen. He worked there for a short time as an electrician and then he became a translator delivering messages to an organization employed by the German Army to dig trenches and tank traps. Kugler worked in an office and was given a bicycle, identity papers and a green ribbon which allowed him to travel through evacuated villages. Kugler had virtually free rein in the office, since the commander was rarely present. He brought prisoners in to work with him instead of in the fields, and secured them wages and identification papers.

In Amsterdam Kleiman was trying to discover whether the warehouseman, van Maaren, was responsible for a series of thefts from the stores during November and December. He visited the police with his suspicions, but a search of van Maaren's home revealed nothing. Remembering van Maaren's boasts about his good relationship with the SD, Kleiman let the matter rest for the time being, but he made sure that he was aware of every move van Maaren made.

Snow had fallen at Auschwitz in November. It lay in great drifts, muting the sounds and movements within the camp. In the hospital compound scores of prisoners were dying of typhus and diphtheria. Edith Frank was one of them. Rosa de Winter remembered, 'I was sent to the hospital barracks, and there I saw Mrs Frank again. I lay down beside her. She was very weak and no longer eating, scarcely in her right mind. Whatever food she was given she collected under her blanket, saying that she was saving it for her husband, because he needed it – and then the bread spoiled under the blanket. I don't know whether she was so weakened because she was starving, or whether she had stopped eating because she was too weak to eat. There was no longer any way of telling . . .'[23] Otto later wrote of his wife's last days, 'The two girls were sent to another camp. From there on my wife was so desperate and so depressed that gradually she lost all will to live.'[24]

Edith Frank died in Auschwitz on 6 January 1945.[25]

The camp's killing centre was being dismantled, stone by stone. Gassings had stopped in November 1944, and the Nazis, wanting to conceal the evidence of their Final Solution, ordered the obliteration of the gas chambers and crematorium. During winter 1944–5, gas chambers four and five were destroyed, the fences surrounding two crematoria were pulled down, the undressing room of crematorium three was dismantled, and all but one of the crematoria were blown up. The last crematorium functioned as an incinerator for those who died in the hospital compound. The ventilating motors and pipes were shipped to Mauthausen and the remaining parts sent to other concentration camps. The cremating pits, containing mounds of human ash, were raked over and planted with grass seed. The dissection rooms were demolished. Only one was left in working order. Twenty-nine clothing stores and buildings were torched and many documents destroyed. In mid-January 1945 the SS abandoned the camp.

Amongst the 32,000 prisoners still living in Auschwitz was Otto Frank. He had been in the camp hospital since November. His health had been weakened by work in a road-building party and then by beatings dealt out by guards who supervised his potato-peeling group. Suffering from starvation and diarrhoea, he became severely depressed. His lowest moment came following yet another brutal assault. 'That had really affected me,' he remembered, 'also in terms of my morale. It was a Sunday morning and I said, "I can't get up," and then my comrades, all Dutchmen of course, because I was the only German, but I was totally accepted by all the others, said to me, "That's impossible – you must get up because otherwise you are lost."' Otto's fellow prisoners called in a Dutch-Jewish doctor. Otto recalled, 'This Dutch doctor came to my barracks. He said, "Get up and come tomorrow morning to the sick barracks and I'll speak to the German doctor and you will be saved." And this is what happened and through that I was saved.'[26]

Peter van Pels had been given a job in the postal department, which enabled him to obtain a few extra rations. When he visited Otto in hospital, the older man did everything he could to persuade Peter to hide there with him, instead of going with the thousands being evacuated from the camp. Terrified of the punishment that would follow in the case of discovery, Peter refused. He was not the only prisoner who had to make that decision: 'Many, who were too weak to move, had to be left behind, and others elected to stay. The Russians were said to be close by (some said they were only ten miles away). Remaining in the camp meant running the risk of being shot by the retreating guards, but that struck many as the lesser evil . . . No doubt, the choice between staying and going was but rarely taken on logical grounds. One stayed, one went, one did not know why.'[27]

On 16 January Peter was taken with thousands of others on a death-march out of Auschwitz. All across Europe, columns of camp survivors were being marched through the countryside under armed guard. Their destinations were the camps and sub-camps of Germany. Belsen, Dachau, Sachsenhausen, Buchenwald and Ravensbruck took in some survivors, but many were turned away. Death-marches were fraught with danger from all sides. Prisoners were sometimes mistaken for German military by Russian soldiers, who would open fire on them. The majority of marchers died of exhaustion, but some were shot; 'the transports left behind them a ghastly trail of prisoners with smashed or bullet-ridden skulls and with faces beaten to a pulp.'[28]

Peter's group eventually arrived at Mauthausen. Completed as a camp in May 1933, built by 40,000 Spanish Republicans and Jews who carried its foundation stones up a mountain path, Mauthausen resembled an ancient hill fort. Wooden barracks housed the inmates, who were mostly Jews, Romanies, Soviet prisoners of war, Spaniards, Jehovah's Witnesses and homosexuals. They were worked to death in the stone quarries of the camp.

Peter van Pels died in Mauthausen on 5 May 1945.[29] Three days later, the camp was liberated.

In Auschwitz Sal de Liema had lost contact with 'Papa Frank'. On 27 January he heard that the Russians were expected, and managed to hobble out of the barracks. In the distance he could see what he thought were small dogs, until bullets began to hail around him. The warning shots had been fired by their liberators.

In another part of the camp Otto also watched the Russians approach. Afterwards his strongest memory was of their 'snow-white fur coats. They were good people, our liberators. We did not care if they were Communists or not. We were not concerned with politics, we were concerned about our liberation. The Russians gave us food, although they did not have much themselves.'[30] The soldiers distributed rations and clothing from old SS stores and separated the chronically ill inmates from those whom they thought might live. Otto was placed in another long barrack in a bunk of his own There were many other male prisoners in the hut, and women from Birkenau came in regularly to search for their relatives and friends. Eva Schloss (then Eva Geiringer) was amongst the female visitors. She and her mother had avoided the death-marches: 'Towards the end, when they were evacuating the camp, we did our best to stay in Auschwitz and not get taken with one of those groups. We thought they would shoot us if we went with them. And that was the right thing to do, because most of those who were taken from the camp died. My father and brother were taken to Mauthausen and there they died.'[31]

At that time, however, Eva did not know the fate of her father and brother, and she had gone to the men's camp to look for them. She noticed Otto sitting on his bunk, staring disconsolately into space. 'He was middle-aged with hardly any face left at all, just a skeleton's skull out of which stared pale brown enquiring eyes. "I know you," I said in Dutch, almost sure in the back of my mind that I had seen him before. He stood up slowly and painfully, tall and dignified still and bowed slightly to me. "I am Otto Frank," he said, smiling weakly. "And you are Eva Geiringer, aren't you? The little friend of Anne." And with that he took me in his arms and hugged me. "Is Anne with you? Have you seen her or Margot?" he asked eagerly, but I had to tell him I had not seen any of my friends from Merwedeplein in the camp . . . I sat on his bunk for a while and told him all the news that I could and he thought it was a good idea to move into Auschwitz where the Russians had permanent headquarters and were going to look after the prisoners. I promised to come back and see him.'[32]

Otto slowly began to regain his health and strength. On 23 February he was able to write to his family in Switzerland:

Dearest Mother,

I hope these lines reach you, bringing you and all my loved ones the news that I have been saved by the Russians, that I am well, full of good spirit, and being looked after in every respect. I don't know where Edith and the children are. We've been apart since 5 September 1944. I only heard that they had been transported to Germany. I hope to see them back safe and healthy. Please tell my brother-in-law[33] and my friends in Holland of my liberation. I long to see you all

again and hope that this will be possible. If only you *are all well.*
Indeed, when will I be able to receive news from you?
    All my love, greetings and kisses,
    Your son,
    Otto.[34]

The last prisoners of war had been shipped out of Bergen-Belsen to make room for the death-march survivors and transports from other concentration camps. The second part of the prisoner of war camp became the women's camp, and another camp for men replaced the original women's camp. Despite the expansion, the problem of overcrowding increased. A British lieutenant-colonel's comment on conditions in one hut during Belsen's liberation illustrates the severity of the problem: 'It would have held eighty-three soldiers by British Army standards, we removed from it 1,426 women and that does not count the dead.'[35]

Anne was always very curious to know who had come in with the transports. Lientje recalled, 'We were taken to another part of the camp. A group of older women and children were also brought there. Anne came excitedly to us, "Let us go there, maybe there are friends among them, they are said to be all Dutch." She wanted to go over immediately. At this moment, I believe, she was the Anne which we know from the diary, mercurial and full of life; at other times I only saw her serious and sad. There were some boys and girls whom Anne knew: Carry Vos, Roosje Pinkhof. But Anne was soon sad again. Her friends had been on exchange lists and should have been sent to a neutral country but despite this they had landed in Belsen. She asked after other friends and learned that Lies, a good friend of hers, was quite near, and she could speak to her in the evening if she was careful. From Lies she got a few little gifts, which pleased her very much. She wanted to share everything with us, but we told her that the gifts were for her and Margot.'[36]

The meeting between Anne and Lies is one of the most remarkable events of the last months of Anne's short life. After her mother's death during childbirth in 1942, Lies had lived in Amsterdam with her remaining family. On 20 June 1943 the family were seized in Amsterdam's last major razzia. They were taken to Westerbork, and then three months later sent to Bergen-Belsen as 'exchange Jews'. They were able to see each other through the day, but in the evening Hans Goslar had to return to the men's barracks. He became seriously ill in the early days of 1945.

At the beginning of February Lies heard that several transports of Dutch women had arrived from Auschwitz. Tramping through the snow one night to find out whether there was anyone amongst them whom she knew, Lies met Mrs van Pels, who told her that Anne was also in the camp. Some minutes later, she heard Anne calling her. Standing against the barbed-wire fence, Lies saw Anne, 'cold, hungry, her head shaved and her skeleton-like form . . . We had only a few moments to talk.'[37] Anne explained that they had never gone to Switzerland, but had been in hiding in Amsterdam. 'She told me that her father had been killed – her mother too, she thought,' Lies remembers. 'It was a pity she thought her father had died when he had not. The way she idolized him perhaps she would have had the hope to live if she knew he still lived.'[38] They talked about the past two years and Anne spoke about the gas chambers in Auschwitz. Then she said that she had nothing to eat. Lies still received Red Cross parcels in her barracks and she promised Anne she would try to help her.

They met again the following night. Lies had packed a woollen jacket, biscuits, sugar and a tin of sardines for her friend. She threw the bundle over, but when it landed, 'I heard an agonized cry from Anne. When I asked what was the matter, she said another woman had caught the bundle and wouldn't give it up.'[39] The next evening Lies threw over another package and this time Anne caught it, but after that the two friends had no more contact. The Goslars thought that they were leaving Belsen, but on the morning of their supposed departure, Lies learned that her father had died during the night. Lies and Gabi were told that their transfer was cancelled. Lies tried to find Anne again, but failed, and at the end of March she suffered another loss when her grandmother died. Lies fell ill with typhus during the last days of the camp.

The mother of Margot's friend Trees also met Anne in Belsen. She recalled, 'I could see Anne beyond the barbed wire across the camp street. Over there conditions were even worse than they were among us . . . I called across the street: "Don't go away, Anne. Wait!" And I ran into the barrack and packed up whatever I could find, packed it into a bundle and ran back to the barbed wire. But it was so far across to the other block, and we women were so weak. While we were wondering how we could throw the bundle across, Mr Brill came by. Mr Brill lived with us. He was very tall and I said to him: "I have an old dress here, and soap and a piece of bread, Mr Brill. Please throw it across. You see the child, standing over there." Mr Brill hesitated at first, not certain whether it was safe, because the guard could see us. But he overcame all his fears at the sight of her . . . he took the bundle and flung his arm far back and then sent it flying in a high arc to the other side.'[40]

In another barracks nearby were a group of Dutch children whom the Nazis treated relatively leniently, unable to decide whether they were Jewish or Gentile. Janny, Lientje, Anne and Margot often visited the children. They sang to them and told them stories to keep their spirits up. Janny and Lientje volunteered to become nurses in a new barracks filled with dying Dutch women and children. They asked Anne and Margot whether they would like to help, but neither girl was strong enough to care for anyone else. The Brilleslijpers stole from the SS pharmacy and distributed the medicines amongst their companions, but lost touch with Anne and Margot, who had been moved from their barracks. Lientje found out where they were from the Daniels sisters. 'Margot had a bad attack of dysentery and could not stand and because of the danger of typhus infection she had to stay in the old block,' Lientje remembered. 'Anne looked after her as well as she could. We were able to bring them a little food which we had organized. A few days later we heard that they were in the sick bay. We went there and urged them not to stay because if they stayed lying they would perish. But it was at least warm there and there were only two of them in the bunk. Anne said, "We are together and we have our peace." Margot said scarcely anything. She had a high fever and smiled contentedly. Her mind was already wandering . . .'[41]

In Auschwitz, Otto continued to write to his family in Switzerland even though he knew that his letters and postcards would not reach his family for a long time. In early March, the survivors of the camp boarded 'large, wide Russian trains'[42] to Katowice. A short note written from Katowice on 15 March shows his determination to think positively, ending, 'It's a miracle that I'm still alive – I've had a lot of luck and should be grateful,'[43] but in another note he writes simply, 'We own nothing more. I hope you are well when you read these lines. I will write more soon. Love, Otto.'[44]

On 18 March he wrote to his cousin Milly in London, '. . . I am a beggar, having lost everything except life. Nothing of my household is left, not a photo, not a letter of my children, nothing, nothing, but I don't want to think what will happen later and if I shall be able to work again. There are as many in the same situation . . . I always was optimistic and I am still trying my best.'[45] In another letter written that day, Otto muses over how much he should tell his mother: 'I still can't decide whether to tell you more comprehensively of some of my experiences, the main thing is you know I am alive and well. I am constantly tormented by not knowing how Edith and the children are. You no doubt understand. I do however, hope to see all well again, and I don't want to lose hope.' In the same letter he expands on some events from the recent past: 'If I hadn't been in hospital due to a weak body – I weighed 52 kg – doubtless I'd no longer be alive. I've had a lot of luck and a lot of friends. Peter van Pels spent two years with us and acted like a son here to help me. Every day he brought me extra food.' Finally, he adds: 'I can hardly imagine normal relationships. I don't want to think about the future yet. Here, I am a beggar and even look like one. But I'm still fresh in my mind and my body has recovered, mainly because we don't have to work here. I hope that I can send you further news . . .'[46]

Otto did send further news only two days later, but it was news that no one, least of all Otto himself, had wanted to hear. Rosa de Winter, who had travelled in the train from Auschwitz with Eva and Fritzi Geiringer, ran into Otto in Katowice. Rosa recalled, 'Mr Frank was sitting alone at a long table when I came in and we recognized one another. I said to him: "I know nothing about the children. They were taken away." After a while, I told him that his wife had died, in bed, right beside me. Mr Frank did not move when I told him. I looked into his face, but he had turned away. And then he made a movement. I no longer remember exactly what it was, but it seems to me he laid his head on the table.'[47] Later Otto made a supreme effort to write to his mother.

> *Dearest Mother,*
>
> *I want to send you a few lines while we're still waiting for transport onward. I can't write much, because Edith's news from the 6.01.45, which I now have, affects me so badly that I'm not quite with it.*

The thoughts on the card cheered me up.[48] *Edith died in hospital of weakness caused by malnutrition, her body couldn't hold out any longer. In reality she is another person murdered by the Germans. If she had managed to survive another two weeks, everything would have been different after the liberation by the Russians. I ask myself whether we can get to Holland via* [illegible word]*, I don't know. I hope, however, that we can get there, despite the fact that Holland is still not liberated.*

I don't wish to write any more today.
I send you all my love.
Otto.[49]

At the beginning of February Victor Kugler was amongst 600 men selected for labour in Germany. The march across the border began on a bright, warm day. Kugler took a bicycle with him and advised a friend of his to do the same. Both men kept to the rear of the line, having made up their minds to escape. In the small town of Zevenaar, near the German border, the column was strafed by British Spitfires. Kugler and his friend ran unnoticed into a field while everyone else took cover. Holding on to their bikes, the two men hid in a farm building until they were sure there were no German soldiers about. Then they began their long journey home, aided by farmers and villagers who gave them bits of food, clothes and shelter. When Kugler arrived in Hilversum, he rang the doorbell of his home, but his wife did not answer. A former neighbour appeared and explained that his wife had been ill and was staying with them. The following day Kugler began to prepare himself a hiding place in case the Germans came looking for him. These measures proved unnecessary; a few days later, German troops stationed at Wageningen surrendered. Victor Kugler was a free man.

At the end of March Otto began his journey home to Amsterdam, travelling by train through Poland. His grief at losing his wife was tempered only by the hope that Anne and Margot were still alive; all his thoughts were on finding them. Many years after the war he recalled, 'I did not find out what happened to the children during this trip. But I always asked about them, especially when we met with other freed prisoners: "Have you perhaps seen my daughters, Anne and Margot Frank?" No one could give me information about them. Once during one of the train's stops I was recognized by a girl who had played with Anne in Amsterdam. This girl introduced me to her mother, who enquired about her husband . . . I tried to find out some sort of information about the children. But it was no use.'[50] The girl and her mother were, of course, Eva and Fritzi Geiringer. Eva remembered, 'I had seen Anne's father, Otto Frank, again during the journey from Katowice to Czernowitz, standing alone at one of the stops. He looked worn out and sad. Mutti was with me then and asked to be introduced to him. She knew he'd just heard from Rosa that his wife had died and she felt great pity for him. I took her over and they exchanged polite words, but there was little to console him and he had no interest in anything. He seemed to want to keep himself apart and remain alone with his grief.'[51]

Otto wrote to his family in Switzerland from Czernowitz on 31 March. His letter reads:

> *My Dears,*
>
> *How often I think of you and long to see you all again. It may be possible that people here can travel on, but nobody can say when we'll be back in Holland. Indeed, it seems that the war is coming rapidly to an end. I am well and am standing up to things well, in spite of the painful news of my wife's death. I only hope to find my children back at home!*
>
> *Otto.*[52]

Between 1 December 1944 and mid-March 1945 25,000 concentration camp evacuees arrived at Bergen-Belsen. Many of the 45,000 prisoners in the camp were suffering from typhus. They were fed on a teaspoon of butter, a slice of cheese or sausage twice a week, and a drop of 'coffee'. Bread was a rarity. Starving prisoners tore up grass and boiled it, and when vats filled with putrid soup were carried to the barracks, 'any spillage was lapped up from the filthy ground by frantic people, and five guards had to accompany the vat carriers to prevent sudden attacks by the starving internees'.[53] There was no water in the camp for days, and by the water-pump 'people died in their hundreds – crawling towards it, raving and shrieking, while the brutal guard there beat the queue; and all the time the other guards went on firing, till in the end this half square mile of soil held more suffering than had ever any spot upon earth.'[54] Lorries thundered about the camp, picking up corpses for the crematorium, but by mid-February, when thousands were dying every day, the incinerator could no longer cope with the demands made on it. Bodies were burned on diesel-soaked wooden pallets, but this led to complaints about the stench from the army training ground nearby, and so the forestry administration forbade the use of wood for corpse-burning. The dead were then simply left where they had died, or were piled up alongside the barracks until 'thousands of bodies were lying about in the camp area – green and swollen by the spring sun, in all stages of decomposition'.[55] As starvation took hold, outbreaks of cannibalism occurred in the camp, and people literally went insane with thirst.

On 6 February Auguste van Pels had been amongst a group of prisoners who were transferred from Belsen to Buchenwald. She was transferred again, either by train or on foot, from Buchenwald to Theresienstadt on 9 April. There are conflicting accounts of her final destination, with some reports placing her at the aeroplane factory in Raguhn, where many concentration camp inmates were put to work.

All that is known for certain is that Auguste van Pels died in Germany or Czechoslovakia some time before 8 May 1945.[56]

Typhus became so widespread in Belsen that inmates who were not suffering from the disease were in the minority. Everyone seemed to be dying from something. Dr Jacob Presser recounts, 'The overwhelming majority wasted away and succumbed to one of the diseases that ravaged the place. The filth was indescribable; towards the end, there was hardly anyone without lice; everywhere people were crawling with them, even on the eyebrows . . . to plague these unfortunates further, the Germans would often amuse themselves by cutting off the water supply. "The accumulation of faeces," wrote a medical expert, "in some of the wash houses was so indescribable that people shunned them altogether; almost everyone suffered from dysentery, until all the barracks were oozing with it." '[57] Thousands of people starved to death while in the camp storeroom hundreds of Red Cross food parcels and as many cans of Ovaltine lay untouched.

In one of the rotting, overcrowded barracks, Margot and Anne lay in agony with typhus. They bore their disease in one of the worst possible places, on the bunk beside the barrack door, where draughts came stinging through night and day. Rachel van Amerongen-Frankfoorder, who had not seen either of them since Westerbork, was aghast at the change in their appearance. 'The Frank girls were almost unrecognizable since their hair had been cut off. They were much balder than we were; how that could be I don't know. And they were so cold, just like the rest of us . . . Day by day they got weaker. Nevertheless, they went to the fence of the so-called free camp every day, in the hope of getting something. They were very determined . . . Sometimes they got a package which had been thrown over to them. Then they would come back elated, very happy and they would sit down and eat what they had gotten with great pleasure. But you could see that they were very sick. The Frank girls were so emaciated. They looked terrible. They had little squabbles, caused by their illness, because it was clear they had typhus . . . They had those hollowed out faces, skin over bone. They were terribly cold . . . You heard them constantly screaming: "Close the door! Close the door! Close the door!", and the voices became weaker every day. You could really see both of them dying . . . that gradual wasting away, a sort of apathy, with occasional revivals, until they became so sick there wasn't any hope.'[58]

Typhus, caused when the bite of an infected louse becomes contaminated with its faeces, spread so swiftly in Belsen because there was nothing with which to fight it. The main symptoms include 'skin rashes, followed by fever, acute headache and pain in the joints, renal failure, blockage of small blood vessels leading to gangrene and reduced resistance to other illnesses such as pneumonia'.[59] When the organism carrying the disease reaches the central nervous system, it produces 'a peculiar agitation followed by delirium, while a falling blood pressure and increasing pulse indicate that the disease has reached the circulatory system. In this state a terrible death, accompanied by convulsions and agonal screaming, follows within twenty-four hours.'[60] Anne and Margot showed all the symptoms of the disease.

Lientje Brilleslijper remembered, 'We visited [Anne and Margot] again, together with Roosje Pinkhof. Margot had fallen from the bunk and was half-unconscious. Anne was already very feverish. She was very friendly and loving, "Margot will sleep well and when she sleeps I don't need to get up anymore" . . . Anne said, "Oh, I'm so nice and warm," and seemed quite happy.'[61]

Margot was too weak to survive the fall on to the cold stone floor. The shock killed her. Her exact date of death is not known, but Margot Frank died in Belsen in mid or late March 1945.[62]

With her sister dead, Anne succumbed to the typhus raging through her own small body. Janny Brilleslijper remembered, 'Anne was sick . . . but she stayed on her feet until Margot died; only then did she give in to her illness . . . At a certain moment in the final days, Anne stood in front of me, wrapped in a blanket. She didn't have any more tears . . . And she told me that she had such a horror of the lice and fleas in her clothes and that she had thrown all of her clothes away . . . she was wrapped in one blanket. I gathered up everything I could find to give her so that she was dressed again. We didn't have much to eat, and Lientje was terribly sick, but I gave Anne some of our bread ration.'[63]

Eva Schloss says, 'I had met my father again in Auschwitz. He came looking for me. At the time I was separated from my mother because there had been a selection and I knew what that usually meant. I didn't know then that she was still alive. So when he asked me, "How is your mother?" I told him, "She's gone to the gas chamber". And I think that's what did it, what broke him. When my brother died, my father was left thinking that he was alone, because he thought my mother was dead and he probably thought that I couldn't survive either. He was alone. And that's why he gave in. If he had known that my mother and I were both alive, I think he would have held on, but he didn't know. You needed that certain spirit, to know that there was someone there for you. This is what happened with Anne, I'm sure. When Margot died, Anne already believed that her mother and father were dead. And so she gave up.'[64]

The death of Margot was more than Anne could stand. She thought she had nothing to live for. Her father was searching frantically for her, but she did not know that. In mid or late March 1945, Anne died in Belsen, alone.[65]

Hilde Jacobsthal, who had attended the River Quarter youth synagogue group with Margot Frank and Peter van Pels, arrived in Belsen in late March. Hilde recalled, 'There were many Dutch children there. I asked if there was anyone from Amsterdam and they said one had been Anne, but she had died a few days before.'[66] When Janny and Lientje visited the barracks again, the bunk on which Anne and Margot had lain was empty. 'We knew what this meant,' Lientje wrote in her memoir. 'We looked for them and found them. Four of us laid the thin bodies on a blanket and carried them to the great open grave. We could do no more.'[67]

On 15 April 1945, only two or three weeks after the death of Anne Frank, British troops liberated Belsen.

Shortly before their arrival, the SS tried in vain to remove the evidence of their gross neglect. Some 2,000 prisoners, themselves half-dead, were made to drag the unburied corpses into mass graves thirty foot deep and sixty foot square, from early in the morning until late at night. Kramer, the camp commandant, insisted that two prisoners' bands play music whilst the procession trailed from barracks to grave. It was, one writer noted, 'a gruesome *danse macabre*, a Dance of Death more nightmarish than even the visionary fantasy of a poet could conjure up'.[68]

Belsen was liberated after a local cease-fire was agreed by both sides who were keen to stop the diseases in the camp from spreading. The inferno of Belsen and several other liberated camps was 'the last major epidemic of typhus in human history'.[69] Some 10,000 corpses were still waiting to be interred. The SS were made to bury them. The liberators could not believe their eyes. Lieutenant-Colonel Gonin of 11 Light Field Ambulance described the scenes: 'One saw women drowning in their own vomit because they were too weak to roll over and men eating worms as they clutched half a loaf of bread purely because they had to eat and could now scarcely tell the difference between worms and bread. Piles of corpses, naked and obscene, with a woman too weak to stand propping herself up against them as she cooked the food we gave her over an open fire. Men and women crouching down just anywhere in the open relieving themselves of the dysentery which was scouring their bodies, a woman standing stark naked washing herself with issue soap in water from a tank in which the remains of a child floated.'[70] The internees were so starved and diseased that in many cases it was impossible to determine their sex. Some lay in their bunks beside companions who had been dead for days.

The gutters outside the huts were clogged with bodies, as were the pathways throughout the camp. It became unfeasible to bury them manually. Bulldozers were brought in to shovel scores of bodies at a time into the deep pits. The brutal process was necessary to prevent the corpses piling up and disease from spreading. Army chaplains and rabbis recited prayers over the dead.

People who lived nearby but claimed to know nothing about the camp were brought in and marched around each and every barrack. They were addressed by Colonel Spottiswoode, who told them: 'What you will see here is the final and utter condemnation of the Nazi Party. It justifies every measure which the United Nations will take to exterminate that Party. What you will see here is such a disgrace to the German people that their name must be eradicated from the list of civilized nations . . .'[71]

On 24 April the evacuation of the camp began. By mid-May it was empty but for 300 former inmates and the British garrison at Belsen. They gathered together while a British officer addressed them: 'This moment is the end of a chapter, the pages of which are filled with the vilest story of cruelty, hate and bestiality ever written by a nation . . .'[72] When he had finished his speech, the huts and edifices of Bergen-Belsen were set alight. Inmates and liberators alike watched as one by one the buildings burned down to the ground. Amongst them were the barracks where Margot and Anne Frank had died. Their bodies lay a few feet away, in a pestilent, unmarked grave.

I Don't
Want to
Have Lived
for Nothing
1945–64

Part Five

Chapter Nine

'I want to publish a book entitled *Het Achterhuis* after the war . . .'

Anne Frank, *Diary*, 11 May 1944

Basel, Switzerland, 20 May 1945
Dearest Mr Kleiman,

They told us that there's another possibility to get in contact with you, so I'm taking a chance. We've waited so long for this opportunity to ask you about our beloved ones. With fear and much sorrow we await your answer, which I hope we won't have to wait long for, and hope that it will bring reassuring news. It goes without saying that our thoughts are always with you, especially where your health is concerned. We are all well here and I try to be as brave as possible. I send you my sincerest greetings, and when it is in your power to do so, please tell my children how much I'm worrying about them. Your last news was from 22 June 1944 – for nearly one year I haven't heard anything. Many thanks for your friendship and lots of good wishes,

Yours, Alice Frank.[1]

By mid-April most of the north-eastern provinces of the Netherlands had been liberated. Arnhem was freed on 14 April, and the rest of the country knew they had only days to wait for their own emancipation.

Many of the camps had been liberated by then: Buchenwald, Nordhausen, Gross Rosen and Belsen among them. Janny and Lientje Brilleslijper were still at Belsen when the British arrived, but Lies and Gabi Goslar had been sent with 7,000 others on a transport headed for Theresienstadt. A fortnight's journey of starvation and terror came to an end on

23 April 1945, at the intervention of Russian soldiers, in the small German village of Trobitz. Lies and her sister were amongst those who had survived.

Berlin surrendered on 2 May. A few days later the Netherlands celebrated its official liberation. As joyous crowds in Amsterdam converged on Dam Square, the Germans opened fire, killing 22 people and injuring over 100. Hitler, by then, had committed suicide with his new wife Eva Braun in his Berlin bunker.

On 25 April the train carrying Otto Frank and his fellow Auschwitz survivors had arrived at the Black Sea port of Odessa where the New Zealand ship *Monoway* awaited them. They set sail for Marseilles on 21 May. Female passengers were given cabins while men slept below decks on hammocks, sharing their quarters with other camp survivors and French and Italian prisoners of war. They were attended by naval officers in crisp white uniforms, who took great pains to ensure that they were looked after and well fed. On 26 May Otto wrote to his mother:

> ... We don't know yet whether we can return to Holland or if we'll have to spend a while in England. The main thing for me is that we've left Russia and with this have the possibility to be with our loved ones again. You would hardly believe how I long to be with you all again. My entire hope lies with the children. I cling to the conviction that they are alive and that we'll be together again, but I'm not promising myself anything. We have all experienced too much ... Only the children, <u>only the children</u> count. I hope continually to find out how they are ... perhaps there are people who have news of the girls ... I'll have to stay in Holland, because I don't have any identification – apart from a number – and can only expect to be with you later on. The most important thing now is that we know we'll see each other again soon. All my best greetings and kisses ...[2]

The next day *Monoway* sailed into Marseilles, where a huge crowd and two military bands were waiting to greet the French prisoners of war. The ship's passengers gave their details to the clerks sitting behind trestle tables on the dockside, and learned which trains they would need to board the following day after spending the night at a hotel in the area. Otto took advantage of the brief interlude to send a telegram to his sister announcing his arrival. On the morning of 28 May he boarded the train bound for the Netherlands. It travelled without mishap through France and Belgium, but stalled at Maastricht, where the bridges had been blown up. During this delay, Rosa de Winter was reunited with her daughter Judy, giving fresh hope to those like Otto who still had no news of their families. After a couple of days temporary bridges were erected and their journey continued by coach to Amsterdam.

Jan Gies had been transferred from his office on Marnixstraat to Centraal Station in Amsterdam, where he met and advised people returning from labour and concentration camps. He frequently enquired about the eight whom he had helped protect for two years. Then on 3 June, a man told him that he had seen Otto Frank. Jan raced home to tell Miep, just as Otto himself disembarked at Centraal Station. He gave his details to another clerk and received money for a taxi to the River Quarter. As they drove through the city, Otto clutched all the belongings he thought he had left in the world: a small bundle of clothing. The taxi pulled up outside Miep and Jan's apartment and Otto slowly made his way to their door. It flew open before he had rung the bell, for Miep had seen him from the window. Otto's first words were: 'Edith is not coming back.' Her eyes swimming with tears, Miep told him to go inside. He added, 'But I have great hope for Margot and Anne.' She nodded at him. He told her he had nowhere else to go. Miep took his bundle of clothes and assured him that he could stay with them for as long as he wished. Over the evening meal, Otto recounted everything that had happened since 4 August 1944.

In his memoir Otto writes of his return to Amsterdam, 'My first path was to Miep and her husband and, because I no longer had a home, I stayed there. It was then that I discovered that she and Bep had never been arrested and that my friends Kleiman and Kugler had come back from the concentration camps to which they had been sent. We all had lots of stories of our sad experiences – they mourned the death of my wife with me – but we were still hopeful that the children would return.'[3]

Otto had his own room at the Gieses', and he returned to work at the Prinsengracht. The annexe was two floors above his private office, but it lay closed off and decaying while he began to piece the remnants of his life together. He was elated by the arrival of his mother's postcard to Kleiman on 8 June and wrote to her immediately, explaining that he had read it and 'really enjoyed seeing [her] handwriting'. He continued:

> *At last we are in touch again! As my various letters haven't arrived here, I don't know what you've received and can only hazard a guess, since after June 1944, only a small line of contact was left. You probably keeled over with shock when you received my telegram. I'm writing from the office. Everything is like a strange dream. In reality, I can't sort myself out yet. I don't even feel like writing much . . . I don't know where Edith and the children are, but I never stop thinking of them . . . I am alone – I don't have to say any more. I found my old friends back here, Kleiman was severely ill whilst I was in jail and at the concentration camp, and Kugler was only freed a fortnight ago. All because of us. Our entire household has been stolen from us. I had kept some things in other places, but not very much. I have neither a hat nor a raincoat, neither a watch nor shoes, apart from those others have lent me, and you can't get anything here, there aren't the supplies. I'm living with Miep Gies. I have enough money at present, I don't need very much anyway. I long to be with you all. Please tell me the boys' addresses.*[4] *I'm waiting to hear from you soon, to learn about everybody – particularly those whom we've heard little about for such a long time. I'm afraid I only wrote a short letter to Robert,*[5] *as I can't go into detail. I'm not yet normal, I mean I can't find my equilibrium. Physically though, I'm fit.*
>
> Otto.[6]

Miep had not yet told Otto that something of his household *did* remain. She was determined that only Anne should receive her diary back from her and that, until then, the diary would stay under lock and key.

It was, of course, Anne's birthday on 12 June. It would have been her sixteenth, and Otto had hoped desperately that she would be back to celebrate it. He still had no news of either daughter, despite extensive efforts on his part to discover their whereabouts. He had heard from his

elder brother Robert, though, who had written concerning a misunder-
standing that arose from Otto's Marseilles telegram of 27 May. It had
been the first communication the family in Switzerland had received from
him, despite the many letters he had sent since his liberation in Auschwitz.
When Otto had written 'we have arrived . . .', they had assumed he meant
himself, Edith and the children, because they did not know that Edith
had died, or that he had been separated from Margot and Anne. Alice
Frank, overwhelmed with joy at the news she *thought* she had been given,
set about informing everyone that her son and daughter-in-law, and both
grandchildren, were safe. Evidently they now knew the truth, for Robert
writes:

> . . . *you can perhaps imagine how we feel after having been informed
> by mother that you were all well . . . I want you to know that we
> are unable to express our feelings about everything that happened.
> How we deplore the loss of Edith, and how we feel with you in your
> anxiety about your children we cannot describe, just as you have
> hardly given us a hint of all you have been through during the last
> few years. May God give that your children will come back to you
> soon and in good health. Every other question seems unimportant
> compared with this one. You say it's a miracle that you are alive and
> I believe you and am thankful for it, and that you are in good health
> and prepared to start a new life. I trust that after all you have been
> through you are not unduly worried about economic questions. They
> will be settled in due course and I can promise you our and Stanfield's[7]
> help . . . Lottie[8] is away . . . you know that she was especially fond
> of Edith and she suffers most terribly thinking of her death . . .[9]*

On 18 June Lottie herself wrote to Otto from the Lake District,
where she was taking a short break:

> . . . *My heart goes out to you, dear Otto, in your great sorrow about
> Edith's death and your anxiety about your children's whereabouts.
> I am deeply grieved about Edith's fate; you know how very fond of
> her I always was and how well we understood each other. I admire
> you for your courage and steadfastness, and I do pray and hope that*

*your dear children will be with you soon. It's no good telling you
that time will help to heal your wounds, but believe me, the horrible
memories you must have will gradually fade, and with the help
of your children and all of us, you will be able to build up a new
life . . . we are longing to hear from you that you are reunited with
your children, and hoping to see you again in the not too distant
future.*[10]

The flurry of letters continued. On 21 June Otto told his sister and
brother-in-law how he was coping without news of Margot and Anne:

*. . . there is never any communication from Russian-occupied terri-
tory and that's why I cannot get any information about the children,
since they might be in Germany. Up to now I was convinced I'd see
them back, but I'm beginning to doubt it. Nobody can imagine how
things were in Germany who has not suffered himself! . . . As regards
the children, I know that nothing can be done. We have to wait,
that's all. I go to the office daily because that's the only way to divert
myself. I just can't think how I would go on without the children,
having lost Edith already. You don't know how they both developed.
It's too upsetting for me to write about them. Naturally I still hope,
and wait, wait, wait. Here all my friends do what they can to help
me and to make life bearable for me. We try to work but as there
are virtually no basic materials, it is difficult. The costs go through
but there's no profit. As long as there is cash the salaries have to be
paid . . . Physically I am very well, weighing again 70 kg. I am
sunburnt too. We haven't seen each other for such a long time that
we'll be surprised at how we grew old . . . Of the 150,000 Jews in
this country, I don't believe there will be more than 20,000 left. I
hope to be able to see you soon, but at the moment, everything is in
chaos . . .*[11]

Otto's brother, Herbert, had survived despite internment at the
notorious Gurs camp in Vichy France. On 23 June Herbert wrote to Otto
for the first time since the war began. He ended his letter:

I think of you all day and half the night. I can't get any sleep. My thoughts are <u>always</u> with you, my dear Otto. I've got a telegram from Julius [Edith's eldest brother], with reply paid, but I never answered and I suppose mother informed him of your terrible fate. He wanted to send money and parcels . . . Give me news as quick as possible . . .

Herbert.[12]

A week later Otto received a letter from Julius, who had been told of his sister's death. His insistence that Otto should join him, and Walter, in America makes it clear that they held their sister's husband in high esteem, and Julius was to repeat his plea after the deaths of Anne and Margot had been confirmed. For now, though, he wrote:

My last hope is that you will find the children. Walter and I will do everything for you. In case you want to come to the USA we have money saved for you three. Send me a cable when you have found the children. There are nine food parcels shipped to you care of Max Schuster. Let me know if you need food. We will send it. Julius.[13]

Every day Otto questioned people, checked lists, called the Red Cross, and placed adverts in the press in the hope of finding his daughters. When he learned that Eva and her mother Fritzi were in Amsterdam again, he paid them a visit – without realizing that he had met Fritzi earlier. Eva recalls, 'I heard a knock at the front door and found Otto Frank standing there. His grey suit hung loose on his tall, thin frame, but he looked calm and distinguished. "We have a visitor," I said, as I took him in to see Mutti. He held out his hand to be introduced to Mutti. "But we've met already," she said. "On the way to Czernowitz." He shook his head. His brown eyes were deep-set and sad. "I don't remember," he said. "I have your address from the list of survivors. I am trying to trace what has happened to Margot and Anne." He was desolated that he had not yet found them but he sat and spoke to Mutti for a long time.'[14]

Otto divided his time between trying to find his children and working at 263 Prinsengracht, now in his former capacity as managing director. A statement was issued by the Dutch government in exile, to the effect that the enforced removal of Jewish persons from their businesses 'must be deemed never to have been promulgated'.[15] Pectacon and Gies & Co. continued trading. The Opekta company, however, was affected by a statutory order of 1944 relating to 'the property of the nationals of enemy powers',[16] because Otto was stateless but of German origin. The problems with Opekta remained unresolved until 1947. There was only one significant change at the Prinsengracht offices in 1945, and that was the dismissal of van Maaren, who had been caught in the act of stealing pectin, salt and soda from the stores.

In July 1945 Janny Brilleslijper visited the Dutch Red Cross. Presented with a list, she placed an 'x' beside the names of those whom she knew to be dead. Some time after her visit, a very dignified gentleman appeared at her door. He told her that he was Otto Frank and that he had seen the Red Cross list on which she had made her marks. Otto then asked her if she could tell him what had become of his children. In shock, Janny spread out her hands and said helplessly, 'They are . . . no more.' She watched in horror as he went white and fell into a chair. There was nothing she could do for him.

Otto had always believed his children would survive. Now a bright summer's day had brought him the darkest news. In his memoir, Otto writes, 'Again and again small groups of survivors returned from different concentration camps and I tried to hear something from them about Margot and Anne. At last I found two sisters who had been with them in Bergen-Belsen, and they told me about the final sufferings and deaths of my children. Both had been so weakened by privation that they fell victim to typhoid. My friends, who had been hopeful with me, now mourned with me . . .'[17]

When Miep heard the news, her first thoughts – other than those of profound anguish – were of Anne's diary. She recalls, 'When we heard, in about July 1945, that Anne, like Margot, had died in Bergen-Belsen, I gave what pieces of Anne's writing I had back to Mr Frank. I gave him everything that I had stored in the desk drawer in my office.'[18]

Miep presented Otto with the diary at the Prinsengracht offices. At the time he was sitting with his head in his hands. He glanced up as she placed the papers on his desk with the words, 'Here is your daughter

Anne's legacy to you.' On top of the pile lay the innocuous, red-checked diary. Miep left the room silently, closing the door behind her.

Otto opened the book, its pages untouched since his daughter's adolescent fingers had turned them over to work from it for her future *Het Achterhuis*. Anne smiled up at him self-consciously from her last school photograph, her upper lip pulled down over the awkward new dental brace: 'Gorgeous photograph, isn't it!!!! I hope I shall be able to confide in you completely, as I have never been able to do in anyone before, and I hope that you will be a great support and comfort to me . . . On Friday, June 12th, I woke up at six o'clock and no wonder; it was my birthday . . .'

After the news of Margot and Anne's deaths had reached his family, Otto received a number of moving condolence letters, from both the Hollanders and the Franks. On 6 August 1945 his mother telegrammed: 'Received sad news we all mourn our dearest ones fondest love and thoughts keep strong and healthy kisses mother – Elias Frank.'[19]

On 9 August 1945 the Americans dropped a second atomic bomb on Nagasaki. The Japanese government capitulated on 2 September 1945. The war was over.

In cinemas and newspapers everywhere, film-reels and photographs of concentration camps left audiences stunned. Some people could not believe what they saw and others could not bring themselves to look. Approximately 110,000 Jews were deported from the Netherlands during the war; only 5,000 returned. Slowly it became clear who had survived and who had not.

Otto tried to contact all those whom he had known before the war. He was especially keen to trace the friends of his children. He learned that the Ledermanns had been told to report to the Hollandse Schouwburg on 20 June 1943. Franz and Ilse, holding hands with their daughters Sanne and Barbara, passed the German sentry at the gate. Barbara suddenly let go of her little sister's hand, turned around and told the soldier to let her out. The man mistook her for a German girl, rather than a German-Jewish girl, apparently on account of her looks and language, and she walked out of the theatre without another word. Sanne and her parents were sent to Westerbork and then on 16 November, to Auschwitz. Ilse

Ledermann wrote to her brother, Paul, whilst aboard the train, 'My dearest, we are now setting off together on our last journey for a long time . . . We are on the way now, farewell dearest, much love, all the best, love and kisses, Ilse.'[20] She threw the note from the train, where someone found and sent it on. They were gassed immediately upon their arrival in Auschwitz.

Lies Goslar had been admitted to a Maastricht hospital upon her return from Trobitz. Her little sister, Gabi, was cared for by a family friend. Otto visited Lies in Maastricht, after travelling for fourteen hours to reach her. Upon seeing him, Lies cried eagerly, 'I've seen Anne! She's alive!' He told her very gently that this was no longer true. They talked for some time, and Lies came to trust him completely. 'He became my father from then on,' she states. 'He took care of everything.'[21]

Otto called on Eva and her mother again when they had moved back into their old apartment on Merwedeplein. Fritzi recalls, 'When he next came, several weeks later, we had already heard that our dear ones had perished in the Austrian camp of Mauthausen and he had received the news that Anne and Margot had died from typhoid fever in Bergen-Belsen. We were all acutely depressed.'[22] Eva remembers, 'It was so hard to be at home again without the family. I was sixteen and I didn't feel like going to school again, but Otto said, "You must go to school, that's the only thing one can give you for this life now: a good education." So I went back, but I couldn't relate to anyone. There was this big thing: those of us who came back, me and everyone else I met, we all wanted to talk about our experiences then, we were desperate to speak out, but no one wanted to hear. It was such a tragedy. I got over it, but I know many people who didn't. It was very hard and this was how it was for a long, long time. Years. Most of our neighbours on Merwedeplein didn't come back. It was empty. Otto did his best to help me overcome the bitterness I felt.'[23]

On 11 August Otto wrote to his family in Switzerland. His letter mainly concerns meetings with old friends. He assures his mother, 'I'm not letting myself go and to the contrary, I do things to help, instead of sitting and thinking.'[24] On 19 August he wrote again to his mother, sharing his memories of Anne:

. . . I've received so much post from everyone and can't always reply immediately. I don't let that trouble me too much, rather, always try to stay occupied with something. I usually succeed in that – only occasionally do I get distressed. I've already written that I have to work at my business . . . I must write to Buddy again. He doesn't know just how often Anne spoke of him and how much she longed to come to you and speak with him about everything possible. The ice-skating pictures that were sent are still here. She had a burning interest in the progress he made, partly because she enjoyed ice-skating so much, but also because she dreamed of going skating with him. Shortly before we disappeared, she received Unstel's skates, her ultimate wish. Buddy's style also reminds me of Anne's way of writing, that's amazing to see. Stephan has a different style . . . I read poems by Goethe and Schiller with Anne, as well as 'The Maid of Orleans', 'Nathan the Wise', 'The Merchant of Venice' and others. She particularly enjoyed reading biographies, e.g., those of Rembrandt, Rubens, Marie Theresia, Marie Antoinette, King Charles I and II, and all the Dutch masters; and 'Gone with the Wind' and many other good novels. Edith and Margot were also very keen readers. Apart from you, I write to virtually nobody about Edith and the children . . .[25]

Otto did write about his lost family to Julius and Walter in New York. His letter of 20 August indicates some of the practical difficulties he was having to overcome in everyday life:

Dear Julius and Walter,

What news could I tell you that would be interesting after the passing of my dear ones? Everything seems unimportant, senseless. But life goes on and I try not to think too much and to be angry. We all have to bear our fate. I can imagine your feelings, as you can mine, but we mustn't go on about that. I hope to hear from you soon again, about the life you are leading and the people you are with. I am just as much interested as ever in anything you do. Here I'm surrounded by the people who were with us daily when we were *in hiding, who risked everything for us in spite of all the dangers and the threats of the Germans. How often Edith and myself impressed on the girls to never forget those people, and to help them in case <u>we</u> didn't come back. We knew that we owed them all we had, and before we were discovered we felt sure we would come through safely. Now I'm alone, but I must not complain . . . Everything is scarce here and of bad quality. Robert did send a suit (not arrived yet) but if you can do so too, it would be very nice, as I have not much to wear. I received underclothes from London. Of course, I would like to help my people here who have no relations, so if you can get some women's wear and stockings, send them. Cigarettes and tobacco are welcome too. We don't get any meat except the tinned 'meat with vegetables', and very little butter. Tea and coffee are still 'surrogate', milk we get, but not enough, so if there is milk-powder, it is welcome. You see I'm not bashful, but I don't want to exaggerate and I don't know what the parcels you already sent contain . . . How lucky that you could get away in time! . . . I want to keep up regular correspondence with both of you and I am longing for news from you. I hope to hear soon about yourselves and remain as ever,*

yours,
Otto.[26]

Two days later, Otto wrote to his mother again and in this letter he mentions the existence of Anne's diary for the first time:

Dearest mother,

Now I've got your letter of the fourth. I know how great your sorrows are, how much your thoughts are with me, and how you share in my own sadness. I don't let myself go and try to keep busy as much as possible. I don't have photos from the last years of course, but Miep by chance saved an album and Anne's diary. But I didn't have the strength to read it. There's nothing left from Margot anymore, except her Latin works, because our whole household was plundered, and that's why all the little things we used so often and all the nice little things of Edith's and the children's are gone. I'm

sure there's no sense in thinking about them, but a human being
doesn't exist only in the mind, but in the heart also.[27]

Despite his efforts not to think too much, occasionally something penetrated the fragile shell of Otto's optimism. One such incident was the arrival of a letter from Betty Ann Wagner in America, who, along with her sister Juanita, was eager to continue writing to the Frank sisters now that the war was over. Otto wrote to his mother, 'Some days ago, a long letter from America arrived for Margot and Anne from a girl with whom they had had no actual contact. This girl wanted to start their correspondence again. I wrote to her in floods of tears. Things like that upset me very much. But it doesn't matter . . .'[28] Betty Ann Wagner recalls her feelings on receiving Otto's letter: 'He told us how the family had died during the war. I just sat and cried. I was then teaching, and when I read the details [of Otto's letter], I read it to my students and tried to impress upon them what had happened.'[29]

Apart from such instances, Otto tried to convince his mother that he was not brooding on the past:

One has to carry on for the people who are still alive. The others
you can't help anymore. You know this was always my belief. It's
so difficult to live out one's destiny now, but it has to be . . . I hope
that Berndt[30] *will have his success. A career in his chosen profession*
[acting] has many pitfalls. I can never mention his name without
thinking of Anne. I can understand Stephan wanting to go away.
Does he speak much English? The boys are now for me the only
ones that count as the younger generation. I'm always exchanging
letters with Julius and Walter. Edith constantly worried about Julius'
eyes . . . One cannot dwell on thoughts of people who have died.
Life asks for more.[31]

Despite his protestations, Otto's subsequent letters to his mother began to dwell more and more on memories of his wife and children. Stephan developed a serious illness which led to septicaemia, and, as Otto worried over his nephew, he thought about his lost daughters. On 14 September, he wrote:

I always see [Stephan] in my mind as a little boy, soft and dreamy ... You are right about my children and him. How much I could tell you ... On New Year's Day[32] I was with Hanneli. I will not go to the synagogue. The Liberal service doesn't exist or I <u>would</u> have gone, but the orthodox one means nothing to me. I know Edith was not so narrow-minded in her thoughts. She never expected or wanted me to fast, and she understood that I went to synagogue only because of her. I would have gone with her or the children, but to go alone makes no sense and would only be hypocrisy. I'll stay at home, for I have certain plans which I'll tell you about later ...[33]

Otto's plans were for Anne's diary. He had now begun to read it and found it difficult to tear himself away. On 26 September Otto wrote to his sister, Leni:

In Anne's diary I found a description of an ice-waltz which she performs with [Buddy] in a dream. What I'm reading in her book is so indescribably exciting, and I read on and on. I cannot explain it to you! I've not finished reading it yet, and I want to read it right through before I make some excerpts or translations for you. She writes about her growing up with an incredible self-criticism. Even if it hadn't been written by her, it would have interested me. What a great pity that this life had to go ...[34]

In his memoir Otto reflects, 'I began to read slowly, only a few pages each day, more would have been impossible, as I was overwhelmed by painful memories. For me, it was a revelation. There, was revealed a completely different Anne to the child that I had lost. I had no idea of the depth of her thoughts and feelings ... I had never imagined how intensely Anne had occupied her mind with the problem and meaning of Jewish suffering over the centuries, and the power she had gained through her belief in God ... How could I have known how important the chestnut tree was to her when she had never seemed interested in nature ... She had kept all these feelings to herself ... Occasionally she would read humorous episodes and stories out to us ... but she never read out anything which was about herself. And so we never knew to what extent she went on to develop her character, and she was more self-critical than any of us . . . I also read how important her relationship with Peter had been . . . I was very saddened sometimes to read how harshly Anne wrote about her mother. In her rage over some kind of conflict she let her feelings out without restraint. It hurt to read how often Anne had judged wrongly her mother's views. But I was relieved to read in later entries that Anne realized that it was sometimes her fault that she frequently didn't get on with her mother. She even regretted what she had written . . . Through Anne's accurate description of every event and every person, all the details of our co-habitation become clear to me again.'[35]

On 30 September Otto wrote to his mother,

I have just been in the synagogue for a children's festival. Anne and Margot always went to this event together, even when they were in Aachen. On the outside, I was smiling, but inside I was crying bitterly. I can't put Anne's diary down. It's just so incredibly exciting. Somebody has begun copying out the 'fairytales book' that she wrote because I don't want to let it out of my hands for a moment, and it is being translated into German for you. The diary I never allow out of my sight because there is so much in it that no one else should read. But I will make excerpts from this . . .[36]

Otto tried to persuade Miep to read the diary, but she refused at first, feeling completely unable to cope with the experience. She remembers how Otto 'started re-typing in German, in his room, certain parts from the diary. He worked on this every evening. He sent these sections to his mother in Basel.'[37] Otto had found a new sense of purpose. He worked from Anne's original diary and the version she re-wrote with a view to publication, combining the two. He omitted some of the less interesting, more intimate and wrathful entries, and added four passages from the book of tales, typing the whole thing out on pieces of paper which he then cut and pasted together until he was satisfied with the result.[38] He enlisted the help of his friend Anneliese Schutz in translating Anne's words from Dutch into German, because his mother knew no Dutch. Otto mailed the translations in batches to Switzerland. His family there were astounded by it. Buddy recalls, 'We were stunned. I couldn't believe what she wrote.

There was so much wisdom and humanity in it. But I must say, tremendous though Anne's diary was, I had no idea what would happen to it. I mean, if someone had said to me, "This is going to be one of the world best-sellers," I would have told them not to be ridiculous, it could never be that! I thought it was wonderful, but I could not foresee how others would react to it. I saw Anne in it because I knew her, but her writing was not what I expected. It was really a phenomenal thing, this transformation.'[39]

Otto began to tell everyone about the diary in his excitement. Eva and Fritzi Geiringer were amongst the first to see it. Eva recalls, 'One day, Otto came to us with the diary. He told us that when he had come back, he had no idea that it had been saved, because Miep had looked after it. He showed it to us, and then he read a few pages from it, and he burst into tears.'[40] Fritzi remembers, 'It took him a long time to read it because he found it such an overwhelming emotional experience. When he finished it, he told us that he had discovered that he had not really known his daughter.'[41]

In October 1945 Otto had received a letter from his old friend Nathan Straus, who was now president of the radio station WMCA in New York. Straus made arrangements to send Otto five hundred dollars from his own bank account, telling him, 'I hope this will be of some assistance to you in what, despite your unwillingness to speak of it, must be difficult financial circumstances. Don't trouble to acknowledge it. You just forget about it.'[42] Otto was moved by his friend's generosity, but he did not keep the money entirely for himself; he used some of it for children he knew who were trying to join families abroad or emigrate to Palestine. In his letter of thanks to Straus he added, 'Apart from business, I am very busy in copying the diary of my youngest daughter (which was found by chance), and to find an editor for it. I am going to let you know more about it later.'[43]

When Otto mentioned the diary to one of his acquaintances, Werner Cahn, a German refugee with connections in publishing, Cahn asked him if he might see it. Otto agreed, lending him a few of the type-written pages. Cahn showed the material to his wife, and they both asked to read more. Eventually, they read the entire typescript. Otto wrote to his mother:

> *. . . on Friday I was with Jetty Cahn at her house, and I started to read out some of Anne's diary, to get Werner's opinion about it. He's been with the publisher Querido for ages, where Jetty was too. Next Friday is the big decision, but already I have the impression: publish without a doubt – quite a big item! You can't imagine what this means. The diary would come out in German and English, telling everything that went on in our lives when we were in hiding – all the fears, disputes, food, politics, the Jewish question, the weather, moods, problems of growing-up, birthdays and reminiscences – in short, everything. Frau Schutz, whose house I was at yesterday, wants to translate a story called 'Blurry the Explorer'. The story of a hero . . . Anne was always so excited about everything . . .*[44]

Werner Cahn approached Alice von Eugen-Nahys of Querido before Otto had found an editor for the typescript, but she rejected it. He then tried a German publisher in Amsterdam, but they also turned it down. Cahn decided to wait until the typescript had been 'polished' before approaching anyone else. Otto took the diary typescript to his friend Ab Cauvern, a dramatist at the Workers Broadcasting Channel, in Laren.

Otto asked him to look out for 'grammatical errors and to remove Germanisms, that is, to correct expressions my daughter had borrowed from the German language and which were therefore bad Dutch'.[45] Cauvern remembers the task: 'I read through the typescript and only corrected typing errors (in the margin). Finally, I added the afterword. So I must have known even then that Otto Frank was planning to publish it. After that Otto Frank took it and I don't know what he did with it then. I didn't have anything to do with further preparation for publication.'[46] In fact, there were a number of changes – punctuation and grammatical improvements, phrasing and deletions – made to the manuscript after Cauvern's evaluation of it, but no additions to Anne's own words. Some of these were made in another, as yet unidentified hand; Miep and Jan Gies thought these might be attributable to Kleiman, who had grown even closer to Otto after the war.[47] Cauvern's epilogue to the diary read simply, 'Anne's diary ended here. On 4 August, the Green Police made a raid on the Secret Annexe . . . in March 1945, two months before the liberation of our country, Anne died in the concentration camp at Bergen-Belsen.'[48]

Otto mentioned the work being done to the typescript, and the on-going translations of Anne's 'Tales', in a letter to his mother on 12 December 1945:

> *. . . Frau Schutz will no doubt send you a translation of Anne's poem 'Eva's Dream', the one Anne gave me last year on my birthday . . . Tomorrow I'm going to Laren and taking Anne's diary for corrections and re-wording. I have got so far with it now, and I would like to have it finished so that I can show it to publishers. Attached is a short translation of a letter Anne wrote about her grandmother. She wrote of you too, if only a little, about your soft, wrinkly skin, which she believed she had virtually touched. She also wrote about receiving your letter exactly on her birthday in 1942. I can hardly get away from it all – and do not want to either . . .[49]*

When the adjustments to the diary typescript were complete, Isa Cauvern reprised her earlier role as Otto's secretary and typed up the revised text. Otto showed it to family and friends, canvassing them for their opinions on publishing the diary. Although he was enthusiastic about seeing it in print, he did have reservations. The reactions of friends were mixed. Margot's physics teacher at the Jewish Lyceum was amongst those Otto consulted. He remembers, 'At the end of 1945 Otto Frank took us to the annexe on the Prinsengracht and showed us the place where the diary papers of Anne were found by people who had helped them in hiding. We did not see the diaries, nor did we ask if we could read them. We knew that Otto Frank wanted to publish the diary, but I don't know who he was in contact with or who helped or advised him. Rabbi Soetendorp told me in the 1960s that Otto Frank had let him read the diary for his advice. Soetendorp had said there was no point in publishing it because nobody would be interested in such a diary.'[50]

Lies Goslar had already left the Netherlands for Switzerland by then, so Otto could not talk to her about it. Anne's other best friend, Jacqueline van Maarsen, still lived in the River Quarter, and she remembers Otto bringing the diary to her home: 'He came with it one day, but more to show it to my mother, I think. I didn't read it at that time, I just looked at it. And perhaps he didn't want me to read it, I don't know. I felt I shouldn't read it anyway, because it was Anne's writing and she had never wanted people to read it when I knew her. He had no intention of publishing it then. When he said later that he was thinking about it, I thought, how crazy, who would want to read a book written by such a young child?'[51]

Otto had given the new typescript to Werner Cahn, who wanted a second opinion on it himself. Cahn now worked at ENSIE-Encyclopedia, where the editor was Dr Jan Romein, a renowned historian. Cahn remembers, 'I took the typescript to Annie Romein-Verschoor [Jan Romein's wife], whose opinion I valued highly. Jan Romein saw the typescript lying there that evening. He read it through in one sitting and immediately wrote his piece in *Het Parool* [Dutch newspaper], which was printed the next day.'[52]

The article appeared on 3 April 1946 under the title 'A Child's Voice' and read in part:

> ... *When I had finished* [reading the diary] *it was night-time, and I was astonished to find that the lights still worked, that we still had bread and tea, that I could hear no aeroplanes droning overhead and no pounding of army boots in the street – I had been so engrossed in my reading, so carried away back to that unreal world, now almost a year behind us ...*
>
> ... *This apparently inconsequential diary by a child, this 'de profundis' stammered out in a child's voice, embodies all the hideousness of fascism, more so than all the evidence at Nuremberg put together ...*
>
> ... *If all the signs do not deceive me, this girl would have become a talented writer had she remained alive. Having arrived here at the age of four from Germany, she was able within ten years to write enviably pure and simple Dutch, and showed an insight into the failings of human nature – her own not excepted – so infallible that it would have astonished one in an adult, let alone in a child. At the same time she also highlighted the infinite possibilities of human nature, reflected in humour, tenderness and love, which are perhaps*

*even more astonishing, and from which one might shrink, especially
when they are applied to very intimate matters, were it not that
rejection and acceptance remain so profoundly childlike.*[53]

A number of publishers had been approached before this article
appeared, including Querido for a second time, but none of them wanted
the book. Immediately after the publication of Jan Romein's article,
however, publishers began to contact him. Romein referred them to
Werner Cahn. The enthusiasm of Fred Batten, an editorial consultant at
Contact, Amsterdam, led to Cahn giving him the typescript on approval.
Contact wanted to publish the diary, but only on condition that a number
of changes were made. These mainly concerned sections dealing with
sexuality and slight differences to the typescript style; in all, twenty-five
passages were dropped at the request of the managing director of Contact,
G. P. de Neve. In June 1946 five excerpts from the diary were published
in Jan Romein's left-wing publication, *De Nieuwe Stem*.

Otto still had misgivings about publishing his daughter's diary. The
rabbi of the Liberal Jewish congregation was against it and told him so.
'Otto Frank was what I call a good man, but also sentimental and weak.
He told me for the first time about his daughter Anne's diary when the
manuscript was already with the publisher, Contact. He didn't come to
me for advice, but rather to unburden himself, as he always was emotional
when he spoke about the diary. He discussed the relationship between
Peter and his daughter . . . I didn't read *Het Achterhuis* until it was in the
shops. Nor did he ever speak to me about the whole commercial hullabaloo
which went on, and I have never appreciated the Anne Frank House. The
same goes for all thinking Jews in the Netherlands.'[54] The rabbi's wife
thought likewise: 'One morning Frank came to see my husband with the
diary . . . He was pretty upset. He said that he was going to publish it. At
that point I asked him how he could do that. I didn't understand (and
still don't) how he could have copied out the thoughts of his adolescent
daughter to show them to the whole world. I was against publication,
and Anne herself would have been too. We must let the dead rest in peace.
That was my view with respect to Frank's plans. I can't remember now
how he reacted to this.'[55]

In the end Otto decided to go ahead with publication because he felt certain that it *was* what Anne would have wanted. Eva recalls, 'When the piece appeared in the paper, and the professor said this was such a valuable document and it should not be kept from the public, then Otto thought, I *will* publish. There were Anne's words on the subject to consider, the fact that she had said, "I want to go on living after my death . . ." It was difficult though, because it was such an intensely personal document. Otto left out some of Anne's harsher words about her mother, and her most intimate thoughts. That was right, I think, to do it that way, right for that time.'[56]

In his memoir Otto himself explains how he reached his decision: 'Anne would have so much loved to see something published . . . After reading everything, I felt the need to speak with close friends, above all with our helpers, about Anne's diary . . . My friends' opinion was that I had no right to view this as a private legacy as it is a meaningful document about humanity. Initially, I was very reluctant to publish, but then again and again I saw that they were right. One morning I read in the paper a leading article with the headline, "A Child's Voice" . . . Then a publisher approached me and so the first edition of the diary appeared in 1947. Anne would have been so proud.'[57]

On Wednesday, 25 June 1947, Otto Frank wrote in his pocket diary: 'BOOK.'[58]

The book to which he referred came out in an edition of 1,500 copies, with a foreword by Annie Romein-Verschoor, and an excerpt from 'A Child's Voice' on the jacket. Its title was *Het Achterhuis: Dagboek-brieven van 14 Juni 1942–1 Augustus 1944*. The author was Anne Frank. Her title. Her book.

Chapter Ten

'. . . By dying young Anne Frank shared the fate of
a number of other great writers . . . That the name "Anne Frank" has
since become a registered trademark on a par with "Coca-Cola", "IBM",
or "Michael Jackson", does nothing to diminish this eminent status . . .'

Gerrold van der Stroom, 'Anne Frank and her Diaries', address,
Institute of Jewish Studies, London, June 1997

When the diary was published, Otto gave copies to family and friends, with personal dedications pasted into each one. Jetteke Frijda's read: 'Finally, *Het Achterhuis* has appeared and I'm sending it to you in remembrance of Margot and Anne. You'll understand why I don't write much about it, but I hope we'll have a chance to talk soon.'[1] Otto was still in touch with Werner Peter Pfeffer and sent him the book, but it was some time before Pfeffer could bring himself to look at it: 'I think I laid it on my bookshelf or desk probably for months. I was afraid to open it. And as the story became more well-known, I said, "Okay, I'll read it." I read it and I could not, I did not, at that time put myself into my father's position . . . My father's part in it was [Anne's] description and I don't think I ever empathized to that point . . . I don't think I was mature enough, or maybe I was too afraid.'[2]

The first Dutch edition sold out after six months and a second was printed to meet demand. Encouraged, Otto submitted the manuscript to publishers in Germany, but without success. He remembered, 'Generally I waited until publishers in other countries contacted me, but one country I did try: Germany. I thought they should read it. But in Germany in 1950, I had difficulty. It was a time when Germans didn't want to read about it. And Schneider of Heidelberg wrote to me. He said, "I have read the book and feel it has to be published, but I don't think it will be a financial success"'[3] Schneider's instinct was not entirely accurate; when the first German print run of 4,500 was issued in 1950, it took a lot of persuasion to convince booksellers to promote it, but it sold well when they did. The diary was published in France that same year by Calmann-Levy, where its reception was positive, both critically and commercially.

In Britain the book was turned down by Allen & Unwin, Gollancz, Heinemann, Macmillan, and Secker & Warburg before Vallentine, Mitchell published it in May 1952. The following month, it was published by Doubleday in America, having been rejected by Knopf, Simon & Schuster and Viking, amongst others. In both countries, Barbara M. Mooyaart-Doubleday's translation was accompanied by a foreword by Eleanor Roosevelt. Mooyaart-Doubleday never saw the original diary, but worked from a typescript, translating three pages every day for four months. 'I was very, very deeply interested and moved,' she recalled, 'I started in the afternoon while my little boys were asleep and again in the evening after I got them to bed. My husband [Dutch Second World War pilot Eduard Mooyaart] always told me to stop at 9 o'clock because otherwise I couldn't sleep. I was almost in a trance, entirely taken up with it.'[4] She met Otto on several occasions, once at the secret annexe. Whenever he spoke about the diary, 'he was always moved, often almost in tears'.[5] Her son Leslie, then five, remembered Otto calling on them: 'I can still picture him in my mind. This man who was on the one hand so nice and so sad. He looked as if he would never smile in a million years.'[6] In America, heralded by Meyer Levin's ecstatic review in the *New York Times*, the book became an instant best seller. The response in Britain was rather cooler; in 1953 it was unavailable for purchase. Pan Books, after some hesitation, published a pocket paperback edition in 1954, and from then on, sales rapidly increased.

The diary was published in Japan in 1952 and met with considerable acclaim. The Japanese 'desperately required Anne Frank . . . sales in Japan after its publication in 1952 were spectacular. Over 100,000 copies were sold by early 1953 as the Diary reached its thirteenth printing . . . To the Japanese, Anne Frank, although European, had become an acceptable and accessible cultural figure of the war – a young victim, but one who inspired hope for the future rather than a sense of guilt for the past. Her sex further emphasized the stress on innocence . . .'[7] Otto had written to Meyer Levin that Anne's book 'is not a war book. War is the background. It is not a Jewish book either, though Jewish sphere, sentiment and surrounding is in the background.'[8] None the less, the Japanese publisher's marketing strategy was to sell the diary as a war book with the accent on the tragedies war caused, an approach which proved highly successful.

By 1955 Otto was spending several hours a day answering the letters he received from captivated readers. Rabbi David Soetendorp recalls, 'Otto Frank visited my parents at home in De Lairessestraat, around the time that Anne's diary was starting to become world famous. He would sit at our dining table full of stories of how children in far-flung nations were becoming inspired by the diary and what a force for good in impressionable young minds it had turned out to be . . . he and my parents would break down in tears at the silently shared thought, "If such a force for good had been in existence in the years leading up to the Second World War . . ." '[9]

With his mission clearly set out before him, Otto agreed with the voices now urging him to allow the diary to be adapted for the stage. Meyer Levin hoped to convince Otto that he was the right person for the task, but after years of impassioned pleading, threats and promises, Levin lost out to the scriptwriting duo Frances Goodrich and Albert Hackett.[10] The play, *The Diary of Anne Frank*, officially opened at New York's Cort Theatre on 5 October 1955. Its premiere was attended by Marilyn Monroe, whose young friend Susan Strasberg was the star. In a letter to the cast and crew, Otto explained that he would not be in the audience: 'For me, this play is part of my life and the idea that my wife and children and I will be presented on the stage is a painful one to me. Therefore it is impossible for me to come and see it.'[11] Otto never went back on his word, though in this instance it might have been better if he had, for despite the accolades heaped upon the production (it won the 1956 Pulitzer Prize and the Tony Award, along with almost all the major critics' prizes), Goodrich and Hackett had depicted his daughter as 'a universal figure whose Jewishness could almost be ignored – Anne Frank had become Everyperson, she was accessible to all . . . impeccably American.'[12] The representations of the other members of the annexe 'family' were also far from faithful, with Pfeffer in particular singled out for something close to character assassination; his incensed widow later wrote to the playwrights about their portrayal of her husband as a 'psychopath'.[13] Otto had read the script, and was uneasy about the interpretations, but on the one hand, he had asked Levin, when he was still being considered as writer, not to 'make a Jewish play out of it. In some way of course it must be Jewish, even so that it works against anti-Semitism. I do not know if I can express what I mean . . .'[14] Otto's hope was that the audience would be able to relate to the people on stage, which he feared they would not if the play was not 'universal' enough. His aim was 'to bring Anne's message to as many people as possible',[15] but the Goodrich and Hackett adaptation flattened out all complexities with its 'non-Jewish Jews and ultimate redemption'.[16]

Despite the bland inaccuracy of the script, enough of 'Anne's message' remained intact to stir the consciences of theatre-goers who had not yet read the diary. The European premiere was held in Sweden in August 1956, but it was the German production which made headlines in the international press. In the country of Anne's birth, the play 'released a wave of emotion that finally broke through the silence with which the Germans had treated the Nazi period'.[17] A correspondent for the *New York Times* reported that in one German city there were 'audible sobs and one strangled cry as the drama struck its climax and conclusion – the sound of the Germans hammering at the door of the hideout. The audience sat for several minutes after the curtain went down and then rose as the royal party left. There was no applause.'[18] More than a million people saw the play in Germany and sales of the diary rocketed. Youth groups were established in Anne's name, schools and streets dedicated to her, a 2,000-strong crowd of teenagers made the journey from Hamburg to Bergen-Belsen to commemorate her death, and at her former home on Ganghoferstrasse a plaque was attached to the wall: 'In this house lived Anne Frank, who was born 12 June 1929 in Frankfurt-am-Main. She died as a victim of the National Socialist persecutions in 1945 in the concentration camp at Bergen-Belsen. Her life and death – our responsibility. The Youth of Frankfurt.'

The Dutch premiere took place on 27 November 1956, in the presence of the Royal Family. Otto attended the opening ceremony (though not the performance), with Jacqueline van Maarsen, Jetteke Frijda, Miep and Jan, Bep and her husband, and Kleiman and his wife. Jetteke remembers, 'Afterwards, I went up to one of the actors and asked them if it was strange for them that night. They said that it was, very much so, because everyone in the audience had some connection with the persons portrayed in the piece, or with the Jews of Holland. They found it very intense.'[19] The play was subsequently performed throughout the world.

It was a natural transition from stage to screen, and in 1957 Twentieth Century Fox's version of *The Diary of Anne Frank* began shooting. George Stevens, who as an American soldier had participated in the liberation of Dachau, directed the film on a specially constructed studio lot. The annexe was entirely recreated but for the outer wall, allowing a camera on a crane to travel into every room. The exterior shots were filmed in Amsterdam. Otto and Kleiman were advisors on the film. Kleiman told a journalist, 'The film people are very precise, I had to send all sorts to America. Pencils, milk-bottles, rucksacks, stamps. Mr Stevens, the director, asked for photographs and exact descriptions of the spice mills. Everything in the film had to be right.'[20] Stevens insisted, 'The film will be devoid of Nazi horrors. It will tell the valiant, often humorous story of a wonderful family hiding out in a time of great stress; the story of a teenage girl's magnificent triumph over fear. Anne Frank was the kind of girl responsible for the survival of the human race.'[21] After a nationwide search for an actress to play Anne, nineteen-year-old Millie Perkins, a model from New Jersey, landed the part. Otto had hoped that Audrey Hepburn would take on the role, but she refused; having lived through the war in the Netherlands as a child, she felt that it would be too painful to act out on screen.[22] Van Hoeven, the real-life grocer on the Leliegracht, played himself in the film. Joseph Schildkraut reprised his stage role as Otto Frank, and Shelley Winters won the Oscar for Best Supporting Actress as Mrs van Daan. The film was also awarded the Oscar for Best Black and White Cinematography and Best Black and White Art Direction. An alternative ending had been shot depicting Anne in the concentration camp, but this was spurned in favour of the play's penultimate line: 'In spite of everything, I still believe people are really good at heart.' The premiere was held in Amsterdam on 16 April 1959, and Miep, Bep and Mrs Kleiman were presented to the Queen and Princess Beatrix. An East German film, *A Diary for Anne Frank*, was made at around the same time. It detailed the deportation of the annexe occupants and unmasked former Nazis. Gemmeker, the commandant of Westerbork, was amongst the men who had their full addresses revealed. It received cautiously approving notices, but was 'rejected by the British Board of Film Censors in the same year as the Hollywood film was on general release'.[23]

On 4 May 1960 the annexe opened as a museum. Ever since the earliest publication of the diary, people had knocked on the door of 263 Prinsengracht to ask if they could look around. Kleiman had acted as an unofficial guide. There had been many changes at the premises in the intervening years. Both Miep and Bep had left the business in the late 1940s. Bep had married her long-term boyfriend Cornelius van Wijk and had begun a family, while Miep wanted to devote herself to her home life, having moved into a new apartment on Jekerstraat in January 1947. Otto continued to live with Miep and Jan (who became parents in 1950) for some time, but after his retirement from Opekta in April 1953, he emigrated to Switzerland. He had his own spacious room in his sister and brother-in-law's house in Basel. It was an emotional year for Otto; his mother, Alice, died on 20 March in Switzerland, and his older brother, Robert, died on 23 May in London, but there was also an addition to the family: Otto married Fritzi Geiringer. Otto had told friends at the end of 1952 that he would marry the following year. Fritzi's daughter, Eva, was not in the least surprised: 'He loved her very much. When their relationship began, Otto would ride to work on his bicycle and my mother went the same way on the tram. Every time the tram stopped, Otto would stop too and talk to her. He was very romantic.'[24]

Otto and Fritzi married on 10 November 1953 in Amsterdam. Fritzi shared his room on the top floor of the house in Basel. The marriage was a strong one, and Fritzi helped him with the vast amount of correspondence produced by Anne's diary, which was stored in a bank safe in Basel. Eva remembers, 'He found great happiness with my mother. They were a real team. When they came to stay here, they had their own room with a bed-settee and a table, and every morning my mother would sit at the table, typing, while Otto paced around, thinking what to put in these letters. I was a bit jealous, because I wanted my mother to come out with me and my children, shopping or some such, but Otto insisted that she stay and help him with the letters. In a way, my life was overshadowed by Anne. Otto was wonderful, but his whole life was his lost daughter, and he could talk about her twenty-four hours a day. I was suppressed by Anne, and upset about the situation. But I loved Otto, he was so kind. We always spent Christmas together, and often went on holiday.'[25]

In 1955 Otto and Kugler retired from Pectacon, and, with Jan Gies, from Gies & Co. The business was sold and Kugler emigrated to Canada after the death of his first wife. He remarried and worked in Weston, Toronto, as an electrician and an insurance agency clerk before his retirement. Kleiman died on 30 January 1959. Otto read a line from Anne's diary at his funeral: 'When Mr Kleiman comes in, the sun begins to shine.'

Kleiman's widow attended the opening ceremony of the 'Anne Frank House' on 4 May 1960, with Otto, Bep, Miep and Jan. The survival of the annexe was something of a triumph over adversity in itself. In 1953 an estate agent purchased the houses on the corner of the Prinsengracht and Westermarkt, and the owner of 263 offered to sell to him as well. Otto persuaded Opekta to buy the building instead, and a meeting of the shareholders decreed that Otto or 'a foundation appointed by him' would take over the property in the near future. Unfortunately, the building was in complete disrepair and the renovation costs would be astronomical. In 1954 a broker bought the property and, with the intended demolition of the neighbouring houses, it looked as though nothing more could be done. The Dutch press reported the threat to the hiding-place and spoke out vehemently against it: 'The Secret Annexe . . . has become a monument to a time of oppression and man-hunts, terror and darkness. The Netherlands will be subject to a national scandal if this house is pulled down . . . There is every reason, especially considering the enormous interest from both inside and outside the country, to correct this situation as quickly as possible.'[26] The Anne Frank Stichting came into being on 3 May 1957 to spearhead the campaign to stop the planned demolition and oversee the urgent appeal for funds to buy and renovate the building. In October 1957 the owner of the property, Berghaus, presented it to the Stichting. An extensive restoration project was launched, and the adjacent buildings up to the Westermarkt corner were purchased with the funds raised by a second campaign. The additional properties would be used for student housing and the establishment of a youth centre where courses and conferences could be held. At 263 Prinsengracht, substantial changes were made to the front house, but the annexe was kept as near as possible in its original state. Otto insisted that it should remain empty; that was how it had been left after the arrest. Two models were constructed to give visitors an idea of how it looked during the war. There were also proposals for the 'other' Anne Frank house, at 37 Merwedeplein, to be made into a museum, but it is still a private property. The Montessori school on Nierstraat was renamed the 'Anne Frank School' on 12 June 1957. The Stichting continues to maintain the property on the Prinsengracht, and to challenge and educate against racism and discrimination.

Otto once told an interviewer why he had left the Netherlands and how he felt when he visited the annexe: 'I live in Basel today because I can no longer live in Amsterdam. I often go there, but I can't stand it for more than three days. Then I go to the Prinsengracht where we hid for two years . . . Sometimes I look at our hiding place; it has not been changed. The rooms are almost empty because everything was removed after our deportation. But the map on the wall with the pins showing the advance of the Allied troops is still there. On a wall I can still see the lines I drew to show how the children grew. The pictures of film stars that Anne hung up for decoration are still on the wall in her room, as well as her other pictures. I look around and then I leave. I cannot bear the sight any longer.'[27] In 1962 Otto and Fritzi moved to a large, lovely house in the Basel suburb of Birsfelden, where Otto became a keen gardener. He set up the Anne Frank-Fonds in Basel in 1966 to protect his daughter's name and to administer the royalties from the sales of the diary, which gained dedicated readers wherever it was published. The profits benefited a host of charities and continue to do so today. With such a vast readership, it was inevitable that Holocaust revisionists and neo-Nazis would try to discredit the diary. Otto had to fight various lawsuits over the years against those who saw his daughter's work as a threat to their own feeble ideology. Any damages incurred were usually donated to the Stichting in Amsterdam.

Otto stayed in touch with his helpers and the friends who had survived the war. He and Fritzi often visited Lies in Israel, where she had married an army major and had three children, and he wrote regularly to Edith's brothers in America. Walter and Julius had 'saved up enough money for a comfortable retirement which they did not live long enough to enjoy'.[28] Julius died in October 1967, and Walter in September 1968.

Fourteen members of the Hollander family besides Edith had perished in the camps.

Otto worked harder than anyone to propagate the ideals, as he saw them, expressed in his daughter's diary. If, as Anne's filmic biographer Jon Blair believes, he did not 'always do himself or his daughter's literary legacy the greatest justice because of his single-minded, and quite laudable, determination to spread his interpretation of her story and the story of the victims of the Holocaust to the world' and 'made bad deals',[29] he still achieved what he had set out to achieve: posthumous fame for Anne, recognition for her literary talent, and a means by which she was, in an abstract sense, able to 'work for the world and mankind'. Of his duty as the keeper of the diary's flame, Otto said, 'It's a strange role. In the normal family relationship, it is the child of the famous parent who has the honour and the burden of continuing the task. In my case the role is reversed.'[30]

Otto wrote a number of articles after the war and in one, 'Has Germany Forgotten Anne Frank?' he stated that he had always been, and always would be, optimistic: 'I know many Jews who don't want to have anything to do with Germans, but I like the young Germans. I am a positive man. You can't bring back those who have been murdered . . .'[31] He told an interviewer, 'Whatever I do now is dedicated to Anne. I am not a hater. I never had the feeling, Why should my child die and not others? Out of Anne's diary, so much that is positive has come. I have never been back to Auschwitz or Belsen. There is nothing there. We have to think of the living.'[32]

Otto was in good health until the last year of his life, when he contracted cancer. The illness rapidly took hold, and on the evening of 19 August 1980 he died at home in Basel. He was ninety-one years old. As he had willed it, his body was cremated, and his ashes were interred in a non-Jewish cemetery close to his home. He shares his resting place with his nephew, Stephan Elias, who died unexpectedly only five days later.

In 1981, on 16 December, Victor Kugler died in Canada. Two years later, after a happy marriage which provided her with the children she had always longed for, Bep Voskuijl-van Wijk also died. The death of Jan Gies, on 26 January 1993, left Miep the sole surviving member of the five 'helpers'. Their efforts were recognized by Yad Vashem in Israel, where they are honoured as 'The Righteous of the Nations'.

In his will, Otto left Anne's writings to the Dutch government. In November 1980 Anne's diary returned to Amsterdam. The Netherlands State Institute for War Documentation received it, and in 1986, 'to dispel the attacks made upon the book's authenticity coming from hostile circles',[33] *The Critical Edition* appeared, comprising Anne's original diary (with a few omissions), her own revised version, and the text that had been available since 1947. The Institute's abbreviated report of the investigation into whether or not the diary is genuine was also included. Unqualified proof that the diary is authentic has not, of course, deterred its decriers.

While work was proceeding on the book, an anonymous donor sent the Institute, via the West German magazine *Stern*, letters, photographs, a French grammar book and a pendant that had belonged to Anne Frank as a baby. When the Anne Frank Stichting launched the international exhibition 'Anne Frank in the World' in 1985, many of the photographs illustrating it had been sent, again, by an anonymous donor. The material is thought to have been in the Franks' furniture when the Gestapo had it shipped to Germany. Another stack of photographs, but this time of Pfeffer, was discovered by Joke Kneismeyer, then working for the Stichting, at Waterlooplein fleamarket in Amsterdam. The albums had been amongst the effects found in Lotte Pfeffer's apartment after her death in 1985.

In his memoir Otto writes: 'I once asked my publisher what, in his opinion, are the reasons why the diary has been read by so many. He said that the diary encompasses so many areas of life that each reader can find something that moves him personally. And that seems to be right . . . parents and teachers learn from it, how difficult it is to really know their children or their pupils . . . Young people identify with Anne or see in her a friend. "I want to live on after my death" Anne wrote, and you could well say that her wish has come true, because she lives on in the hearts of so many people.'[34] The incredible success of the published diaries, the number of visitors to the 'Anne Frank House', the travelling exhibition, and the establishment of several other Anne Frank organizations prove this to be the case, yet there are also those for whom the name 'Anne Frank' means business. One company in Spain hoped to sell Anne Frank jeans, while another in Singapore wanted to set up an export and import enterprise under the name 'Anne Frank'.[35]

Even the Anne Frank Stichting itself has been the subject of speculation.[36] The Stichting refused a request for information from the distinguished film-maker Willy Lindwer for his documentary on Anne's incarceration in the camps. Their explanation was that 'supplying this information did not fit in with the image of Anne as preferred by the Stichting'.[37] Gerrold van der Stroom, one of the editors of *The Critical Edition*, contends that 'to deliberately ignore the final chapter in the short life of Anne Frank . . . is tantamount to the falsification of history'.[38] One of the most vociferous critics of the ways in which Anne and her diary have been (mis)represented is Cynthia Ozick, whose article in the *New Yorker* went so far as to claim it might have been better if the diary had been destroyed rather than preserved.[39] To some, Anne Frank is no more than the 'Holocaust poster child',[40] and to others, the number of writers and speakers who like to quote repeatedly the line that 'people are really good at heart' has made her death 'not the murder that it was but an operatic closing of the eyes, an angelic expiration without pain and without degradation'.[41] There are those who balance the humorous, ebullient entries in the diary against the darker, pessimistic entries and find that the latter come out strongest, but there are also those who do the opposite.

When, in her shuttered room, Anne mused, 'will I ever be able to write anything great?'[42] she had no idea just how powerful her written testimony would become. Her diary is now acclaimed as 'the most important source of knowledge in the world today concerning the Holocaust'; 'the most widely read book of World War II'; 'one of the key writings of the twentieth century';[43] and is a set text in schools everywhere. The slim volume of her short stories, which her father characterized as filled with 'childish idealism . . . so typical of Anne'[44] has also become a minor classic.

Her fame, though, rests on her diary, and it must be in part because the absence of its 'real' ending – Anne's death in Bergen-Belsen – leaves the reader with the feeling that, since the written word has survived, so too, in some way, has its author.

'. . . nothing is worse than being discovered.'

Anne Frank, *Diary*, 25 May 1944

Who Killed Anne Frank? asked the provocative title of a CBS television programme shown on 13 December 1963. Otto Frank, Simon Wiesenthal and Dr Louis de Jong, of the Netherlands State Institute for War Documentation, were interviewed for the programme, which was critically praised but in fact failed to answer its central question: who betrayed the eight in hiding on the Prinsengracht?

In *Ashes in the Wind*, Dr Jacob Presser points out how fragile was the balance between concealment and discovery for fugitives during the war: 'It is certain that thousands of Jews lost their lives as a result of denunciation, anonymous or otherwise, sometimes even by their hosts . . . The *Algemeen Politieblad* [Police Gazette] kept publishing lists of missing Jews sent in by various burgomasters and calling for their capture. On one occasion, the Germans published an appeal to Jews in hiding: those who gave themselves up would be pardoned . . . all who did come forward were deported.'[1]

Informants fell into two categories: the professional and the amateur. The former were sharp enough to realize that more mileage could be had from blackmailing hidden Jews rather than turning them in immediately; payments could be increased over time.

The most infamous of this first category were the Henneicke Column, whose activities 'brought about the deaths of hundreds of Jews. The men were paid piece-rates and their blood-money was, in time, raised from seven and a half guilders to thirty-seven and a half guilders per Jewish head.'[2] The Henneicke Column used appropriated Jewish money to reward successful captors. Amateurs were a more difficult group to grasp; their motive was rarely monetary in the sense that, generally, they did not inform regularly enough to profit from it. The drive to betray seemed primarily to be emotional, stemming from anti-Semitism, personal dislike, malice, or adherence to the Nazi doctrine. The Netherlands was 'full of Nazi collaborators. While the number of Dutch rescue efforts appears to have been high, the number of people actually rescued represented only 11 per cent of the Jewish population. Betrayal was commonplace.'[3] Of the 25,000 Jews who went into hiding 8,000 to 9,000 were arrested. Nazi-organized raids, laxity on the part of the fugitives themselves, and slip-ups by their protectors were also factors. Which of these factors, or a combination, can be held liable for the raid on the Secret Annexe?

Kleiman was the first to bring the matter to the attention of the authorities. Shortly after the liberation, he visited the Political Criminal Investigations Department (POD) with a written declaration which strongly implied that Willem Gerard van Maaren, the warehouseman, was guilty of their betrayal. Kleiman summarized all the thefts allegedly committed by van Maaren, and stated: 'To my question whether he had known that people had been hidden away in the building he said that he had merely suspected it, but that the staff of one of the next door businesses had once said something to him to that effect . . .'[4]

The danger that van Maaren might turn informer was one which the eight in hiding had frequently discussed. When he was taken on to replace Bep's father in spring 1943, everyone was initially unconcerned. In her diary Anne had already written about another assistant in the ground-floor stores: 'We are getting a new warehouseman, the old one has to go to Germany, which is a pity but much better for us, because the new one doesn't know the house. We've always been frightened of the warehousemen.'[5] Kugler recruited van Maaren; one cannot imagine that he knew about the trail of bungled business ventures and a reputation for unreliability, particularly where finances were concerned, that dogged van Maaren's past. He had previous experience as a warehouseman with the organization 'Charity According to Ability'. What van Maaren did not tell Kugler was that whilst working there he had been exposed as a thief who stole from his employers.

Problems began to arise soon after his arrival in the warehouse.

Small amounts of sugar, spices and potato flour disappeared, and van Maaren started to ask questions that made Kugler and Kleiman wonder whether he had guessed their secret. On one occasion Kugler caught him scraping the blue paint from the windows overlooking the annexe and muttering, 'Well, I've never been over there.' When van Maaren found van Pels's briefcase[6] in the warehouse (van Pels had accidentally left it there the evening before), he interrogated Kugler about it and also asked him whether 'a certain Mr Otto Frank used to work here'. More worrying still, he set traps in the warehouse at night: pencils laid on the very edge of a desk where any movement would displace them, and potato meal dropped on the floor to preserve footprints. When he was queried about this behaviour, he said, quite reasonably, that he was merely trying to catch the real thief to prove he was not to blame.[7] He did his best to impugn Bep Voskuijl and her father in the thefts. However, Kleiman and Kugler hired a man named J. J. de Kok to assist van Maaren and his co-worker, Hartog, in the warehouse, and after the war de Kok admitted having sold the goods van Maaren stole from the Prinsengracht on the black market. Both de Kok and Hartog had ceased working in the warehouse before the end of 1944.

The occupants of the annexe soon grew to distrust van Maaren. The extent and speed with which their unease took hold is apparent in Anne's diary entry of 16 September 1943 (just six months after van Maaren had begun work): 'the warehouseman, van Maaren, is becoming suspicious about the Annexe. Of course anyone with any brains at all must have noticed that Miep keeps saying she's off to the laboratory, Bep to look at the records, Kleiman to the Opekta storeroom, while Kugler makes out that the "Secret Annexe" is not part of our premises but belongs to the neighbor's building. We really wouldn't mind what Mr van Maaren thought of the situation if he wasn't known to be so unreliable and if he wasn't so exceptionally inquisitive, so difficult to fob off.'[8] A subsequent entry indicates how much his presence disturbed them: 'On Saturday there was a big drama here, which exceeded in fury any that has gone before. It all started with van Maaren . . .'[9] His conduct led to new security measures, for instance, about when it was safe to flush the toilet: 'van Maaren mustn't hear us.'[10] On 21 April 1944 Anne wrote: 'Here we are having one misfortune after another, scarcely had the outside doors been strengthened[11] than van Maaren appeared again. In all probability it was he who stole the potato meal and wants to put the blame on Bep's shoulders . . . Maybe Kugler will have that seedy-looking character shadowed now.'[12] This passage raises a question: Anne refers to van Maaren as 'seedy-looking' but how did she come by her description of him? Was it something the helpers had said, mere dramatization on her part, or had she caught a glimpse of him herself, and if she had, who is to say he had not seen her? But to return to Anne's diary; her entry for 25 April 1944 reads: 'there has been another unpleasant incident, which hasn't been explained so far. Van Maaren is trying to blame Bep for all the things that have been stolen and spreads the most barefaced lies about her. A lot of potato flour has gone and more's the pity, our private chest in the front attic has been almost completely emptied. Van Maaren probably has his suspicions about us as well . . . Bep isn't the last to leave any more; Kugler locks up. Kleiman, who has been here in the meantime, Kugler and the two men have been looking into the question of how to get this fellow out of the place from every possible angle. Downstairs they think it is too risky. But isn't it even riskier to leave things as they are?'[13]

Perhaps it was, for on 4 August 1944 the Gestapo arrived at the Prinsengracht. After the removal of everyone from the Secret Annexe, and Kugler and Kleiman, only Miep remained in the offices that afternoon, while van Maaren continued his work in the warehouse. He had been given the keys on Silberbauer's orders, but it is debatable whether this fact increases the likelihood that he was the betrayer. After all, Silberbauer knew that Miep was well acquainted with the secret annexe, and there was no one else to whom he could consign the keys. She later stated that van Maaren had said he was 'on good terms with the SD',[14] but he denied her allegation. When Kleiman returned to work in winter 1944, van Maaren lost his position as 'administrator'. The thefts increased, and in one instance stores kept deliberately secret from him were plundered. He submitted to a house search, but it proved abortive, and it wasn't until after the liberation that Kleiman was able to dismiss him, having at last caught him red-handed in the act of thieving.

It is commonly believed that Otto did not want the betrayer identified, but this is not entirely correct; he was primarily afraid that the wrong person would be charged. After learning that his daughters had died, Otto and his helpers visited the POD. On 11 November 1945 he wrote to his mother in Switzerland:

> . . . I can tell you about something very serious . . . I was at the Security Police. We did all we could to try to get out of them who had betrayed us. It now seems possible to put the wheels in motion, and so yesterday we all went to the police station to study photographs, to see if we could recognize who arrested us. The photos were astounding – we could identify two of the men. They're still in prison and we're going to confront them. All this is very upsetting as you can imagine. It is these – the murderers – who are responsible for the deaths of Edith and my children. But one has to stay calm in order to get the people to speak, so that we can find out more. If only this might work, but quite often the people themselves don't know who the actual traitors were, and simply did what their whiter-than-white superiors told them. . .[15]

The photograph identifications came to nothing; both men denied all knowledge of the raid. No further action was taken until May or June 1947, when Otto called at the Political Investigation Branch (PRA) of the police. Kleiman re-submitted his letter from 1945 with a covering note mentioning Otto's visit. In January 1948 the PRA interviewed Kleiman, Kugler and Miep.

Kleiman told them that on 4 August 1944 the SD officer and his men had 'seemed to know precisely what they were doing, for they went straight to the hiding place and arrested all eight persons present there'.[16] He also told them about an incident that had occurred in July 1944. The wife of van Maaren's assistant in the warehouse, Hartog, had asked the wife of one of Kleiman's brother's employees, Genot, if it was true that there were Jews hiding at 263 Prinsengracht. Genot's wife did not respond, other than to warn Hartog's wife to be careful with such talk. She related the conversation to Kleiman's brother, who then told Kleiman. There was nothing he could do, except hope that the rumour had died, but he now knew that the warehouse staff had either seen or guessed the secret of the back house.

On 2 February 1948 van Maaren himself visited the PRA to deposit a written declaration of his innocence. In it he claimed to have 'held a position of trust within the business' and to have had nothing to do with the warehouse thefts. He also said he had twice gone to see Kugler at the Euterpestraat on Miep's orders, once to get a chemical formula for a preservative, which he had succeeded in obtaining from Kugler. This was clearly untrue; Kugler and Kleiman had already been transferred to another prison. Van Maaren said that he had known nothing about the secret annexe and, on seeing the entrance to it, had been 'dumbfounded by its technical ingenuity . . . the SD would never have been able to find out anything about this secret door without inside information.' He added, 'I was told that on arrival the SD went straight upstairs to the bookcase and opened the door.'[17] He was not asked to clarify his statement.

On 10 March 1948 the Genots were interviewed at their home in Antwerp. Asked about Kleiman's account of the conversation between Mrs Hartog and Mrs Genot, they confirmed that this had indeed occurred. Genot had cleared out the annexe prior to its clandestine habitation. In 1942 he had realized that Kleiman was harbouring Jews on the premises, having noticed the amounts of food delivered to the offices. Although he judged van Maaren 'a very odd sort of fellow' and 'didn't know what to make of him',[18] he thought it unlikely that he was the betrayer. Ten days later, the police visited Hartog, who said that he had also noticed the food deliveries, but had never suspected anything until 'van Maaren told me about fourteen days before the Jews were taken away that there were Jews hidden in the building'. Hartog said of the arrest: 'I was struck by the fact that the detectives who raided the place were not just on the lookout for hidden Jews but were, you might say, completely in the picture.'[19]

On 31 March van Maaren was questioned. He admitted that, prior to the arrest, he had 'suspected that something peculiar was going on in the building, without, however, hidden Jews ever coming to mind'. His suspicions – like those of Genot and Hartog – were roused by the substantial quantities of food brought to the offices. He said his 'traps' were to catch the office thief and had been placed with Kugler's full knowledge. He continued: 'It's not true that I ever spoke to the staff of the Keg company[20] . . . about Jews being hidden at our place. Admittedly I did so after the Jews had been carried off . . . After the arrest, I did indeed receive the keys from Mrs Gies, but I did not know that it was done on the orders of the SD.' He denied 'very emphatically' that he was the betrayer.[21]

The PRA compiled their report the following day and reached a conclusion of 'no case to answer'.[22] On 22 May the public prosecutor decided that no further action would be taken, but in November that same year the case was re-opened, perhaps because van Maaren felt that his name had not been sufficiently cleared. He was granted a conditional discharge, effectively putting him on probation for three years, and lost his civil rights. Again he appealed and this time won his case. At his examination on 8 August 1949, he maintained his innocence; five days later, he was cleared and his rights were restored.

And there the matter might have rested, were it not for the resonance which the name 'Anne Frank' evoked by the early 1960s. Anne was now known to millions: there had been a celebrated play and film of her diary, which was a best seller throughout the world; her father had been received at the Vatican by the pope, who praised the diary; President John F. Kennedy had spoken glowingly of her; schools and villages bore her name; plaques and statues had been erected in her memory; the house where she hid was rapidly becoming one of the most visited sites in the Netherlands; and a shoot from the Dutch chestnut tree she had gazed at from her window had even been planted in Israel, where a forest of 10,000 trees already grew in her honour.

In October 1958, after anti-Semitic demonstrations disrupted a Viennese performance of the play, Nazi-hunter Simon Wiesenthal overheard a young man telling his friends he was sorry he had missed the protest. When Wiesenthal questioned him, the student shrugged off the diary as a fake and said that in all probability, Anne Frank had never existed. Arguing with the boy and his friends proved fruitless, but one of the youths challenged Wiesenthal to find the man who had arrested her. Then, they said, they might listen to what Wiesenthal had to say.

Wiesenthal took up the challenge, using an appendix to the diary as his starting point. There he found the name of the Austrian SD officer given as 'Silbernagel'. This misnomer had been put into the public domain at Otto's insistence; Silberbauer was a common name in Austria and Otto was keen not to draw attention to innocent people who happened to share SS-Oberscharführer Silberbauer's surname. Wiesenthal consulted the telephone directories and compiled a list of eight 'Silbernagels', all of whom had been members of the Nazi Party. He soon realized that the man he wanted was not amongst them. In 1963 Wiesenthal travelled to the Netherlands for a television interview. He visited the Anne Frank House where, he remembers, 'I laid my hand on the wall the young girl had touched, as if I could draw strength from it for my researches.'[23] On a second visit he discussed his search with two Dutch friends. One was a senior Dutch police officer, who gave him a photocopy of the wartime telephone directory for the Netherlands' SD. Flying back to Vienna, Wiesenthal opened the book, which contained more than 300 names. He was almost asleep when one name leapt out at him from a page headed 'IV B4 Joden': Silberbauer.

In Vienna Wiesenthal turned again to the telephone directories. He knew that most of the men who had worked for 'IV B 4' had been recruited from the German and Austrian police. He had a strong suspicion that Silberbauer was amongst the latter and had returned to his post after the war. He enlisted the help of his friend Dr Josef Wiesinger, an official at the Austrian Ministry of the Interior. It was not difficult for Wiesinger to trace Silberbauer, whose history was just as Wiesenthal had suspected. Karl Josef Silberbauer, son of a police officer, was born in Vienna in 1911. He served briefly in the Austrian Army before joining the police force in 1935. Although not previously a member of the Nazi Party, he entered the Gestapo in 1939. He was transferred to the SD and moved to The Hague in November 1943, where he worked for the notorious IVB4 section. In April 1945 he returned to the city of his birth, and, after fourteen months in prison, was reinstated in the Vienna police in 1954.

On 15 October 1963 Wiesenthal called Wiesinger to find out whether there was any news about Silberbauer. He was told there was none. In fact, on 4 October Silberbauer had been suspended from his job while enquiries were made into his wartime activities. His revolver and warrant card were confiscated and he went into hiding. The story of 'Anne Frank's Nazi' broke in the press on 11 November, with the publication of an article in the Communist newspaper *Volksstimme*. Silberbauer had been ordered to keep quiet about his suspension, but he had told a colleague that he was 'having some bother because of that Anne Frank',[24] and the colleague, a Communist Party member, went straight to *Volksstimme* with the information. Wiesenthal's contact, Wiesinger, had also been warned to say nothing about the whole thing; the first Wiesenthal knew about it was from the press. Angry at claims made by Russian journalists that resistance fighters and vigilantes had brought about Silberbauer's suspension, Wiesenthal gave an interview to a Dutch journalist, explaining that it was through his tenacity Silberbauer had been exposed. Otto was unhappy with the turn of events; he had always known Silberbauer's true identity, and was quoted as saying that the S D officer had merely carried out orders. Wiesenthal had 'always doubted that Frank was being truthful'[25] and disagreed that Silberbauer was simply doing his duty. But he had at least achieved his goal: Silberbauer had been found.

Newspapers everywhere seized upon the story. On 21 November, the *New York Herald Tribune* reported: 'An Interior Ministry official said Silberbauer declared "that for him, the Frank family was just one of many Jewish families who were rounded up by the Gestapo" . . . Silberbauer's wife said, "We are all very upset about this affair . . . Why can't you leave us alone?" '[26] On the same date the *Los Angeles Times* claimed that Silberbauer had said that 'since no Jews had the right to live in freedom, it was only logical that orders were issued for the arrest of the Franks'.[27] The following day journalists announced that Silberbauer had identified van Maaren as the betrayer. The *New York Times* wrote: 'The former Nazi officer who arrested Anne Frank and her family has said that the Franks were betrayed to the Gestapo by a Dutchman who worked in their drugstore in Amsterdam.' The adjacent column read: 'Dutch Seek Informer: The Dutch said today that they were looking for a mysterious "M van M", the alleged pro-German informer whose tip led to the arrest of Anne Frank. The name "M van M" cropped up in Vienna yesterday when authorities there announced the suspension of Karl Silberbauer from the police force after he had confessed making the arrest.'[28]

After 23 November the story was temporarily relegated following the assassination of John F. Kennedy, but by the end of the month it was again commanding acres of print. One newspaper caught up with van Maaren at his home, spoke with him, and even printed his address. The article, entitled 'Arrest Starts New Anne Frank Inquiry', proclaimed:

'Willem van Maaren, 68, is hiding behind closed doors once again. He refuses to see visitors . . . The case has been re-opened in Holland, following the arrest in Vienna of police inspector Karl Silberbauer, 52, who admits he arrested the girl, acting, he says, on information given by van Maaren. And the accusations against van Maaren have started again . . . [van Maaren] now lives quietly with his wife. He is silver-haired, wears glasses and a patient, resigned air. Of the latest accusations he says, "It's horrible. They have caused me so much distress . . . and now that fellow in Vienna . . . it's unimaginable. Let him show proof, papers . . . I should like nothing better than that the real traitor be found." The Dutch Prosecutor in charge of war cases, Mr G. R. Nube, who has ordered the new investigation, will send a police inspector this week to question Silberbauer. He said, "The Frank case is a very important case, although it's only one of thousands for us. We very much want to find who betrayed those people." ' The newspaper also quoted Otto as having said, 'When we were arrested, Silberbauer was there. I saw him. But van Maaren was not there, and I have no evidence about him.'[29]

The Dutch authorities had indeed decided to hold another investigation. On 26 November van Maaren's assistant for a short period in 1943, J. J. de Kok, was traced and interviewed. He readily confessed to having sold the goods van Maaren stole on the black market, but said of his former co-worker, 'I never saw any signs that he was interested in National Socialism or even sympathized with the occupying power.'[30]

Four days later an interview with Silberbauer appeared in the Dutch press. His mother had given journalist Jules Huf her son's address, saying, 'He'll really like that, he used to live in the Netherlands himself.'[31] Huf spoke to Silberbauer at his home in Vienna and noted that he 'looked like a nervous wreck, his whole body was trembling, and he seemed to have the greatest difficulty in hiding his fear of what might happen.' Silberbauer's wife was also present, complaining, 'For God's sake, what have we got to do with Anne Frank, we've been through enough, we just want to be left in peace. What's the point of coming back to this twenty years later – my husband doesn't earn that much . . . tomorrow everything will be in the papers. What do you think the neighbours will say about that? And it'll be in the newspapers that my husband is accused of being a criminal.' Silberbauer disagreed, 'Nobody is saying I'm a criminal . . . But what's behind all this? It's probably Wiesenthal, or someone in the ministry who wants to butter up the Jews. On 4 October 1963 our world caved in . . .' His wife explained that they were having a hard time financially, 'and that's all because of Anne Frank. My husband never knew anything.'

At this point in the interview, Silberbauer reached for his copy of Anne's diary. He said, 'It stops before the arrest. I haven't seen the film or the play, and I only realized that it was me who arrested her after reading the newspapers. In 1943 I was transferred from the Gestapo in Vienna to the SD in Amsterdam. My boss there was Willi Lages. Lages got on my nerves right from the start . . .' His wife interrupted, 'How can you say that, this man will put it in his newspaper. And then we'll be back to Germans cursing Germans.' After telling her to keep quiet, Silberbauer went on, 'In [Lages'] eyes I was a typical Austrian drip who was always too soft on his men. Let me tell you, I'd much rather have stayed at home in Vienna with my wife.'[32]

Silberbauer talked about the arrest: 'It was a sunny, warm August day. I was just about to go and eat when I had a phone call saying that there were Jews hidden in a house on the Prinsengracht. I got together eight[33] Dutch SD men who were always at our beck and call and drove to the Prinsengracht. The door opened and there was this aroma of seasonings wafting towards me, which always lingers around places that store those sorts of goods. One of my Dutchmen wanted to speak to the storeman, but this man silently indicated upstairs with his thumb, as if he meant, "They're upstairs." One by one, we went up the narrow stairs until we reached the offices of the company belonging to Mr Frank.'[34] He described the scenes in the annexe: 'People were rushing around, stuffing their belongings into bags. Because there was no room, I had to remain standing in the doorway. When I saw that one man wasn't doing anything, I said to him, "Come on, get a move on." Then he came over and introduced himself as Frank and said he had been a reserve officer in the German Army. I was interested to know how long the people had been in hiding there. "Twenty-five months", he answered. When I said I didn't believe him, he took the girl standing next to him by the hand – that must have been Anne – and placed her against the door jamb,[35] where there were lines which clearly showed how she had grown. I could in fact see that she was much taller than the last line.' Silberbauer glanced at the photograph of Anne in the diary. 'She was much nicer-looking than her photo, and older. I said to Frank, "What a lovely daughter you have." Her mother was not particularly attractive.'[36]

Huf asked him why he had not sent Otto, as a former member of the German Army, to Theresienstadt. Silberbauer replied, 'We never knew what was happening to the Jews. I've no idea how Anne Frank came to write in her diary that the Jews were being gassed. We never knew that ... In those days, nobody was interested in the Jews anymore, it was all going downhill for us then, and if Frank hadn't gone into hiding, nothing would have happened to him. For me, the whole thing was dealt with in an hour. The eight were put on a transport and I never bothered about them again. And I don't know what happened to them after that.'

At the end of the interview, Silberbauer stood with Huf on the doorstep and declared, 'Just look at this. I built it all with my own hands. I mixed the concrete myself, did all the painting, and now this happens. I don't know what to do. Please write about us objectively, because unfortunately I can't do anything until the disciplinary investigation is completed. But my motorbike and sidecar are standing there so that, if the communists come, I can still get to the border.'[37]

On 2 December 1963 Otto was interviewed by the State Criminal Investigation Department in Amsterdam. He was unable to add anything to his previous statements, but he did say that he and his helpers had become 'increasingly convinced that van Maaren was the only likely suspect'.[38] A week later, Bep was questioned, but she, too, had nothing new to say, except that she had been 'terribly afraid of [van Maaren] at the time and considered him capable of anything'.[39] Miep was interviewed on 23 December and said that she now thought she might have sent van Maaren to the Gestapo headquarters, but only so that the authorities would think he was in charge at 263 Prinsengracht and not appoint someone else 'administrator'. She also said that van Maaren 'gave me the clear impression that in one way or another he had some influence with the Germans' but she was 'unable to name any facts and/or circumstance that would make it clear beyond doubt that he was the man who betrayed the hiding place of the eight Jewish persons to the SD'.[40]

The investigation continued in 1964. The wartime head of the

Amsterdam Bureau of the Security Police and Security Service, Willi P. F. Lages (whom Silberbauer had mentioned in conversation with Jules Huf), was interviewed in Breda, where he was in prison. Lages, a trained policeman, had been transferred to Amsterdam as the personal representative of Wilhelm Harster, chief of the Gestapo, and was put in charge of the Zentrallstelle. One acquaintance described him as 'an intellectual criminal'. He had little of interest to say, apart from his statement that: 'You ask me whether it makes sense that having received a phone call giving away the hiding place of one or more people, we should have immediately gone to the building in question and arrested those concerned. My reply to you is that it makes little sense to me, unless the tip came from someone who was well-known to us as an informer and whose reports had always been based on the truth.'[41] This would appear to support van Maaren's claim of innocence, for certainly he was not a well-known informer.

In March a Dutch detective travelled to Vienna to attend the examination of Silberbauer by a leading Austrian police officer. This, and his earlier written depositions, do not differ significantly in their account of the events of 4 August 1944 from that he gave to Jules Huf. However, in his interview of March 1964 he stated that the person who made the telephone call had said there were eight people hiding in the annexe. If this was correct, then evidently whoever turned informer had all the facts at their fingertips. Silberbauer said his chief, Julius Dettmann, had taken the call and then notified Abraham Kaper, head of the Dutchmen employed by IV B4, to accompany him (Silberbauer) to the Prinsengracht. Repeating the anecdote of the warehouseman pointing upstairs, when asked where the Jews were hidden, Silberbauer said, quite rightly, that the gesture could have been indicating the head of the company. He described the moment when Kugler revealed the entrance to the annexe, claiming that Kugler had done so freely, although Kugler later, understandably, gave a slightly different version of events. Silberbauer said he had no recollection of Miep, whose story of visiting the Gestapo headquarters on her friends' behalf was, in his view, an invention, and he was unable to identify van Maaren from a photograph shown to him.

Although the judicial inquiry against Silberbauer was discontinued in June 1964 owing to a lack of evidence, the disciplinary proceedings went ahead. He was subsequently acquitted of the charge of keeping his past a secret, and his suspension was lifted. There was an appeal against the outcome, but it was unsuccessful and in October 1964 Silberbauer was once more working for the police in Vienna.

Van Maaren was questioned again on 6 October. That summer two extensive articles in the press named him as the betrayer; one included a full-page photograph of him at the door of his home.[42] During his examination van Maaren denied all the allegations put to him. He admitted stealing, but only small quantities. He said he hadn't known that there were Jews hidden in the building where he worked, although he had once seen the annexe when he and Kugler were on the roof repairing a leak. He had noticed 'an air of secrecy in the building before the arrests',[43] which he had never been able to understand. He said that his gesture in response to the Dutch Nazi's question had simply been intended to show where the offices were. He claimed that a worker from a nearby business had once asked him if there was anything hidden at 263, to which he had replied that he didn't know what the man was talking about. The man then said that 'they' had better take care because 'they' went out in the evenings to visit the chemist on the Leliegracht; van Maaren told the man he must mean his employer. On looking into the matter, the detectives discovered that the man to whom van Maaren referred had been a member of the NSB, and was 'repeatedly urged by his block warden, a brother of Abraham Kaper [the head of the Dutchmen employed by IBV4] to "show greater initiative".'[44] Unfortunately, the men in question had died by the time of the investigation.

Van Maaren also said Miep had voluntarily given him the keys and he had gone to the Euterpestraat on her orders. He said a friend of his who worked for the Resistance had contacts in the SD, but he himself had none. This friend had moved to Germany after the war and the detectives were unable to locate him. They questioned other members of the Resistance who said that although van Maaren was not liked, his friendship with the Resistance leader had been genuine, and they thought it highly improbable that he was the betrayer. Someone else told the detectives that van Maaren had been employed by the Wehrmacht as a purchasing agent and had received handouts from the Nazi-run Winter Aid Netherlands organization. Van Maaren refuted the assertions. He also told his examiners that he had hidden his own son at home throughout the war.

On 4 November 1964 the State Criminal Investigation Department declared the case closed. They sent the file to the public prosecutor with a letter concluding that 'the inquiry did not lead to any concrete results'.[45] In the chapter 'The Betrayal' in *The Diary of Anne Frank*, Harry Paape remarks that the investigations failed because the detectives concentrated on van Maaren too much; had they widened their net, they might have caught more fish. But Paape feels certain that 'van Maaren knew that Jews were hidden in the back of the building'.[46] There can be no further questions asked of van Maaren; he died in Amsterdam in 1971 and took the truth of whether or not he was the betrayer with him to the grave.

Otto Frank barely touches on the subject of their betrayal in his memoir, except to say, 'There was doubtless a traitor, but it could never be established who it was.'[47] But he gave the matter more consideration in an article for *Life Magazine*, written the year before he died: 'We do not know whether we were betrayed because of anti-Semitism or because of money. We never found out who betrayed us. We had our suspicions. A man who'd been in the police during the occupation was suspected and questioned. But we never had proof. I do have a theory, though. It was said that a woman made the telephone call that led to our capture. I therefore assume that the policeman who had been cross-examined might have spoken to someone about us. But as long as I cannot prove this, I have no right to accuse anyone. Those who are truly guilty are those who manipulated the strings at the top. Not much can be achieved with punishment. What has taken place can never be erased.'[48] Thus Otto introduced into the equation two entirely new suspects, but no more has ever been said about them and no actions have been taken.

During their research for *The Critical Edition* of Anne's diaries, workers at the State Institute for War Documentation made full use of the file for the 1963 investigation, but acknowledged that the file was incomplete. Two letters, written by Victor Kugler in 1963, were missing. Both have recently come to light. One of them has nothing substantial to say about the arrest. The other is much more interesting, and excerpts from it are reproduced here for the first time. Kugler was clearly writing in response to a letter he had received from Otto Frank about the betrayal:

> . . . I share your opinion about Silberbauer. He is less important in the sense that he arrested us, and twenty years have passed under the bridge since then, but he is the only person who can put pressure on van Maaren.
>
> I am also writing to you about the window panes that were painted *blue* [in the front house overlooking the annexe]. *I have often thought about why he asked me what was going on up there when he looked through an opening in the blue panes. He said that he had never been up there and asked why he wasn't allowed there. I replied to him that we weren't allowed either and we knew nothing of what went on up there. He was, however, only content with this answer for a very short time, because he asked the same question only a few weeks later and I said to him that I didn't even know where the entrance to the other building was. 'But there is a door upstairs, the one to the skylight,*[49] *so you must be able to get in there,' [said van Maaren; Kugler replied,] I'm very sorry, but when we rented the house we only rented the rooms known to us and nothing else. With that, I hoped to put an end to all further questions.*
>
> *He left pencils on the edges of our desks more than once. On top of that, he often left a short wooden pole on the packing table so that the pole stuck out a little over the table. As the gap between the table and the barrels on the other side was not very wide, it was quite possible for a person passing by to dislodge the pole. He would also inspect the dust for footprints. Every time he set such a trap, the first thing he would ask in the morning was, 'Have you been into the warehouse?' My immediate reply was always, 'Yes, I have,' or, 'I must have done, but I don't remember.' I was committed to these answers and Kleiman always double-checked them with me.*
>
> *Once, when I went downstairs he showed me a wallet and asked did it belong to me? Without a second thought I said that it did and that I had been missing it for some time. When I mentioned this upstairs, van Pels said that it was in fact his wallet, with ten guilders inside it. He explained that a few days before he had climbed on to*

the weighing machine in the grain room, taken off his jacket and lain it down on a pile of sacks opposite the door to the grain room. It must have fallen out of his jacket then. I had put the wallet in my bag without saying anything except thanks. The ten guilders had gone. On the same day, or perhaps it was a couple of days later, a second man came up to me and made it known that he had seen van Maaren pick up the wallet between empty baskets somewhere on the V- [indecipherable word]. When I then asked van Maaren where he had found it, he replied in a very confused, argumentative way. The young man insisted that he had found it there and van Maaren said that this would have been impossible. He [van Maaren] said that he had found a briefcase down there.[50] I still have this briefcase. Quite a simple thing, sewn together on two sides and open on two sides. You will certainly know the type of thing, since they're very common. Moreover, he often laid things down on the packing table and marked where he had placed them. If they had then been moved, even if only very slightly, he would ask me the same questions I mentioned before.

About Silberbauer's statement: once the men who were conducting the arrests arrived, he [van Maaren] pointed to the people upstairs. That's how it appeared in the papers at the time. That's what I believe too, because when we were all taken downstairs, he even stood there and stared at us, all 'over the moon',[51] as we liked to say in Amsterdam. I can never forget his face. I see it continually before me. We can expect him to deny everything; he's unlikely to say, 'I'll be happy to relieve myself from the strain of having the deaths of seven people on my conscience.' According to the newspapers he is still complaining, 'I don't have anything to do with any of these things and they've caused me so much stress.' Silberbauer is, in fact, the only person who can put any pressure on him. According to the press he still hasn't been interrogated by the Vienna police. He's made his announcements at press conferences. The police will have done something meanwhile though, surely. Have the police in Amsterdam been to their place [van Maaren's home] and are they going, or have they been, to Vienna to speak to Silberbauer?

And then we come to the final question: Are we still going to punish van Maaren in this case? In the meantime, far worse criminals have been convicted. Van Maaren has only swirled up dust because he is connected to the 'Anne Frank story' . . .[52]

Evidently, Kugler thought van Maaren was guilty. Unfortunately, Otto's earlier letter, and his subsequent answer to Kugler's missive, have not been found. There is nothing in Kugler's letter that leads the objective reader to share, categorically, his belief that van Maaren was the traitor, but it does serve to reinforce the impression that van Maaren was excessively curious about the annexe and that he probably had guessed its secret.

There are other suggestions, besides van Maaren. Sounds from the annexe could have filtered through to the adjacent building. Might one of the Keg workers have betrayed them? The NSB man who spoke to van Maaren (and there seems no reason to doubt his account of their conversation) obviously had some idea what was going on. He may have informed Abraham Kaper's brother or gone to the police himself. Visitors to the offices noticed that something was amiss; they could have acted on their suspicions. Even the fugitives, as Jan Gies had assumed, could have been careless, while the helpers might have passed a remark in earshot of someone less trustworthy than themselves.

There were several burglaries on the premises during the relevant period. Any of the culprits could have tipped off the police without confessing to their own crimes. One of the thieves almost certainly saw Hermann van Pels. On 28 February 1944 van Pels had gone downstairs after hours to perform his routine check-up and was surprised to see papers scattered over the desks and the floor. He tried the lock on the front door, but it was still in place. He went back up to the annexe, puzzling over it, but did not mention his observations to anyone. The following morning, Peter returned to the annexe after his rounds downstairs and said that the front door was open and the projector not in its usual spot in the cupboard. Van Pels told them then of his findings the previous night. Kugler's new portfolio had also disappeared. It seemed the thief must have had a key and had secreted himself in the building after being disturbed by van Pels. The fugitives were haunted by the thought that someone else had a key – and could come back, perhaps with the police, and might then discover the bookcase door. In her diary Anne wrote: 'It's a mystery. Who can have our key? And why didn't the thief go to the warehouse? If the thief is one of the warehousemen, then he now knows that someone is in the house at night . . .'[53]

Even more dangerous was the break-in of 8 April 1944. That evening Peter had frightened intruders in the warehouse and rushed upstairs to tell everyone. After Peter and his father had frightened them off, they returned to the hiding place, convinced that the thieves would put in another appearance. The occupants of the annexe were sitting huddled together in the darkness when they heard a door slam downstairs. No one said a word, each listening to the footsteps passing below, through the rooms in the main building, and then on the stairs that led from the offices to the hallway where the bookcase stood. More footsteps, closer, and then they stopped. Suddenly the bookcase rattled; someone was pulling at it violently. Anne breathed, 'Now we're lost.' The tugging continued and something fell down, then the noise stopped. The footsteps moved away from the cupboard and through the house until they died away completely. The eight in hiding could see a light burning on the other side of the bookcase. There were no further disturbances, but the night-watchman had seen the hole in the warehouse door left by the burglars and notified the police of a break-in. Van Hoeven, their green-grocer, had also seen the ruined door but shrewdly did not call the police, knowing their presence would not be welcomed.

Another possible suspect was the NSB man who lived behind the secret annexe on the Westermarkt. A woman who knew him at that time told the Netherlands State Institute for War Documentation, 'I had an aunt who lived at Westermarkt No 4. From her house you could see the annexe. And next door at No 6 lived a man called A —,[54] a well-known NSBer (he worked with the Germans), but he died at the end of 1943. The windows of the annexe were obscured . . . In mid-1943 A— asked me if there were people still living in there. I answered, "Of course not, nobody in their right mind would want to live in a house like that." At that time I didn't know there were people living there.'[55] Although the man died in 1943, he could have passed his suspicions on to someone else.

There were others, too, living in the houses around the lawn-and-gravel courtyard during those years who thought that something was going on in the annexe. Two young boys, out of sheer mischief, climbed through the window into the warehouse on the evening of 24 March 1943. One of the boys, Wijnberg, came forward many years later and admitted they 'simply went in and out and did not go into the office'.[56] Whilst they were in the warehouse, they heard the toilet flushing above them in the supposedly abandoned building and scrambled out in alarm. Wijnberg's interviewer noted: 'Mr Wijnberg did not say that there were people living in the house, because he had learnt to keep quiet about it; there were more people in hiding in the neighbourhood that he knew about.'[57] Interviewed again for the Jon Blair documentary, *Anne Frank Remembered*, Wijnberg also claimed to have seen Anne gazing from the window of Otto's office: 'I saw a face which later I knew, because I saw the pictures, which must have been Anne Frank . . . I even know what position I was in when I saw her first, because I was coming up that wall so I was first sitting down then standing up. So you see the face from different angles. And that face I still see here.' Asked whether she had seen him, Wijnberg replied, 'Yes. She backed away. I now know why. I was not supposed to see her . . . I think I told my sister.'[58] Anne had written about the break-in at length in her diary. Perhaps, as children do, the boys had told someone that the old, deserted house was haunted, and someone had put two and two together.

There is no doubt that the occupants of the annexe grew careless over the years. Anne saw the dangers, she realized that they had become less circumspect about the strict security measures they were supposed to observe. In winter 1943 they began to light the stove in the main room at half-past seven instead of half-past five on Sunday mornings. Anne wrote: 'I think it's a risky business. What will the neighbours think of our smoking chimney? Just like the curtains . . . sometimes on an irresistible whim one of the gentlemen or ladies decides to take a look outside. Consequence: a storm of reproaches. Reply: "But no one can see." That's how every careless act begins and ends. "No one can see, no one can hear, no one pays any attention," is easily said, but is it the real truth?'[59] In April 1944, Peter forgot to unbolt the front door one morning, which meant Kugler and the warehousemen could not get in when they arrived for work. One of the Keg employees had already fetched a ladder and was half-way up to Peter's window when Kugler saw him and managed to persuade him that the ladder was too short. Kugler had to force open the kitchen window while the others watched. Anne worried, 'What can they be thinking? And van Maaren?'[60]

All paths seem, eventually, to lead back to him.

In *The Critical Edition* Harry Paape concludes his assessment of the known facts: 'It took a good two years before someone picked up the telephone and called the SD. That this someone was van Maaren does not strike us as an improbability. To what lengths could frustration and rancour drive a man? That it could have been someone else, however, is we feel, at least as likely.'[61]

There is no decisive evidence. But on 4 August 1944 someone dialled the number of Julius Dettmann in Amsterdam, knowing their call would send a group of people to almost certain death. Perhaps that same someone watched curiously on that bright summer morning as the eight prisoners and two of their helpers stepped into a barred police truck. Eight lives shipped to Westerbork, Auschwitz, Belsen . . . To hard labour, starvation, gas chambers, madness, typhus and death. Their betrayer escaped justice. But, as Otto Frank said, 'It will not bring my wife and daughters back.'

'... it seems to me that neither I – nor for that matter
anyone else – will be interested in the unbosomings
of a thirteen-year-old schoolgirl ...'

Anne Frank, *Diary*, 20 June 1942

In the spring of 1998, whilst immersed in the research for this book, I was told that a number of hitherto unknown pages of Anne's diary had come to light. These papers were in the possession of a MrCornelius Suijk, who claims he was given them by Otto Frank, a long-time friend of his. Otto had apparently handed him the material in 1980, when two German neo-Nazis, Ernst Romer and Edgar Gaiss, were on trial for denouncing the diary as a forgery. Both men were found guilty, and when their case came to appeal, a team of historians was sent by the German Federal Government to assess the authenticity of the diary notes. Otto allowed them to examine his daughter's works, but not before he had removed from the archive five pages which he wanted to remain a private matter. These he then handed to Cornelius Suijk, who claims that Otto's purpose in entrusting him with the papers was to be able truthfully to tell any interested parties that he held no further diary pages in his possession.

After Otto's death in 1980, Suijk retained the five pages and made no mention of them to RIOD (the Netherlands State Institute for War Documentation) during the preparation of the *Critical Edition* of the diary, even though, under the terms of his will, Otto had bequeathed all of Anne's writings to the institute. Suijk's decision to remain silent about the unpublished material was motivated, he has said, out of a desire to protect Fritzi, Otto's widow, from being confronted with it. The editors of the *Critical Edition* did indeed consult Fritzi Frank in the course of their work. She asked them to excise a number of lines from Anne's original entry for 8 February 1944; the passage begins with another argument between Anne and Edith, in which Anne records saying to her mother 'by way of a joke', 'You know you're a real Rabenmutter' (a cruel mother). At the end of the paragraph are a series of ellipses, and the footnote reads: 'In the 47 lines omitted here Anne Frank gave an extremely unkind and partly unfair picture of her parents' marriage. At the request of the Frank family this passage has been deleted.'[1] David Barnouw, one of the editors of the *Critical Edition*, now assumes that the pages in Suijk's custody are an extension of the erased entry: 'The archive had been numbered after the five pages were removed, so we didn't know they had gone. However, I believe these five pages are actually a rewritten version of a shorter entry from 8 February 1944 which was also critical of her parents' marriage.'[2]

In the summer of 1998, news of the missing pages broke in the world's press. Public interest was immense, and newspapers gave the story extensive coverage. However, months before, after having had the opportunity to read these missing pages, I had come to the conclusion that the existence of the 'new' diary fragments was of great importance because they were written by Anne Frank, but that the actual material they contained was in no sense revelatory. There is nothing in the pages (written on loose sheets in February 1944) which Anne has not said, in one form or another, elsewhere in her diary. The main theme – and the one which caused the most excitement – concerns the marriage of Otto and Edith, which Anne believed fell far short of the ideal image her parents tried to project. She thought that the relationship was romantically unequal, that her mother was being broken by the lack of passion and love shown to her by Otto. In Anne's eyes, Otto's emotions towards his wife were those of respect and love, but not what Anne termed 'full' love, by which she meant romantic love. She hinted (as she had before) at a relationship in her father's past, before his marriage to Edith, perhaps implying that this was the great love of Otto's life. Anne wrote that she admired her mother for coping so well with a marriage which existed in name only, and wondered whether she could help her in some way, before concluding that the gulf between herself and her mother was too wide to allow such a move on her part.

As with other aspects of the diary, one should bear in mind the circumstances under which Anne's dissection of her parents' marriage was written. Anne's notions of love had not then been tempered by actual experience, and she was always at her most critical when describing herself and the people with whom she lived in almost unendurable, constant proximity. Anne's judgement may or may not have been fair, but the marriage must have been under strain because of the situation in which the Franks found themselves: the close confinement, stress, fear, and the lack of privacy (Margot shared her parents' bedroom) would have done little to help any couple. In any case, Otto was thirty-six years old when he married. It is both unrealistic and naïve to imagine he had never looked at another woman before meeting Edith. What, then, can be deemed revelatory or shocking about Anne's adolescent speculations?

Much has been made of the idea that Anne was more sympathetic towards her mother in the missing pages than anywhere else in the diary; I do not feel this is the case. In both the *Definitive* and *Critical* editions as they now stand, there is an easily traceable, if gradual, maturation in Anne's attitude towards her mother. At one point she decides that it is better to write down her less charitable thoughts about her mother than to speak of them openly; she also resolves not to point out the problems in their relationship, confiding to Kitty: 'I want to save her the unhappiness it would cause her.'3 Had the diary continued beyond August 1944, then in all probability Anne's occasional anger toward her mother, which was clearly lessening as she grew older, would have petered out, as most teenagers' rebellion does.

In the remainder of the missing pages, Anne wrote that she would be careful to preserve her papers from the eyes of her family, feeling that their secrets were hers alone. This has given rise to feverish conjecture that Anne would not have wanted her diary published. Again, one should remember that Anne was mercurial, and her opinions and ideas changed from one day to the next. Near the beginning of her diary, she states: 'I don't intend to show this cardboard-covered notebook, bearing the proud name of "diary," to anyone . . .'4 It's impossible to say now whether she would have gone on to have her work published in the form in which it first appeared, but there can be little doubt that Anne's greatest wish – self-proclaimed – was to be a writer. Whatever her frame of mind on different dates, she *did* begin to rewrite the entire document with a view to publication, and she was still working on these diary revisions when the Gestapo arrived.

So why did Otto Frank conceal these pages for so long? I don't think Otto's aim was to preserve his own image in the eyes of the diary's readers, nor do I think that Fritzi Frank would have been shocked by their content – she was no child bride when she married Otto, after all. The real answer, I believe, lies in these lines from Otto's memoir: 'I was very saddened sometimes to read how harshly Anne wrote about her mother. In her rage over some kind of conflict she let her feelings out without restraint. It hurt to read how often Anne had judged wrongly her mother's views. But I was relieved to read in later entries that Anne realized that it was sometimes her fault that she frequently didn't get on with her mother. She even regretted what she had written.'5 I am convinced that it was these feelings of distress over the relations which had existed between his wife and youngest daughter that led Otto to omit these entries from the published diary. He wanted to preserve the image of his daughter not only for her readers, but also for himself. He knew perfectly well that Anne was no saint, but, as her father, he followed his instincts in excluding those passages where Anne's anger was at its most vehement, particularly when that anger was directed towards the wife he had lost.

As things stand at the time of writing, in December 1998, Cornelius Suijk still has the pages in his possession, and it is not possible to quote from them. Suijk has said that he will hand over the pages to RIOD, who had already planned to update the *Critical Edition*, but he has refused to say when. The pages will eventually be included in this, and in all new editions of the diary. David Barnouw explains: 'Ten years have passed since we had those discussions [*about the omissions*], and we feel it's time. We also won't enclose a footnote. It will be for the readers to make up their own minds.'6

Prologue

1 / Karl Josef Silberbauer interviewed by Jules Huf, in Simon Wiesenthal, *Justice Not Vengeance: The Test Case* (London: Weidenfeld & Nicolson, 1989), p. 340.

2 / Those involved in the raid on the Prinsengracht who survived the war have given countless interviews, written statements and sworn testimonies about the events. There are a number of discrepancies in the different versions, mainly due to lapses in time, memory and perspective. The accounts given here are based on events as they have been most frequently reported. All direct quotations are, of course, duly credited.

3 / Bep Voskuijl in Ernst Schnabel, *The Footsteps of Anne Frank* (London: Pan Books, 1976), p. 101.

4 / Bep Voskuijl in Harry Paape, 'The Arrest', David Barnouw and Gerrold van der Stroom (eds), *The Diary of Anne Frank: The Critical Edition* (London: Viking, 1989), p. 21.

5 / Ibid.

6 / Schnabel, *Footsteps*, p. 104. It has never been established exactly how many Dutch Nazis accompanied Silberbauer. *The Critical Edition* places the figure at four or five.

7 / Miep Gies-Santrouschitz, declaration before various notaries of Amsterdam, 5 June 1974. Collection of RIOD (Netherlands State Institute for War Documentation).

8 / Victor Kugler in Eda Shapiro, 'The Reminiscences of Victor Kugler, the "Mr Kraler" of Anne Frank's Diary' *Yad Vashem Studies* XIII (Jerusalem: 1979), p. 358.

9 / Ibid.

10 / Ibid., pp. 358–9.

11 / Gies-Santrouschitz, declaration, 5 June 1974.

12 / Miep Gies, interview transcripts for the Jon Blair documentary *Anne Frank Remembered* (BBC2, 6 May 1995). Private collection of Jon Blair.

13 / Otto Frank in Schnabel, *Footsteps*, p. 105.

14 / Kugler in Shapiro, 'Reminiscences', pp. 359–61.

15 / Otto Frank in E. C. Farrell, 'Postscript to a Diary', *Global Magazine*, 6 March 1965.

16 / Miep Gies and Alison Leslie Gold, *Anne Frank Remembered* (New York: Bantam Press, 1987), p. 156.

17 / Otto Frank in Jane Pratt, 'The Anne Frank We Remember', *McCalls Magazine*, January 1986.

18 / Gies and Gold, *Anne Frank*, p. 156.

19 / Otto Frank in Schnabel, *Footsteps*, p. 111.

20 / Johannes Kleiman's testimony in Schnabel, *Footsteps*, p. 111.

21 / 'This is a photograph . . .' *Diary*, 10 October 1942 (a), p. 282; 'This is June 1939 . . .' *Diary*, 28 September 1942 (a), p. 190. All quotations from Anne's diary are from *The Diary of Anne Frank: The Critical Edition* (London: Viking, 1989). The letters in brackets indicate which version of the diary is quoted: (a) is Anne's original version, (b) her revised draft, and (c) the published diary, edited by her father.

22 / The Franks' photograph album, May 1941. Courtesy of Anne Frank-Fonds, Basel.

23 / *Diary*, 29 October 1943 (b), p. 411.

24 / *Diary*, 17 April 1944 (a), p. 612.

Chapter One

1 / Anne Frank in Ernst Schnabel, *The Footsteps of Anne Frank* (London: Pan Books, 1976), p. 89; also 2 May 1943 (a), *The Diary of Anne Frank: The Critical Edition* (London: Viking, 1989), p. 306.

2 / Amos Elon, *Founder: Meyer Amschel Rothschild and His Time* (London: Harper Collins, 1996), p. 20.

3 / Information from Landau town archives, and the pamphlets *Some Historical Facts About the House* and *Facts Relating to the Jews of Landau* available from the Frank-Loeb'sches House. In 1940 those Jews still remaining in Landau were billeted at the house until their deportation to Gurs and, from there, to Auschwitz. After the war there was talk of calling it 'The Anne Frank House'. It was formally opened, under its current name, on 7 May 1987, and today hosts a permanent exhibition on the history of the Jews of Landau, displays fine art and serves as a cultural centre.

4 / *Diary*, undated, but probably 28 September 1942 (a), p. 190.

5 / *Diary*, 8 May 1944 (a), p. 636.

6 / Otto Frank in Schnabel, *Footsteps*, p. 17.

7 / Otto Frank in Cara Wilson, *Love,*

Otto: The Legacy of Anne Frank (Kansas: Andrews & McMeel, 1995), pp. 136–7.

8 / *Diary*, 8 May 1944 (a), p. 636. Anne was mistaken here. There was no Hermann in Luxembourg. She is almost certainly referring to Otto's cousins Arnold and Jacob.

9 / At this time, Nathan Straus was still known by his birth name, Charles Webster Straus (he was named after an early partner at Macy's), but around the age of twenty-one, he wanted to go into politics, so he decided to use the more recognized 'Nathan Straus' and had his name legally changed. The Straus family historian writes, 'He gave his family three months to become comfortable calling him Nathan and would not answer to the name Charlie. The only one who kept calling him Charlie was his sister-in-law Flora Stieglitz Straus, who was married to his brother Hugh Grant Straus.' In fact, Flora was *not* the only one to carry on calling Nathan by his birth name. In all their correspondence, Otto addresses Nathan as 'Charley', but his friend always signed himself 'Nathan'. To avoid confusion, I have used the name Nathan Straus Jun. throughout the text. Information courtesy Straus family historian, e-mail to author, 16 January 1998.

10 / Straus family historian, e-mail to author, 3 December 1997.

11 / The family cannot recall the cause of Michael Frank's death.

12 / Otto Frank's letters, 1909–10. Private collection of Buddy Elias.

13 / Ibid., August 1915.

14 / Ibid., 1915–18.

15 / Ibid., 18 February 1916.

16 / Ibid., 21 June 1917.

17 / Otto Frank, letter, 1975, in *Anne Frank Magazine 1998* (Amsterdam: Anne Frank Stichting, 1998), p. 39.

18 / Otto Frank, quoted in the exhibition *Anne Frank: A History for Today*, Anne Frank Educational Trust UK, 1996.

19 / Otto Frank in Schnabel, *Footsteps*, p. 16.

20 / Miep Gies and Alison Leslie Gold, *Anne Frank Remembered* (New York: Bantam Press, 1987), p. 36.

21 / Otto Frank, letter, 11 February 1966, in Wilson, *Love, Otto*, pp. 26–7.

22 / Information on the Hollander family courtesy of family tree, Dr Trude K. Hollander, Eddy Fraifeld and Dick Plotz.

23 / Eddy Fraifeld, e-mail to author, 2 December 1997.

24 / Dr Trude K. Hollander, letter to author, 25 March 1997. Dr Hollander goes on to say that Edith was 'known to be an intelligent person, faithful to the family tradition which believed in true values', and contends that the Hollanders were 'grossly neglected in all editions of Anne's books . . . after corrections, editions and self-serving additions by Anne's father, who was by then the one living family member, Otto had become Anne's mentor, role-model and undisputed influence in her life. This may sound like sour grapes now, but it is common family knowledge – of a family who has by now no voice in this world any more.'

25 / Later, Margot also addressed him as 'Berndt', while Anne addressed him 'Bernd'.

26 / Margot's baby book, 14 March 1926. Courtesy Anne Frank-Fonds, Basel.

27 / Ibid., 12 May 1926.

28 / Ibid., 14 June 1926.

29 / Ibid., December 1927.

30 / Straus family historian, e-mail to author, 16 January 1998.

31 / Nathan Straus Jun., postcard, 23 July 1928. Private collection of Buddy Elias.

32 / Schnabel, *Footsteps*, p. 19.

33 / Quoted in A. C. Roodnat and M. de Klijn, *A Tour of the Anne Frank House in Amsterdam* (Amsterdam: Anne Frank Stichting, 1971), p. 20.

34 / Kathi Stilgenbauer in Schnabel, *Footsteps*, p. 24.

35 / Ibid.

36 / Milly Stanfield in Carl Fussman, 'The Woman Who Would Have Saved Anne Frank', *Newsday*, 16 March 1995.

37 / Ibid.

38 / Buddy Elias, author interview, Cheltenham: October 1997.

39 / Ibid.

40 / Ibid.

41 / Ibid.

42 / Anne Frank, 'Paula's Plane Trip' in *Tales from the Secret Annexe* (London: Penguin, 1982), p. 25.

43 / Ibid., pp. 33–4.

44 / Ibid., p. 28.

45 / Schnabel, *Footsteps*, p. 19.

46 / Ibid., pp. 19–20.

47 / Margot's photo album, 1930s. Courtesy of Anne Frank-Fonds, Basel.

48 / Schnabel, *Footsteps*, p. 21.

49 / The signature is illegible.

50 / Otto Frank, letter, 2 April 1932. Private collection of Buddy Elias.

51 / Schnabel, *Footsteps*, p. 27.

52 / I have been unable to find the original source for this quote.

53 / Otto Frank in Schnabel, *Footsteps*, pp. 24–5; and Anna G. Steenmeijer and Otto Frank (eds), *A Tribute to Anne Frank* (New York: Doubleday, 1971), p. 13.

54 / Otto Frank, 'You cannot . . .' in R. Peter Straus, article in *Moment*, December 1977; 'The world around me collapsed . . .' Otto Frank, letter, 19 June 1968, in Wilson, *Love, Otto*, p. 50.

55 / Buddy Elias, author interview, Cheltenham: October 1997.

56 / Harry Paape, 'Originally from Frankfurt-am-Main', *Diary*, p. 4.

57 / Elias, author interview, October 1997.

58 / Eva Schloss, author interview, London: January 1998.

59 / Elias, author interview, October 1997.

60 / Ibid.

61 / Schloss, author interview, January 1998.

62 / Gertrud Naumann in Schnabel, *Footsteps*, p. 24.

63 / Quoted in Karen Shawn, *The End of Innocence: Anne Frank and the Holocaust* (New York: Anti-Defamation League of B'nai B'rith, 1989), p. 11.

64 / Edith Frank, letter, undated, in Schnabel, *Footsteps*, p. 25.

65 / Gies and Gold, *Anne Frank*, p. 10.

66 / Ibid., p. 13.

67 / Ibid., pp. 16–20.

68 / *Diary*, 15 June 1942 (a), p. 182. Margot Frank turned eight years old in February 1934.

69 / Edith Frank, letter, March 1934, in Schnabel, *Footsteps*, p. 25.

Chapter Two

1 / 'The Merry': Anne is referring to Merwedeplein, the street in Amsterdam where the Frank family lived.

2 / Van Gelder in Ernst Schnabel, *The Footsteps of Anne Frank* (London: Pan Books, 1976), pp. 40–41.

3 / 15 June 1942 (a), *The Diary of Anne Frank: The Critical Edition* (London: Viking, 1989), p. 179.

4 / Hanneli Pick-Goslar in Willy Lindwer, *The Last Seven Months of Anne Frank* (New York: Pantheon, 1991), p. 14.

5 / Anne Frank in Schnabel, *Footsteps*, p. 33.

6 / Pick-Goslar in Lindwer, *Last Seven Months*, p. 15.

7 / Edith Frank, letter, undated, in Schnabel, *Footsteps*, p. 26.

8 / Miep Gies and Alison Leslie Gold, *Anne Frank Remembered* (New York: Bantam Press, 1987), pp. 17, 22.

9 / Julianne Duke, 'Anne Frank Remembered', *New York Times*, 11 June 1989.

10 / Ibid.

11 / Otto Frank, letter, 9 April 1934, in Harry Paape, 'Originally from Frankfurt-am-Main', *Diary*, p. 8.

12 / Otto Frank, postcard, 1934, from the exhibition *Anne aus Frankfurt*, Anne Frank Youth Centre, Frankfurt, March 1998.

13 / I have been unable to find my original source for this quote.

14 / Lucy S. Dawidowicz, *The War against the Jews 1933–1945* (London: Penguin, 1987), pp. 100–101.

15 / Ibid., p. 99.

16 / From 26 November 1935, gypsies and black people were included in the prohibition of 'mixed' marriages.

17 / Edith Frank, letter, 26 March 1935, *Anne aus Frankfurt* exhibition.

18 / Margot Frank, letter, 1935, *Anne aus Frankfurt* exhibition.

19 / Edith Frank, letter, undated, in Schnabel, *Footsteps*, p. 26.

20 / Ibid.

21 / Edith Frank, letter, undated, *Anne aus Frankfurt* exhibition.

22 / Otto Frank, 'Anne was always . . .' and 'But Anne . . .' in E. C. Farrell, in 'Postscript to a Diary', *Global Magazine*, 6 March 1965; 'a normal, lively . . .' in 'The Living Legacy of Anne Frank', *Journal*, September 1967; 'Margot was . . .' and 'She was ebullient . . .' in R. Peter Straus, article in *Moment*, December 1977.

23 / Otto Frank, memoir. Private collection of Buddy Elias.

24 / Edith Frank, letter, undated, in Schnabel, *Footsteps*, p. 26.

25 / Pick-Goslar in Lindwer, *Last Seven Months*, p. 17

26 / *Diary*, 27 November 1943 (b), p. 422.

27 / Alison Leslie Gold, *Memories of Anne Frank: Reflections of a Childhood Friend* (New York: Scholastic Press, 1997), pp. 15–16. The information here is taken from Lindwer, *Last Seven Months*, p. 17, unless otherwise stated.

28 / Gold, *Memories*, pp. 29–30.

29 / Pick-Goslar in Lindwer, *Last Seven Months*, pp. 16–17.

30 / Gold, *Memories*, p. xii.

31 / Pick-Goslar in Lindwer, *Last Seven Months*, pp. 16–17.

32 / Anne Frank, letter, 18 December 1936, in *Stern*, 21 May 1982.

33 / Quoted in Ruud van der Rol and Rian Verhoeven, *Anne Frank: Beyond the Diary* (London: Penguin Books, 1993), p. 25.

34 / Gies and Gold, *Anne Frank*, p. 21.

35 / Ibid., pp. 22–3.

36 / Ibid., p. 23.

37 / *Diary*, 6 January 1944 (a), p. 448.

38 / Sol Kimmel, 'Heart to Heart', *Hadassah Magazine*. I have been unable to find the date of this article.

39 / Pick-Goslar in Lindwer, *Last Seven Months*, pp. 16–17.

40 / Otto Frank in Anna G. Steen-meijer and Otto Frank, *A Tribute to Anne Frank* (New York: Doubleday, 1971), p. 18.

41 / Buddy Elias, 'I had no idea . . .' author interview, Cheltenham: October 1997; 'I never dreamed . . .' in 'Past Lives Again Because of Little Girl', *Dayton Daily News*, 2 October 1960.

42 / Elias, 'the serious one . . .' in 'Past Lives Again', *Dayton Daily News*; 'She was very different . . .' author interview, October 1997.

43 / Buddy Elias, 'I Knew the Real Anne Frank', *Mail on Sunday: You Magazine*, 2 February 1997.

44 / Elias, author interview, October 1997.

45 / Elias in 'I Knew', *Mail on Sunday*.

46 / Otto Frank in Wolf von Wolzogen, *Anne aus Frankfurt* (Frankfurt: Historical Museum, 1994), p. 102.

47 / Edith Frank, letter, 1937, *Anne aus Frankfurt* exhibition.

48 / Quoted in Anne Frank Stichting, *Anne Frank in the World 1929–1945*, exhibition catalogue (Amsterdam: Bert Bakker, 1985), p. 47.

49 / Dawidowicz, *War against the Jews*, p. 136.

50 / Gies and Gold, *Anne Frank*, p. 29.

51 / Ibid.

52 / Ibid.

53 / Ibid., p. 30.

54 / Anne Frank's photo album, 1938. Courtesy of Anne Frank-Fonds, Basel.

55 / Milly Stanfield in Carl Fussman, 'The Woman Who Would Have Saved Anne Frank', *Newsday*, 16 March 1995.

56 / *Anne Frank Magazine 1998* (Amsterdam: Anne Frank Stichting, 1998), p. 8.

57 / Hermann Röttgen in 'On the Occasion of the "Habimah" Production: My Last Meeting with Anne Frank and her Family'. I have been unable to trace further details of this article.

58 / Anne Frank, 'My First Article' in *Tales from the Secret Annexe* (London: Penguin, 1982), p. 128.

59 / Henny van Pels, Hermann's sister, had lived in Amsterdam since 1935, and their father, Aron, arrived to live with her in 1938. He died in 1941.

60 / Gies and Gold, *Anne Frank*, p. 30.

61 / Ibid.

62 / Max van Creveld in *Anne Frank Magazine 1998*, pp. 12–13.

63 / Ibid.

64 / Bertel Hess in ibid., p. 13.

65 / Gies and Gold, *Anne Frank*, p. 30.

66 / Pfeffer and Lotte, who had been living together as a couple, found that marriage became an impossibility after the Nazi occupation of the Netherlands and the application of the 'race' laws (Lotte was not Jewish). They continued to live together, making various unsuccessful attempts to marry. In 1953, eight years after Pfeffer's death, Lotte had their marriage officially registered in Berlin.

67 / Lotte Pfeffer in Schnabel, *Footsteps*, p. 49.

68 / Conversation with Bep van Wijk-Voskuijl, 25 February 1981. Collection of RIOD (Netherlands State Institute for War Documentation).

69 / Bep Voskuijl in Schnabel, *Footsteps*, p. 89.

70 / Edith did not accompany them, for some unknown reason.

71 / Buddy Elias, 'That was . . .' author interview, October 1997; 'She had such a sense of comedy' in Mary E. Campbell, 'Cousin of Anne Frank Remembers the Holocaust Well', *The Times*, 17 July 1985.

72 / Conversation with Miep Gies, 19 and 27 February 1985. Collection of RIOD.

73 / Nazi list of Jews living in Aachen 1935, courtesy of Dick Plotz, e-mail to author, 6 December 1997.

74 / Dr Trude K. Hollander, letter to author, 25 March 1998.

75 / *Diary*, 28 September 1942 (a), p. 191.

76 / Otto Frank, letter, May 1939, from ibid.

77 / Ibid.

78 / Ibid., p. 190.

79 / Illustration in Lindwer, *Last Seven Months*.

80 / Dawidowicz, *War against the Jews*, p. 143.

81 / Neville Chamberlain in Robert Kee, *The World We Left Behind: A Chronicle of the Year 1939* (London: Weidenfeld & Nicolson, 1984).

82 / Van Gelder in Schnabel, *Footsteps*, p. 41.

83 / Van Gelder in 'In Those Days She was Called Annelies', *De Telegraaf*, 8 June 1957.

84 / Mrs Kuperus, 'Anne was a . . .' in Matthieu van Winsen, 'How I remember Anne Frank', *PRIVE*, 16 June 1979; 'I was so . . .' in Schnabel, *Footsteps*, pp. 42–3.

85 / Otto Frank, memoir.

86 / Margot Frank, letter, 27 April 1940. Collection of Simon Wiesenthal Centre USA.

87 / Anne Frank, letter and postcard, 29 April 1940. Collection of Simon Wiesenthal Centre USA.

88 / Juanita Wagner, affidavit in *Autographs, Including Anne Frank Correspondence*, auction pamphlet from the Swann Galleries, USA, 25 October 1988.

89 / Betty Ann Wagner, 'We often talked . . .' in 'American Pen-Pals to Auction Anne Frank Correspondence', *Los Angeles Times*, 24 July 1988; 'To be very . . .' in Richard F. Shepard, 'Letter by Anne Frank is Being Sold', *New York Times*, 22 July 1988.

90 / Milly Stanfield in Fussman, 'Woman Who Would Have Saved', *Newsday*.

91 / Anne Frank verse in Peggy Isaak Gluck, 'Anne Frank's Signature', *Jewish Journal*, 20–26 April 1990, and in 'Antique Judaica, Rare Anne Frank Autograph Verse', *Holy Land Treasures*, 1990. The poetry album was auctioned at Christie's in New York in 1990. Antique Judaica collector Rabbi Irvin D. Ungar bought it and donated it to the Simon Wiesenthal Centre USA. Ungar paid a five-figure sum for it.

92 / Gies and Gold, *Anne Frank*, pp. 36–7.

93 / *Diary*, undated (a), p. 222.

94 / *Diary*, 10 October 1942 (a), p. 282.

Chapter Three
1 / I have been unable to find the original source for this quote.

2 / Jetteke Frijda, author interview, Amsterdam: March 1998.

3 / Eva Schloss, author interview, London: January 1998.

4 / Ibid.

5 / Eva Schloss with Evelyn Julia Kent, *Eva's Story: A Survivor's Tale* (London: W. H. Allen, 1988), p. 30.

6 / Ibid., p. 32.

7 / Schloss, author interview, January 1998.

8 / Schloss, 'Anne was definitely . . .' in ibid.; 'They were . . .' in Schloss and Kent, *Eva's Story*, p. 31.

9 / Schloss, author interview, January 1998.

10 / Schloss, 'We were sitting . . .' in Schloss and Kent, *Eva's Story*, p. 32; 'Anne had to . . .' in author interview, January 1998.

11 / Fritzi Frank in Jane Pratt, 'The Anne Frank We Remember', *McCalls Magazine*, January 1986.

12 / Schloss, author interview, January 1998.

13 / Ibid.

14 / Laureen Nussbaum in 'Life and Death', *Sunday Oregonian*, 4 October 1992.

15 / Ibid.

16 / Otto Frank in Ernst Schnabel, *The Footsteps of Anne Frank* (London: Pan Books, 1976), p. 50.

17 / 28 September 1942 (a), *The Diary of Anne Frank: The Critical Edition* (London: Viking, 1989), p. 190.

18 / *Diary*, 6 January 1944 (a), pp. 448–9.

19 / Hanneli Pick-Goslar in the Jon Blair documentary, *Anne Frank Remembered* (BBC2, 6 May 1995).

20 / Dr Jacob Presser, *Ashes in the Wind: The Destruction of Dutch Jewry* (London: Souvenir Press, 1968), p. 12.

21 / Schnabel, *Footsteps*, p. 51.

22 / Presser, *Ashes in the Wind*, p. 21.

23 / Schnabel, *Footsteps*, pp. 51–2.

24 / Information on Pectacon and Opekta from Harry Paape, 'Originally from Frankfurt-am-Main', *Diary*, pp. 5–20.

25 / The day after the move, Otto sent a letter to the Bureau of Economic Investigation, apologizing for the delay in sending them the enclosed information about his businesses.

26 / Miep Gies and Alison Leslie Gold, *Anne Frank Remembered* (New York: Bantam Press, 1987), p. 64.

27 / Lies's younger sister Gabi.

28 / Margot Frank, letter, December 1940. Unless otherwise stated, all the Frank family correspondence quoted in this chapter is in the private collection of Buddy Elias.

29 / Schnabel, *Footsteps*, p. 52.

30 / The area was later partially re-opened.

31 / Anne Frank, letter, 13 January 1941.

32 / This probably refers to a photo of Buddy dressed as a clown in his ice-show.

33 / Anne Frank, letter, 22 March 1941.

34 / Quoted by Paape, 'Originally from Frankfurt', *Diary*, p. 13.

35 / Edith's mother.

36 / Because of the anti-Jewish measures.

37 / Anne Frank, letter, June 1941.

38 / Anne Frank, postcard, June 1941, in Anne Frank Stichting, *Anne Frank 1929–1945* (Heidelberg: Lambert Schneider, 1979), Figure 28.

39 / A business associate of Otto Frank.

40 / The couple who ran the camp.

41 / The baby son of Heinz and Eva.

42 / Anne Frank, letter, June 1941.

43 / One of several nonsense names Anne used for her father.

44 / Anne Frank, letter, June 1941.

45 / Gies and Gold, *Anne Frank*, p. 48.

46 / Presser, *Ashes in the Wind*, p. 75.

47 / Ibid., p. 93.

48 / Schnabel, *Footsteps*, p. 52.

49 / Presser, *Ashes in the Wind*, p. 35.

50 / Mrs Kuperus, 'There were . . .' in Matthieu van Winsen, 'How I remember Anne Frank', *PRIVE*, 16 June 1979; 'For a while . . .' in Schnabel, *Footsteps*, p. 43.

51 / Otto Frank, memoir. Private collection of Buddy Elias.

52 / Nussbaum in 'Life and Death', *Sunday Oregonian*.

53 / Jacqueline van Maarsen, author interview, Amsterdam: February 1998.

54 / Jacqueline van Maarsen, *My Friend Anne Frank* (New York: Vantage Press, 1996), p. 6.

55 / Ibid.

56 / Ibid.

57 / Van Maarsen, author interview, February 1998.

58 / Jacqueline van Maarsen, 'the kitchen where . . .' in van Maarsen, *My Friend*, p. 6; 'We did our homework . . .' van Maarsen, author interview, February 1998.

59 / Van Maarsen, *My Friend*, p. 18.

60 / Photograph in Jacqueline van Maarsen, *Anne en Jopie* (Amsterdam: Balans, 1990).

61 / Jacqueline van Maarsen in the Jon Blair documentary, *Anne Frank Remembered*.

62 / Ibid.

63 / *Diary*, 6 January 1944 (a), p. 443.

64 / Van Maarsen, *My Friend*, p. 24.

65 / Ibid., p. 21.

66 / *Diary*, 24 January 1944 (a), p. 463.

67 / *Diary*, 18 March 1944 (a), p. 545.

68 / Otto Frank, 'This was . . .' in 'The Living Legacy of Anne Frank', *Journal*, September 1967; 'Anne was lively . . .' in Hazel K. Johnson, 'Father Won't Watch Anne Frank Portrayal', April 1959. I have been unable to trace further details of this latter publication.

69 / Jacqueline van Maarsen, 'always very sweet . . .' in Van Maarsen, *My Friend*, pp. 21–2; 'Margot was very nice . . .' Van Maarsen, author interview, February 1998.

70 / Van Maarsen, *My Friend*, pp. 46, 23.

71 / Mrs van Maarsen in Schnabel, *Footsteps*, pp. 37–8.

72 / Van Maarsen, *My Friend*, p. 24.

73 / Mrs van Maarsen in Schnabel, *Footsteps*, p. 39.

74 / Otto Frank, postcard, 14 September 1941.

75 / Ibid.

76 / Laureen Nussbaum, interview transcripts for the Jon Blair documentary, *Anne Frank Remembered*.

77 / Laureen Nussbaum, 'She was thin . . .' in 'Life and Death', *Sunday Oregonian*; 'she had a . . .' interview transcripts for the Jon Blair documentary, *Anne Frank Remembered*.

78 / *Diary*, 20 June 1942 (a), p. 183.

79 / Hilde Jacobsthal in Art Myers, *A Survivor's Story*. I have been unable to find further details of this publication.

80 / Ibid.

Chapter Four

1 / Lucy S. Dawidowicz, *The War against the Jews 1933–1945* (London: Penguin, 1987), p. 169.

2 / Ibid., p. 170.

3 / Ibid., p. 171.

4 / Ibid., p. 180.

5 / Letters in possession of Anne Frank Stichting, Amsterdam.

6 / Alice Frank, letter, 12 January 1942. Unless otherwise stated, all Frank family correspondence quoted in this chapter is in the private collection of Buddy Elias.

7 / Ibid., 20 January 1942.

8 / Ibid., 12 April 1942.

9 / Otto Frank in Ernst Schnabel, *The Footsteps of Anne Frank* (London: Pan Books, 1976), pp. 59–60.

10 / Hermann Röttgen in 'On the Occasion of the "Habimah" Production: My Last Meeting with Anne Frank and her Family'. I have been unable to trace further details of this article.

11 / Information taken from Harry Paape, 'Originally from Frankfurt-am-Main', *The Diary of Anne Frank: The Critical Edition* (London: Viking, 1989), p. 16. Lewinsohn went into hiding during the war and survived.

12 / Otto Frank, letter, 10 June 1971.

13 / Victor Kugler, 'To leave Holland . . .' in Maxine Kopel, 'The Man Who Hid Anne Frank'. I have been unable to trace further details of this publication; 'Certainly we could . . .' in 'The Man Who Hid Anne Frank', *Hamilton Spectator*, 23 March 1974.

14 / Miep Gies and Alison Leslie Gold, *Anne Frank Remembered* (New York: Bantam Press, 1987), pp. 64–5.

15 / Kleiman's brother was also informed about the hiding plan.

16 / Dr Jacob Presser, *Ashes in the Wind: The Destruction of Dutch Jewry* (London: Souvenir Press, 1968), pp. 222–3.

17 / *Diary*, 22 May 1944 (a), p. 657.

18 / *Diary*, 9 October 1942 (b), p. 274.

19 / Eva Schloss, author interview, London: January 1998.

20 / *Diary*, 20 June 1942 (a), p. 183.

21 / Jacqueline van Maarsen, author interview, Amsterdam: February 1998.

22 / Toosje in Schnabel, *Footsteps*, p. 58.

23 / Anne Frank, *Tales from the Secret Annexe* (London: Penguin, 1982), p. 93.

24 / Anne Frank, letter, 1942.

25 / Otto Frank, memoir. Private collection of Buddy Elias.

26 / Quoted in Presser, *Ashes in the Wind*, p. 101.

27 / Ibid., p. 112.

28 / Ibid., p. 118.

29 / Ibid., p. 120.

30 / Miep Gies in Schnabel, *Footsteps*, p. 66.

31 / Schloss, author interview, January 1998.

32 / Ibid.

33 / *Diary*, 20 June 1942 (a), p. 183.

34 / Anne Frank, letter, in *Diary*, p. 117.

35 / Hanneli Pick-Goslar in Willy Lindwer, *The Last Seven Months of Anne Frank* (New York: Pantheon, 1991), p. 18.

36 / Jacqueline van Maarsen, *My Friend Anne Frank* (New York: Vantage Press, 1996), p. 25.

37 / Van Maarsen, author interview, February 1998.

38 / *Diary*, 20 June 1942 (b), p. 185.

39 / Jacqueline van Maarsen, 'We never sat . . .' author interview, February

1998; 'We always ran . . .' Van Maarsen, *My Friend*, p. 22.

40 / Anne Frank, letter, May 1942.

41 / Buddy Elias, author interview, Cheltenham: October 1997.

42 / Otto Frank, letter, May 1942.

43 / Margot Frank, letter, May 1942.

44 / Quoted in Presser, *Ashes in the Wind*, pp. 325–6.

45 / Ibid., pp. 128–9.

46 / *Diary*, 14 June 1942 (a), p. 178.

47 / *Diary*, 12 June 1942 (a), p. 177.

48 / *Diary*, 28 September 1942 (a), p. 177.

49 / Pick-Goslar in Lindwer, *Last Seven Months*, pp. 17–18.

50 / Van Maarsen, *My Friend*, p. 27.

51 / Ibid., p. 54.

52 / Ibid., p. 68.

53 / Hanneli Pick-Goslar in Alison Leslie Gold, *Memories of Anne Frank: Reflections of a Childhood Friend* (New York: Scholastic Press, 1997), p. 31.

54 / *Diary*, 19 June 1942 (a), p. 189.

55 / Van Maarsen, author interview, February 1998.

56 / Edmond Silberberg, author interview, telephone: June 1998.

57 / Ibid.

58 / Edmond Silberberg, 'The word that . . .' ibid.; 'I think I was probably . . .' in Tina Traster, 'Holocaust Survivor Discloses his Courtship of Anne Frank', *The Record, Hackensack*, 18 April 1996.

59 / *Diary*, 30 June 1942 (a), p. 203.

60 / Silberberg, author interview, June 1998.

61 / *Diary*, 30 June 1942 (a), p. 201.

62 / *Diary*, 5 July 1942 (b), p. 205.

63 / Pick-Goslar in Lindwer, *Last Seven Months*, p. 18.

64 / *Diary*, 1 July 1942 (b), p. 205.

65 / Mrs van Maarsen in Schnabel, *Footsteps*, p. 36.

66 / Ibid., p. 57.

67 / Otto Frank in Schnabel, *Footsteps*, p. 67.

68 / Victor Kugler in Schnabel, *Footsteps*, p. 81.

69 / Victor Kugler, 'Nazis Located Anne Frank in Hiding Place 14 Years Ago', *New Haven Evening Register*, 4 August 1958.

70 / Otto Frank, letter, 4 July 1942.

71 / Presser, *Ashes in the Wind*, p. 140.

72 / *Diary*, 8 July 1942 (b), p. 207.

73 / Ibid., p. 208.

74 / Johannes Kleiman in Schnabel, *Footsteps*, p. 67.

75 / Otto Frank in ibid.

76 / Gies and Gold, *Anne Frank*, p. 70.

77 / *Diary*, 8 July 1942 (b), p. 208.

78 / Gies and Gold, *Anne Frank*, p. 70.

79 / Otto Frank, postcard, 5 July 1942.

80 / Anne Frank, ibid.

81 / Bicycles were by then forbidden to Jews, so Margot must have kept hers clandestinely, or borrowed one.

82 / Gies and Gold, *Anne Frank*, p. 70.

83 / *Diary*, 8 July 1942 (b), p. 209.

84 / Gies and Gold, *Anne Frank*, p. 71.

85 / Ibid., p. 73.

86 / Toosje in Schnabel, *Footsteps*, p. 60.

87 / Silberberg, author interview, June 1998.

88 / Jetteke Frijda, author interview, Amsterdam: March 1998.

89 / Pick-Goslar in Lindwer, *Last Seven Months*, pp. 19–20.

90 / Mrs van Maarsen in Schnabel, *Footsteps*, pp. 60–61.

91 / Van Maarsen, *My Friend*, pp. 27–8.

Chapter Five

1 / Dr Jacob Presser, *Ashes in the Wind: The Destruction of Dutch Jewry* (London: Souvenir Press, 1968), p. 141.

2 / Ibid., p. 392.

3 / Ibid., p. 383.

4 / Eva Schloss, author interview, London: January 1998.

5 / Bruno Bettelheim, 'The Ignored Lesson of Anne Frank' in Michael R. Marrus, *The Holocaust in History* (London: Penguin Books, 1989), pp. 131–2.

6 / For general information about 'helpers', I have relied mainly on Presser, *Ashes in the Wind*, and Eva Fogelman, *Conscience and Courage: Rescuers of Jews During the Holocaust* (London: Cassell, 1995).

7 / Presser, *Ashes in the Wind*, p. 388.

8 / Fogelman, *Conscience and Courage*, p. 159.

9 / Ibid., pp. 162–3.

10 / Ibid., p. 59.

11 / Kleiman also cites the instance of his daughter's loyalty to Anne (see Ernst Schnabel, *The Footsteps of Anne Frank*, London: Pan Books, 1976, pp. 84–5), and in her diary Anne mentions visits paid to the annexe by Mrs Kleiman, i.e. on 26 September 1942.

12 / Miep Gies, 'I never felt . . .' in Angela Lambert, 'A Portrait of Anne Frank', *Independent*, 4 May 1995; 'but when . . .' Miep Gies in the Jon Blair documentary, *Anne Frank Remembered* (BBC2, 6 May 1995).

13 / Miep Gies in *Anne Frank Magazine 1998* (Amsterdam: Anne Frank Stichting, 1998), pp. 26–8.

14 / Presser, *Ashes in the Wind*, p. 387.

15 / *Diary*, 11 July 1943 (b), p. 366.

16 / Fogelman, *Conscience and Courage*, pp. 150–51.

17 / *Diary*, 28 January 1944 (c), pp. 472–3.

18 / *Diary*, 1 October 1942 (b), p. 261.

19 / *Diary*, 5 October 1942 (a), p. 268.

20 / Presser, *Ashes in the Wind,* p. 389.

21 / Van Maaren's behaviour and possible part in their betrayal is discussed in full in the Epilogue.

22 / *Diary,* 9 November 1942 (b), p. 300.

23 / Ibid.

24 / *Diary,* 9 August 1943 (b), p. 389.

25 / *Diary,* 15 January 1944 (a), p. 458.

26 / *Diary,* 14 March 1944 (a), p. 528.

27 / *Diary,* 25 May 1944 (a), p. 659.

28 / *Diary,* 27 September 1942 (a), p. 258.

29 / *Diary,* 29 September 1942 (b), p. 257.

30 / Otto Frank, memoir. Private collection of Buddy Elias.

31 / Otto Frank, letter, 10 June 1971. Private collection of Buddy Elias.

32 / *Diary,* 22 December 1943 (b), p. 428.

33 / Fritz Pfeffer, letter, 15 November 1942, in Anneke Visser, 'Discovery of Letters Written by Man Who Hid in Anne Frank's Annexe', *Handelsblad,* 7 November 1987.

34 / *Diary,* 22 December 1942 (b), p. 330.

35 / Werner Peter Pfeffer in the Jon Blair documentary, *Anne Frank Remembered.*

36 / *Diary,* 5 February 1943 (b), p. 335.

37 / Otto Frank, memoir.

38 / *Diary,* 30 September 1942 (a), p. 262.

39 / Miep Gies and Alison Leslie Gold, *Anne Frank Remembered* (New York: Bantam Press, 1987), p. 130.

40 / Gies and Gold, *Anne Frank,* pp. 132–3.

41 / *Diary,* 17 October 1943 (b), p. 409.

42 / Otto Frank, memoir.

43 / The wife of a business acquaintance.

44 / *Diary,* 30 September 1942 (a), p. 261.

45 / *Diary,* 1 October 1942 (b), p. 262.

46 / *Diary,* 17 November 1942 (b), p. 312.

47 / *Diary,* 10 December 1942 (b), p. 326.

48 / Otto Frank, memoir.

49 / Peter's beloved cat.

50 / Gies and Gold, *Anne Frank,* p. 95. There may also have been photographs of the Franks and their friends in hiding. When Miep was showing Cara Wilson around the annexe in 1977, she said, 'Here is where Anne would write in her diary. Right here by the window. In the room where we stand. I remember once taking a picture of her as she was writing. She looked up at me, slammed her book shut, and stormed out of the room. She was very angry with me for doing that. Yes, she had a temper.' Miep Gies in Cara Wilson, *Love, Otto: The Legacy of Anne Frank* (Kansas: Andrews & McMeel, 1995), p. 118. Furthermore, in an interview with the *Holland Herald* in the 1970s, Victor Kugler shows the journalist conducting the interview several photographs, including, apparently, one he took of Anne in the annexe. Unfortunately, despite repeated research, no photographs from this period have yet been discovered.

51 / Ibid., p. 100.

52 / *Diary,* 28 November 1942 (b), p. 319.

53 / *Diary,* 11 July 1942 (b), p. 216.

54 / *Diary,* 11 July 1942 (b), p. 218.

55 / Otto Frank, memoir.

56 / *Diary,* 19 November 1942 (b), p. 316.

57 / *Diary,* 13 January 1943 (b), p. 332.

58 / *Diary,* 2 May 1943 (a), p. 307.

59 / *Diary,* 25 September 1942 (a), p. 243.

60 / *Diary,* 28 September 1942 (a), p. 192.

61 / Jacqueline van Maarsen, author interview, Amsterdam: February 1998.

62 / *Diary*, undated entry 1942 (a), p. 283.

63 / Buddy Elias in the Jon Blair documentary, *Anne Frank Remembered*.

64 / Ibid.

65 / *Diary*, 14 August 1942 (b), p. 221.

66 / Buddy Elias, author interview, Cheltenham: October 1997.

67 / Ibid.

68 / Ibid.

69 / *Diary*, 24 December 1943 (b), pp. 430–31.

70 / *Diary*, 15 July 1944 (a), p. 694.

71 / *Diary*, 26 May 1944 (a), p. 662.

72 / *Diary*, 26 May 1944 (a), p. 661.

73 / *Diary*, 23 February 1944 (a), p. 497.

74 / *Diary*, 23 February 1944 (a), p. 498.

75 / Schnabel, *Footsteps*, p. 91.

76 / Johannes Kleiman in ibid., p. 97.

77 / *Diary*, 21 September 1942 (a), p. 237.

78 / *Diary*, 20 October 1942 (a), p. 286.

79 / *Diary*, 18 October 1942 (a), p. 272.

80 / *Diary*, 17 April 1944 (a), p. 611.

81 / *Diary*, 14 October 1942 (a), p. 276.

82 / Otto Frank, memoir.

83 / Footnote quoting BBC news, in *Diary*, p. 273.

84 / *Diary*, 4 October 1942 (a), p. 267.

85 / Miep Gies, in *Anne Frank Magazine* 1998, pp. 28–9.

86 / Victor Kugler in Maxine Kopel, 'The Man Who Hid Anne Frank'. I have been unable to find further details of this article.

87 / Bep Voskuijl in Schnabel, *Footsteps*, p. 97.

88 / Otto Frank, 'I remember . . .'

letter, 19 June 1968 in Wilson, *Love, Otto*, p. 50; 'Only with . . .' in his memoir.

89 / *Diary*, 20 November 1942 (b), p. 317.

90 / Otto Frank letter, 1975, in *Anne Frank Magazine 1998*, p. 39.

91 / Lotte Pfeffer, letter in Judith E. Doneson, *The Holocaust in American Film* (New York: Jewish Publication Society, 1987), p. 81. Lotte was writing to Albert Hackett and his wife Frances Goodrich, who adapted the diary for stage and screen, condemning their portrayal of Pfeffer as a Jewish man uneducated about his religion.

92 / Otto Frank, all quotes taken from his letter to the Hacketts, 2 February 1954, in Lawrence Graver, *An Obsession with Anne Frank: Meyer Levin and the Diary* (London: University of California Press Ltd, 1995), pp. 78–9, p. 58. The last part of the quotation, 'Anne had never shown . . .' is from Otto's memoir.

93 / *Diary*, 2 May 1943 (a), p. 306.

94 / *Diary*, 16 February 1944 (a), pp. 491–2.

95 / *Diary*, 7 March 1944 (a), p. 518.

96 / *Diary*, 19 November 1942 (b), p. 316.

97 / *Diary*, 27 February 1943 (b), p. 337.

98 / *Diary*, 27 November 1943 (b), p. 422.

99 / *Diary*, 29 December 1943 (a), p. 436.

100 / *Diary*, 12 March 1944 (a), p. 526.

101 / *Diary*, 11 April 1944 (a), p. 600.

102 / Fritzi Frank in Jane Pratt, 'The Anne Frank We Remember', *McCalls Magazine*, January 1986.

103 / *Diary*, 12 July 1942 (a), p. 223.

104 / *Diary*, 2 January 1944 (b), p. 439.

105 / Otto Frank, memoir.

106 / *Diary*, 5 February 1943 (b), p. 335.

107 / *Diary*, 14 August 1942 (b), p. 219.

108 / 'A little wretch . . .' *Diary*, 7 November 1942 (a), p. 292; 'I keep teasing . . .' *Diary*, 30 September 1942 (a), p. 263.

109 / Johannes Kleiman in Schnabel, *Footsteps*, p. 83.

110 / *Diary*, 30 January 1943 (b), pp. 333–4.

111 / *Diary*, 28 September 1942 (a), p. 260.

112 / Corrie was in the same hockey club as Jacqueline van Maarsen.

113 / Johannes Kleiman in Schnabel, *Footsteps*, p. 84.

114 / Victor Kugler, 'They were probably . . .' in 'The Man Who Hid Anne Frank', *Hamilton Spectator*, 23 March 1974; 'When we bought . . .' in Kopel, 'The Man Who Hid Anne Frank'.

115 / Victor Kugler in Schnabel, *Footsteps*, p. 82.

116 / Otto Frank, memoir.

117 / *Diary*, 6 January 1944 (a), pp. 442–3.

118 / Ibid., p. 442.

119 / *Diary*, 28 February 1944 (a), p. 501.

120 / *Diary*, 24 January 1944 (a), p. 468.

121 / *Diary*, 6 January 1944 (a), p. 451.

122 / Ibid.

123 / *Diary*, 12 February 1944 (a), p. 483.

124 / *Diary*, 14 February 1944 (a), p. 484.

125 / *Diary*, 16 February 1944 (a), p. 490.

126 / *Diary*, 17 March 1944 (a), p. 543.

127 / *Diary*, 2 May 1944 (a), p. 624.
128 / *Diary*, 5 May 1944 (a), p. 630.
129 / *Diary*, 7 May 1944 (a), p. 635.
130 / Otto Frank, memoir.
131 / *Diary*, 28 April 1944 (a), p. 623.
132 / *Diary*, 3 May 1944 (a), pp. 628–9.

133 / *Diary*, 15 July 1944 (a), p. 693.

134 / Otto Frank, 'Anne Frank Would Have Been Fifty This Year', *Life*, March 1979.

135 / Kitty Egyedi, in 'In Search of Kitty, the Friend of Anne Frank', *Day In, Day Out*, 14 June 1986.

136 / Otto Frank, 'Anne Frank Would Have Been Fifty', *Life*.

137 / Fritzi Frank in Pratt, 'The Anne Frank We Remember', *McCalls*.

138 / Victor Kugler, 'Little things . . .' in Kopel, 'The Man Who Hid Anne Frank'; 'between the pages . . .' in Kugler, 'Nazis Located Anne Frank in Hiding Place 14 Years Ago', *New Haven Evening Register*, 4 August 1958.

139 / *Diary*, 4 October 1942 (a), p. 268.

140 / Gies and Gold, *Anne Frank*, p. 113.

141 / *Diary*, 20 October 1942 (a), p. 286.

142 / Bep Voskuijl, in Harry Paape, 'The Arrest', *Diary*, p. 25.

143 / *Diary*, 7 August 1943 (b), p. 387.

144 / Anne Frank, 'Villains!' in *Tales from the Secret Annexe* (London: Penguin, 1982), p. 101.

145 / *Diary*, 3 February 1944 (a), p. 481.

146 / Anne Frank, 'the finest thing . . .' in *Diary*, 23 February 1944 (a), p. 497; 'I have nothing . . .' in *Diary*, 19 March 1944 (a), p. 548.

147 / *Diary*, 25 March 1944 (a), p. 569.

148 / *Diary*, 5 April 1944 (a), p. 587.
149 / *Diary*, 3 May 1944 (a), p. 629.
150 / *Diary*, 13 June 1944 (a), p. 678.

151 / Ibid.
152 / Ibid.
153 / Gerrit Bolkestein in Gerrold van der Stroom, 'The Diaries, *Het Achterhuis* and the Translations', *Diary*, p. 59.

154 / *Diary*, 29 March 1944 (a), p. 578.

155 / *Diary*, 5 April 1944 (a), pp. 586–8.

156/ *Diary*, 14 April 1944 (a), p. 603.
157/ *Diary*, 21 April 1944 (a), p. 616.
158/ *Diary*, 11 May 1944 (a), p. 647.
159/ *Diary*, 20 May 1944 (a), p. 653.
160/ *Diary*, 17 April 1944 (a), p. 612.
161 / Photograph of list in Van der Stroom, 'The Diaries', *Diary*, p. 60.
162 / Bep Voskuijl in Schnabel, *Footsteps*, p. 90.
163 / Gies and Gold, *Anne Frank*, p. 147.
164 / *Diary*, 1 August 1944 (a), p. 699.
165 / Ibid.

Chapter Six

1 / Dr Jacob Presser, *Ashes in the Wind: The Destruction of Dutch Jewry* (London: Souvenir Press, 1968), p. 164.
2 / There were many Resistance groups in the Netherlands during the war; unfortunately, their work falls outside the scope of this book, but the interested reader should take note of the relevant chapter in Presser's work, and may wish to visit the Museum of Resistance housed in the former synagogue at 63 Lekstraat, Amsterdam.
3 / *Vrij Nederland* in Presser, *Ashes in the Wind*, p. 162.
4 / Presser, *Ashes in the Wind*, p. 273.
5 / P. S. Gerbrandy in ibid., p. 264.
6/ Grete Weil in Jan Stoutenbeek and Paul Vigeveno, *A Guide to Jewish Amsterdam* (Amsterdam: De Haan, 1985), p. 128.
7 / As noted in the Prologue, all those who survived the raid on the Prinsengracht have given countless interviews, written chronicles and sworn testimonies about the events that followed; the accounts given here are based on events as they have been most frequently reported.
8 / Miep Gies in Harry Paape, 'The Betrayal', *The Diary of Anne Frank: The Critical Edition* (London: Viking, 1989), pp. 29–30.

9 / Jan Gies in Ernst Schnabel, *The Footsteps of Anne Frank* (London: Pan Books, 1976), p. 114.
10 / Miep Gies in Harry Paape, 'The Arrest', *Diary*, p. 24.
11 / Jan Gies's testimony to officials in Lübeck, 29 September 1959. Collection of RIOD (Netherlands State Institute for War Documentation).
12 / Information from a report of two conversations with Jan Gies and Miep Gies-Santrouschitz in Amsterdam on 19 and 27 February 1985. Collection of RIOD.
13 / Miep Gies and Alison Leslie Gold, *Anne Frank Remembered* (New York: Bantam Press, 1987), pp. 157–8.
14 / Ibid., p. 158.
15 / Stoutenbeek and Vigeveno, *A Guide*, p. 127.
16 / Schnabel, *Footsteps*, pp. 115–17.
17 / Victor Kugler in Eda Shapiro, 'The Reminiscences of Victor Kugler, the "Mr Kraler" of Anne Frank's Diary', *Yad Vashem Studies* XIII (Jerusalem, 1979), p. 360.
18 / Ibid.
19 / Ibid., pp. 360–61.
20 / Ibid., pp. 361–2.
21 / Ibid.
22 / Eva Schloss, author interview, London: May 1998.
23 / Ibid.
24 / Based on Gies and Gies-Santrouschitz, conversations, 19 and 27 February 1985; Paape 'The Arrest', *Diary*, p. 25; Gies and Gold, *Anne Frank*, pp. 160–62; Schnabel, *Footsteps*, pp. 119–20.
25 / Miep Gies in Paape, 'The Betrayal', *Diary*, p. 36.
26 / Van Maaren in ibid., p. 34.
27 / Otto Frank, memoir. Private collection of Buddy Elias.
28 / Otto Frank in Schnabel, *Footsteps*, p. 117.
29 / Ibid.

30 / Jaap Nijstad, *Westerbork Drawings: The Life and Work of Leo Kok 1923–1945* (Amsterdam: Balans, 1990), p. 27.

31 / Presser, *Ashes in the Wind*, p. 406.

32 / The cabaret was disbanded in 1944.

33 / Presser, *Ashes in the Wind*, p. 450.

34 / Ibid., p. 435.

35 / Vera Cohn and Harold Berman, 'The Day I Met Anne Frank', *Anti-Defamation League Bulletin*, June 1956.

36 / Ibid.

37 / Lenie de Jong-van Naarden in Willy Lindwer, *The Last Seven Months of Anne Frank* (New York, Pantheon Books, 1991), p. 144.

38 / Ronnie Goldstein-van Cleef in ibid., p. 176.

39 / Lientje Brilleslijper-Jaldati, 'Memories of Anne Frank', in the press leaflet for the film *Ein Tagebuch für Anne Frank* (Berlin: VEB Progress Film-Vertrieb, 1959).

40 / Lientje Brilleslijper-Jaldati in Edith Anderson, 'A Sequel to Anne Frank's Diary', *National Guardian*, May 1966.

41 / Rachel van Amerongen-Frankfoorder in Lindwer, *Last Seven Months*, pp. 92–3.

42 / Rosa de Winter in Schnabel, *Footsteps*, p. 127.

43 / Eva Schloss, author interview, London: May 1998.

44 / Rosa de Winter in Schnabel, *Footsteps*, pp. 127–8.

45 / Otto Frank, memoir.

46 / Gies and Gold, *Anne Frank*, p. 162.

47 / Paape, 'The Arrest', *Diary*, p. 26.

48 / Johannes Kleiman in Paape, 'The Betrayal', *Diary*, p. 30.

49 / Gies and Gold, *Anne Frank*, p. 165.

50 / Rosa de Winter in Schnabel, *Footsteps*, pp. 128–9.

51 / Schloss, author interview, May 1998.

52 / Anonymous witness in Presser, *Ashes in the Wind*, p. 462.

53 / Ibid.

54 / Etty Hillesum, *Letters from Westerbork* (London: Jonathan Cape, 1986), p. 56.

55 / Brilleslijper-Jaldati, 'Memories'.

56 / Rosa de Winter in Schnabel, *Footsteps*, pp. 129–30.

57 / Lenie de Jong-van Naarden in Lindwer, *Last Seven Months*, pp. 146–7.

58 / Otto Frank, memoir.

Chapter Seven

1 / Rosa de Winter in Ernst Schnabel, *The Footsteps of Anne Frank* (London: Pan Books, 1976), p. 130.

2 / Eva Schloss, author interview, London: May 1998.

3 / Ibid.

4 / Anton Gill, *The Journey Back from Hell: Conversations with Concentration Camp Survivors* (London: Grafton Books, 1988), p. 26.

5 / Janny Brilleslijper in Willy Lindwer, *The Last Seven Months of Anne Frank* (New York: Pantheon Books, 1991), p. 56.

6 / Schloss, author interview, May 1998.

7 / Gill, *Journey Back from Hell*, p. 35.

8 / Otto Frank in 'Anne Frank's Vater: Ich will Versöhnung', *Welt am Sonntag*, 4 February 1979. There is some confusion over when Hermann van Pels died, but the official Red Cross dossier (number 103586), in the archives of RIOD (Netherlands State Institute for War Documentation), dates his death as the night the Westerbork transport arrived in Auschwitz.

9 / Gill, *Journey Back from Hell*, pp. 26–7.

10 / Victor Kugler in Eda Shapiro, 'The Reminiscences of Victor Kugler, the "Mr Kraler" of Anne Frank's Diary', *Yad*

Vashem Studies XIII (Jerusalem: 1979), pp. 363–4.

11 / Ibid., p. 364.

12 / Ibid., p. 366.

13 / Miep Gies and Alison Leslie Gold, *Anne Frank Remembered* (New York: Bantam Press, 1987), p. 167.

14 / Ibid.

15 / Rosa de Winter in Schnabel, *Footsteps*, p. 135.

16 / Ronnie Goldstein-van Cleef in Lindwer, *Last Seven Months*, p. 186.

17 / Rosa de Winter in Schnabel, *Footsteps*, p. 135.

18 / Bloem Evers-Emden in Lindwer, *Last Seven Months*, p. 129.

19 / Ronnie Goldstein-van Cleef in ibid., p. 187.

20 / Lenie de Jong-van Naarden in ibid., p. 153.

21 / Bloem Evers-Emden in ibid., p. 129.

22 / Lenie de Jong-van Naarden in ibid., p. 155.

23 / Ronnie Goldstein-van Cleef in ibid., pp. 191–2.

24 / Sal de Liema, ' "We should try" ' in the Jon Blair documentary, *Anne Frank Remembered* (BBC2, 6 May 1995); 'The biggest problem . . .' in 'Holocaust Survivors Recall Their Hell on Earth', *Watertown Daily Times*, 5 February 1995.

25 / Sal de Liema in the Jon Blair documentary *Anne Frank Remembered*.

26 / Red Cross International Tracing Service Report. Collection of RIOD.

27 / Lientje Brilleslijper-Jaldati, 'Memories of Anne Frank', in the press leaflet for the film *Ein Tagebuch für Anne Frank* (Berlin: VEB Progress Film-Vertrieb, 1959).

28 / Lientje Brilleslijper-Jaldati in Edith Anderson, 'A Sequel to Anne Frank's Diary', *National Guardian*, May 1966.

29 / Rosa de Winter in Schnabel, *Footsteps*, p. 137.

30 / Ibid., pp. 137–8.

31 / Rosa de Winter, 'Fifteen and eighteen . . .' in Dick Schaap, 'I Knew Anne Frank', *Freedom after Auschwitz* (I have been unable to find further details of this publication); 'Anne encouraged Margot . . .' in Schnabel, *Footsteps*, p. 138.

32 / Rosa de Winter in ibid.

Chapter Eight

1 / Rosa de Winter in Dick Schaap, 'I Knew Anne Frank', *Freedom after Auschwitz*. I have been unable to find further details of this publication.

2 / The selection took place on 30 October; the next transport to leave Auschwitz-Birkenau was on 1 November 1944, which must have been the transport including Margot and Anne Frank. The figure is given in the footnotes of Eberhard Kolb, *Bergen-Belsen, from 1943–1945* (Gottingen: Sammlung Vandenhoeck, 1988), p. 54.

3 / Something of a misnomer; as will become clear, Bergen-Belsen was a detention camp from 1943 until mid-1944, only then did it run along concentration camp lines.

4 / Kolb, *Bergen-Belsen*, p. 24.

5 / Red Cross quoted in ibid., p. 35.

6 / Lientje Brilleslijper-Jaldati, 'Memories of Anne Frank', in the press leaflet for the film *Ein Tagebuch für Anne Frank* (Berlin: VEB Progress Film-Vertrieb, 1959).

7 / Ibid.

8 / Janny Brilleslijper, interview transcripts for the Jon Blair documentary, *Anne Frank Remembered* (BBC2, 6 May 1995). Private collection of Jon Blair.

9 / Kolb, *Bergen-Belsen*, p. 38.

10 / Anita Lasker-Wallfisch, *Inherit the Truth: 1939–1945* (London: Giles de la Mare, 1996), p. 90.

11 / Ibid.

12 / Brilleslijper-Jaldati, 'Memories'.

13 / Christine Lattek, 'Bergen-Belsen: From "Privileged" Camp to Death Camp' in Jo Reilly et al. (eds), *Belsen in History*

and Memory (London: Frank Cass, 1997), p. 57.

14 / Lientje Brilleslijper-Jaldati, 'Anne used to . . .' in Edith Anderson, 'A Sequel to Anne Frank's Diary', *National Guardian*, May 1966; 'We compiled a . . .' in 'Memories', *Ein Tagebuch für Anne Frank*.

15 / Lientje Brilleslijper-Jaldati, 'Our hands began . . .' in ibid.; 'we did better . . .' in Anderson, 'A Sequel', *National Guardian*.

16 / Lientje Brilleslijper-Jaldati in ibid.

17 / Ibid.

18 / Lasker-Wallfisch, *Inherit the Truth*, p. 91.

19 / Lattek, 'Bergen-Belsen', Reilly et al. (eds), *Belsen*, p. 55.

20 / Lientje Brilleslijper-Jaldati, 'Memories', *Ein Tagebuch für Anne Frank*.

21 / Ibid.

22 / Ibid.

23 / Rosa de Winter in Schnabel, *Footsteps*, p. 134.

24 / Otto Frank, memoir. Private collection of Buddy Elias.

25 / Netherlands Red Cross dossier. Collection of RIOD (Netherlands State Institute for War Documentation).

26 / Otto Frank, archive interview in the Jon Blair documentary, *Anne Frank Remembered*.

27 / Dr Jacob Presser, *Ashes in the Wind: The Destruction of Dutch Jewry* (London: Souvenir Press, 1968), p. 526.

28 / Ibid., p. 527.

29 / Netherlands Red Cross dossier. Collection of RIOD.

30 / Otto Frank, 'Anne Frank Would Have Been Fifty This Year', *Life Magazine*, March 1979.

31 / Eva Schloss, author interview, London: May 1998.

32 / Eva Schloss with Evelyn Julia Kent, *Eva's Story* (London: W H Allen, 1988), p. 165.

33 / Otto is referring to Edith's brother Julius here.

34 / Otto Frank, letter, 23 February 1945. Private collection of Buddy Elias.

35 / Quoted in Lattek, 'Bergen-Belsen', Reilly et al. (eds), *Belsen*, p. 57.

36 / Brilleslijper-Jaldati, 'Memories'.

37 / Hanneli Pick-Goslar in Patricia Yaroch, 'Her Best Friend Reveals a Surprising New Side of the Little Girl Whose Diary Touched the Heart of the World', 1957. I have been unable to trace further details of this publication. Interviewed by Willy Lindwer many years later, Lies did not think she had been able to actually see Anne as they spoke together.

38 / Ibid.

39 / Ibid.

40 / Trees's mother in Schnabel, *Footsteps*, p. 145.

41 / Brilleslijper-Jaldati, 'Memories', *Ein Tagebuch für Anne Frank*.

42 / Frank, 'Anne Frank Would Have Been Fifty', *Life*.

43 / Otto Frank, letter, 15 March 1945. Private collection of Buddy Elias.

44 / Otto Frank, undated note. Private collection of Buddy Elias.

45 / Otto Frank, letter, 18 March 1945, in Carl Fussman, 'The Woman Who Would Have Saved Anne Frank', *Newsday*, 16 March 1995.

46 / Otto Frank, letter dated 18 March 1945. Private collection of Buddy Elias.

47 / Rosa de Winter in Schnabel, *Footsteps*, p. 133.

48 / It is unclear to what Otto is referring here. Buddy Elias does not recollect the family contacting Otto until much later in the year.

49 / Otto Frank, undated letter. Private collection of Buddy Elias.

50 / Frank, 'Anne Frank Would Have Been Fifty', *Life*.

51 / Schloss and Kent, *Eva's Story*, pp. 196–7.

52 / Otto Frank, letter 31 March 1945. Private collection of Buddy Elias.

53 / Lattek, 'Bergen-Belsen', Reilly et al. (eds), *Belsen*, p. 55.

54 / Ibid., p. 57.

55 / Kolb, *Bergen-Belsen*, p. 46.

56 / Netherlands Red Cross dossier. Collection of RIOD.

57 / Presser, *Ashes in the Wind*, p. 517.

58 / Rachel van Amerongen-Frankfoorder in Lindwer, *Last Seven Months*, pp. 103–4.

59 / Paul Kemp, 'The British Army and the Liberation of Bergen-Belsen, April 1945' in Reilly et al. (eds), *Belsen*, pp. 146–7.

60 / Ibid.

61 / Lientje Brilleslijper-Jaldati, 'We visited them . . .' in 'Memories', *Ein Tagebuch für Anne Frank*; 'Anne said . . .' in Anderson, 'A Sequel', *National Guardian*.

62 / Netherlands Red Cross dossier. Collection of RIOD.

63 / Janny Brilleslijper in Lindwer, *Last Seven Months*, pp. 73–4.

64 / Eva Schloss, author interview, London: May 1998.

65 / Netherlands Red Cross dossier. Collection of RIOD.

66 / Hilde Jacobsthal in Art Myers, *A Survivor's Story*.

67 / Brilleslijper-Jaldati, 'Memories', *Ein Tagebuch für Anne Frank*.

68 / Kolb, *Bergen-Belsen*, p. 47.

69 / Paul Kemp, 'The British Army' in Reilly et al. (eds), *Belsen*, pp. 146–7.

70 / Quoted in ibid., pp. 136–7.

71 / I have been unable to find the original source for this quote.

72 / I have been unable to find the original source for this quote.

Chapter Nine

1 / Alice Frank, postcard, 20 May 1945. Unless otherwise stated, all correspondence quoted in this chapter is in the private collection of Buddy Elias.

2 / Otto Frank, letter, 26 May 1945.

3 / Otto Frank, memoir. Private collection of Buddy Elias.

4 / He is referring to Buddy and Stephan.

5 / Otto's older brother.

6 / Otto Frank, letter, 8 June 1945.

7 / Cousin.

8 / Robert's wife.

9 / Robert Frank, letter, 12 June 1945.

10 / Lottie Frank, letter, 18 June 1945.

11 / Otto Frank, letter, 21 June 1945.

12 / Herbert Frank, letter, 23 June 1945.

13 / Julius Hollander, letter, 30 June 1945.

14 / Eva Schloss with Evelyn Julia Kent, *Eva's Story* (London: W. H. Allen, 1988), p. 215.

15 / Quoted in Harry Paape, 'Imprisonment and Deportation', *The Diary of Anne Frank: The Critical Edition* (London: Viking, 1989), p. 55.

16 / Ibid., p. 56.

17 / Otto Frank, memoir. There is another version of how Otto discovered that his daughters were dead. Miep recalls that Otto received a letter giving him the news, but since the letter is dated 11 November, and Otto clearly knew by the end of August that his daughters were dead, this seems unlikely. There may, of course, be an earlier letter to that effect, but I have relied upon the version given in Willy Lindwer, *The Last Seven Months of Anne Frank* (New York: Pantheon Books, 1991).

18 / Conversation with Miep and Jan Gies, 18 February 1981. Collection of RIOD (Netherlands State Institute for War Documentation).

19 / Frank-Elias family, telegram, 6 August 1945.

20 / Ilse Ledermann, letter, 16 November 1943, in Miki Shoshan, 'We're on Our Way, Farewell, My Darlings', *Saturday and Sunday*, 4 May 1985.

21 / Hanneli Pick-Goslar in Lindwer, *Last Seven Months*, p. 33.

22 / Fritzi Frank in Schloss and Kent, *Eva's Story*, p. 221.

23 / Eva Schloss, author interview, London: January 1998.

24 / Otto Frank, letter, 11 August 1945.

25 / Otto Frank, letter, 19 August 1945.

26 / Otto Frank, letter, 20 August 1945.

27 / Otto Frank, letter, 22 August 1945.

28 / Otto Frank, letter, 6 September 1945.

29 / Betty Ann Wagner, 'Anne Frank Letter to Iowa Pen-Pal to be Sold', *New York Times*, 22 July 1988.

30 / Buddy.

31 / Otto Frank, letter, 6 September 1945.

32 / The Jewish New Year.

33 / Otto Frank, letter, 14 September 1945.

34 / Otto Frank, letter, 26 September 1945.

35 / Otto Frank, memoir.

36 / Otto Frank, letter, 30 September 1945.

37 / Conversation with Miep Gies-Santrouschitz, 18 February 1981. Collection of RIOD.

38 / Otto's second typescript.

39 / Buddy Elias, author interview, Cheltenham: October 1997.

40 / Eva Schloss, author interview, London: January and May 1998.

41 / Fritzi Geiringer in Schloss and Kent, *Eva's Story*, p. 222.

42 / Nathan Straus, letter, 25 October 1945.

43 / Otto Frank, letter, 14 November 1945.

44 / Otto Frank, letter, 11 November 1945.

45 / Quoted in Gerrold van der Stroom, 'The Diaries, *Het Achterhuis* and the Translations', *Diary*, p. 63.

46 / Conversation with Ab Cauvern, 23 January 1981. Collection of RIOD.

47 / Conversation with Miep and Jan Gies, 18 February 1981. Collection of RIOD.

48 / Quoted in van der Stroom, 'The Diaries', *Diary*, p. 64.

49 / Otto Frank, letter, 12 December 1945.

50 / Conversation with Mr M. G., 8 April 1981. Collection of RIOD.

51 / Jacqueline van Maarsen, author interview, Amsterdam: February 1998.

52 / Statement of Werner Cahn, 12 March 1981. Collection of RIOD.

53 / Jan Romein, 'A Child's Voice', *Het Parool*, 3 April 1945.

54 / Conversation with Rabbi I. H., 23 February 1981. Collection of RIOD.

55 / Conversation with Mrs M. B., 12 January 1981. Collection of RIOD.

56 / Eva Schloss, author interview, London: January 1998.

57 / Otto Frank, memoir.

58 / Otto Frank, diary, 25 June 1947, photocopy. Collection of RIOD.

Chapter Ten

1 / Jetteke Frijda, author interview, Amsterdam: March 1998.

2 / Werner Peter Pfeffer (Peter Pepper), interview transcripts for the Jon Blair documentary, *Anne Frank Remembered* (BBC2, 6 May 1995). Private collection of Jon Blair.

3 / Otto Frank in E. C. Farrell, 'Postscript to a Diary', *Global Magazine*, 1965.

4 / B. M. Mooyaart-Doubleday in *The Jewish Week*, 19 May 1995.

5 / Ibid.

6 / Leslie Mooyaart-Doubleday in ibid.

7 / Tony Kushner, 'I Want to Go on Living after My Death: The Memory of Anne Frank' in Martin Evans and Kenneth Lunn (eds), *War and Memory in the Twentieth Century* (London: Berg Publishers, 1997), p. 10.

8 / Otto Frank, letter, June 1952, in Lawrence Graver, *An Obsession with Anne Frank: Meyer Levin and the Diary* (London: University of California Press, 1995), p. 54.

9 / Rabbi David Soetendorp, *Diary 1997*, Anne Frank Educational Trust UK, p. 3.

10/ The conflict between Otto Frank, Meyer Levin and other involved parties is complex and lengthy. Interested readers are referred to two books dealing with the subject: Graver's *An Obsession*, and Ralph Melnick's *The Lost Legacy of Anne Frank* (Connecticut: Yale University, 1997).

11 / Otto Frank, letter, October 1955, in Anne Frank Stichting, *A History for Today* (Amsterdam: Anne Frank Stichting 1996), p. 84.

12 / Kushner, 'I Want to Go on Living', Evans and Lunn (eds), *War and Memory*, p. 13.

13 / Melnick, *The Lost Legacy*, p. 168.

14 / Graver, *An Obsession*, p. 54.

15 / Otto Frank, letter, in Judith E. Doneson, *The Holocaust in American Film* (New York: The Jewish Publication Society, 1987), p. 71.

16 / Kushner, 'I Want to Go on Living', Evans and Lunn (eds), *War and Memory*, p. 14.

17 / Reader's Supplement in *Anne Frank: The Diary of a Young Girl* (New York: Washington Square Press, 1972), p. 18.

18 / Quoted in ibid., p. 19.

19 / Frijda, author interview, March 1998.

20 / Johannes Kleiman, in *Snapshot: The Anne Frank House*. I have been unable to find further details of this publication.

21 / George Stevens, in *Anne Frank Comes to Hollywood*. I have been unable to trace further details of this publication.

22 / Audrey Hepburn later became a patron for the Anne Frank Educational Trust UK.

23 / Kushner, 'I Want to Go on Living', Evans and Lunn (eds), *War and Memory*, p. 16.

24 / Eva Schloss, author interview, London: May 1998.

25 / Ibid.

26 / 'Anne Frank's Secret Annexe Awaits the Wrecker's Ball', *Het Vrij Volk*, 23 November 1955.

27 / Otto Frank, 'Anne Frank Would Have Been Fifty This Year', *Life Magazine*, March 1979.

28 / Dr Trude K. Hollander, letter to the author, 25 March 1998.

29 / Jon Blair, 'Compulsion', *New York Times Book Review*, 28 September 1997, p. 3.

30/ Otto Frank in Peter Straus, article in *Moment*, December 1977.

31 / Otto Frank in 'Has Germany Forgotten Anne Frank?', *Coronet*, February 1960.

32 / Otto Frank in Farrell, 'Postscript', *Global Magazine*.

33 / Gerrold van der Stroom, 'Anne Frank and her Diaries', paper delivered at the Institute of Jewish Studies, University College, London, June 1997, p. 1.

34 / Otto Frank, memoir. Private collection of Buddy Elias.

35 / Both ideas were vetoed by the Anne Frank-Fonds, Basel.

36 / 'Anne's Legacy', *Reporter*, KRO-TV, 1995.

37 / Van der Stroom, 'Anne Frank', p. 6.

38 / Ibid.

39/ Cynthia Ozick, 'Who Owns Anne Frank?', *New Yorker*, 6 October 1997.

40 / 'The Censoring of Anne Frank', *Life Entertainment Story*, 11 October 1997.

41 / Richard Cohen, 'Anne Frank's Book about Hate', *Washington Post*, 30 October 1997.

42 / *Diary*, 5 April 1944 (a), p. 588.

43 / Kushner, 'I Want to Go on

Living', Evans and Lunn (eds), *War and Memory*, pp. 3– 16.

44 / Otto Frank, letter, April 1954, in Melnick, *The Lost Legacy*, p. 103.

Epilogue

1 / Dr Jacob Presser, *Ashes in the Wind: The Destruction of Dutch Jewry* (London: Souvenir Press, 1968), p. 392.

2 / Ibid., p. 392.

3 / Eva Fogelman, *Conscience and Courage: Rescuers of Jews During the Holocaust* (London: Cassell, 1995), p. 72.

4 / Johannes Kleiman, letter, undated, in Harry Paape, 'The Betrayal', *The Diary of Anne Frank: The Critical Edition* (London: Viking, 1989), pp. 30– 31.

5 / *Diary*, 4 March 1943 (b), p. 339.

6 / Briefcase or wallet; see Victor Kugler's letter, quoted in this chapter.

7 / These matters are all discussed in Kugler's letter.

8 / *Diary*, 16 September 1943 (b), p. 405.

9 / *Diary*, 29 September 1943 (b), p. 408.

10 / *Diary*, 18 April 1944 (a), p. 613.

11 / Following a burglary.

12 / *Diary*, 21 April 1944 (a), p. 616.

13 / *Diary*, 25 April 1944 (a), p. 618.

14 / Miep Gies in Paape, 'The Betrayal', *Diary*, p. 30.

15 / Otto Frank, letter, 11 November 1945. Private collection of Buddy Elias.

16 / Johannes Kleiman in Paape, 'The Betrayal', *Diary*, p. 31.

17 / All statements by van Maaren in ibid., p. 33.

18 / P. J. Genot in ibid., p. 32.

19 / All statements by L. Hartog in ibid., p. 33.

20 / One of the neighbouring businesses.

21 / All statements by van Maaren in Paape, 'The Betrayal', *Diary*, pp. 33– 4.

22 / Quoted in ibid., p. 34.

23 / Simon Wiesenthal, *Justice Not Vengeance: The Test Case* (London: Weidenfeld & Nicolson, 1989), pp. 335– 40.

24 / Quoted in ibid.

25 / Hella Pick, *Simon Wiesenthal: A Life in Search of Justice* (London: Weidenfeld & Nicolson, 1996), p. 173.

26 / *New York Herald Tribune*, 21 November 1963.

27 / *Los Angeles Times*, 21 November 1963.

28 / *New York Times*, 22 November 1963.

29 / Peter Hann, 'Arrest Starts New Anne Frank Inquiry'. I have been unable to discover which newspaper this article appeared in.

30 / J. J. de Kok in Paape, 'The Betrayal', *Diary*, p. 35.

31 / Jules Huf, 'I Went Through a Lot of Misery', *Haagse Post*, 30 November 1963.

32 / Karl Josef Silberbauer and his wife in ibid.

33 / As noted in the Prologue, no one was able to agree on the exact number of men accompanying Silberbauer on the raid.

34 / Huf, 'I Went Through a Lot', *Haagse Post*.

35 / Silberbauer is mistaken; the height marks were on the wall, but near the door to Anne's room.

36 / Huf, 'I Went Through a Lot', *Haagse Post*.

37 / Ibid.

38 / Otto Frank in Paape, 'The Betrayal', *Diary*, p. 35.

39 / Bep Voskuijl in ibid.

40 / Miep Gies in ibid., pp. 35– 6.

41 / Willi Lages in ibid., p. 44.

42 / The articles were by Carole Kleesiek and Simon Wiesenthal, and both appeared on 26 July 1964.

43 / Van Maaren in Paape, 'The Betrayal', *Diary*, p. 38.

44 / Ibid., p. 39.

45 / Quoted in ibid., p. 40.

46 / Ibid., p. 43.

47 / Otto Frank, memoir.

48 / Otto Frank, 'Anne Frank Would Have Been Fifty This Year', *Life Magazine*, March 1979.

49 / This is probably the unusual door/window in Peter's room, which can be seen from the front house.

50 / In the warehouse, probably.

51 / Jubilant.

52 / Victor Kugler, letter, undated but for the year 1963. Private collection of Buddy Elias.

53 / *Diary*, 1 March 1944 (a), p. 504.

54 / His name is on the document in the archives of RIOD (Netherlands State Institute for War Documentation).

55 / Conversation with Mrs B., 6 February 1981. Collection of RIOD.

56 / Conversation with Mr H. Wijnberg, 13 October 1981. Collection of RIOD.

57 / Ibid.

58 / Mr H. Wijnberg, interview tran- scripts for the Jon Blair documentary, *Anne Frank Remembered* (BBC2, 6 May 1995). Private collection of Jon Blair.

59 / *Diary*, 3 November 1943 (b), p. 412.

60 / *Diary*, 15 April 1944 (a), p. 604.

61 / Paape, 'The Betrayal', *Diary*, pp. 44–5.

Afterword

1 / 8 February 1944 (a), *The Diary of Anne Frank: The Critical Edition* (London: Viking, 1989), p. 482.

2 / David Barnouw in Jay Rayner, 'Anne Frank's Father Censored Her Diaries to Protect the Family', 23 August 1998.

3 / *Diary*, 12 January 1944 (a), p. 454.

4 / *Diary*, 20 June 1942 (b), p. 180.

5 / Otto Frank, memoir. Private collection of Buddy Elias.

6 / David Barnouw in Rayner, 'Anne Frank's Father'.

Anne Frank Stichting, *Anne Frank 1929–1945* (Heidelberg: Lambert Schneider, 1979)

—, exhibition catalogue in Dutch and English, *Anne Frank in the World 1925–1945* (Amsterdam: Bert Bakker, 1985)

—, exhibition catalogue in Japanese, *Anne Frank in the World* (Amsterdam, Anne Frank Stichting, 1985)

—, exhibition catalogue in English, *Anne Frank: A History for Today* (Amsterdam, Anne Frank Stichting, 1996)

—, *Anne Frank Magazine 1998* (Amsterdam: Anne Frank Stichting, 1998)

David Barnouw and Gerrold van der Stroom (editors), *The Diary of Anne Frank: The Critical Edition* (London: Viking, 1989)

Janrense Boonstra and Jose Rijnder, *The Anne Frank House: A Museum with a Story* (Amsterdam: Anne Frank Stichting, 1992)

Lucy S. Dawidowicz, *The War against the Jews 1933–1945* (London: Penguin, 1987)

Judith E. Doneson, *The Holocaust in American Film* (New York, Jewish Publication Society, 1987)

Amos Elon, *Founder: Meyer Amschel Rothschild and his Time* (London: Harper Collins, 1996)

Martin Evans and Kenneth Lunn (editors), *War and Memory in the Twentieth Century* (London: Berg Publishers, 1997)

Eva Fogelman, *Conscience and Courage: Rescuers of Jews During the Holocaust* (London: Cassell, 1995)

Anne Frank, *Tales from the Secret Annexe* (London: Penguin, 1982)

Miep Gies and Alison Leslie Gold, *Anne Frank Remembered* (New York: Bantam Press, 1987)

Martin Gilbert, *Auschwitz and the Allies* (London: Mandarin, 1991)

—, *Holocaust Journey* (London: Orion Publishing Group, 1997)

—, *The Holocaust* (London: Harper Collins, 1987)

Anton Gill, *The Journey Back from Hell: Conversations with Concentration Camp Survivors* (London: Grafton Books, 1988)

Alison Leslie Gold, *Memories of Anne Frank: Reflections of a Childhood Friend* (New York: Scholastic Press, 1997)

Frances Goodrich and Albert Hackett, *The Diary of Anne Frank* (London: Blackie & Son, 1970)

Lawrence Graver, *An Obsession with Anne*

Frank: Meyer Levin and the Diary (London: University of California Press Ltd, 1995)

Joachim Hellwig and Gunther Deicke, *Ein Tagebuch für Anne Frank* (Berlin: Verlag der Nation, 1959)

Etty Hillesum, *Letters from Westerbork* (London: Jonathan Cape, 1986)

Laurel Holliday (editor), *Children's Wartime Diaries* (London: Piatkus, 1995)

Louis de Jong and Simon Schema, *The Netherlands and Nazi Germany* (Connecticut: Harvard University Press, 1990)

H. R. Kedward, *Resistance in Vichy France* (Oxford: Oxford University Press, 1978)

Eberhard Kolb, *Bergen-Belsen from 1943–1945* (Gottingen: Sammlung Vandenhoeck, 1988)

Anita Lasker-Wallfisch, *Inherit the Truth: 1939–1945* (London: Giles de la Mare, 1996)

Isaac Levy, *Witness to Evil: Bergen-Belsen 1945* (London: Peter Halban, 1995)

Willy Lindwer, *The Last Seven Months of Anne Frank* (New York, Pantheon, 1991)

Jacqueline van Maarsen, *My Friend Anne Frank* (New York: Vantage Press, 1996)

Jane Marks, *Hidden Children: Secret Survivors of the Holocaust* (London: Transworld Publishers, 1995)

Michael R. Marrus, *The Holocaust in History* (London: Penguin Books, 1989)

Ralph Melnick, *The Lost Legacy of Anne Frank* (Connecticut: Yale University Press, 1997)

Bob Moore, *Victims and Survivors: The Nazi Persecution of the Jews in the Netherlands 1940–1945* (New York: St Martin's Press, 1997)

Dirk Mulder, *Kamp Westerbork* (Westerbork: Herinneringscentrum Kamp Westerbork, 1991)

Jaap Nijstad, *Westerbork Drawings: The Life and Work of Leo Kok 1923–1945* (Amsterdam: Balans, 1990)

Hella Pick, *Simon Wiesenthal: A Life in Search of Justice* (London: Weidenfeld & Nicolson, 1996)

Dr Jacob Presser, *Ashes in the Wind: The Destruction of Dutch Jewry* (London: Souvenir Press, 1968)

Jo Reilly, David Cesarani, Tony Kushner and Colin Richmond (editors), *Belsen in History and Memory* (London: Frank Cass, 1997)

Ruud van der Rol and Rian Verhoeven, *Anne Frank: Beyond the Diary* (London: Penguin Books, 1993)

A. C. Roodnat and M. de Klijn, *A Tour of the Anne Frank House in Amsterdam* (Amsterdam: Anne Frank Stichting, 1971)

Lord Russell of Liverpool, *The Scourge of the Swastika: A Short History of Nazi War Crimes* (Chivers Press, 1989)

Leopold Diego Sanchez, *Jean-Michel Frank* (Paris: Éditions de Regard, 1980)

Eva Schloss with Evelyn Julia Kent, *Eva's Story: A Survivor's Tale by the Step-sister of Anne Frank* (London: W. H. Allen, 1988)

Ernst Schnabel, *The Footsteps of Anne Frank* (London: Pan Books, 1976)

Eda Shapiro, 'The Reminiscences of Victor Kugler, the "Mr Kraler" of Anne Frank's Diary', *Yad Vashem Studies* XIII (Jerusalem: 1979)

Karen Shawn, *The End of Innocence: Anne Frank and the Holocaust* (New York, Anti-Defamation League of B'nai B'rith, 1989)

Anna G. Steenmeijer and Otto H. Frank (editors), *A Tribute to Anne Frank* (New York, Doubleday, 1971)

Jan Stoutenbeek and Paul Vigeveno, *A Guide to Jewish Amsterdam* (Amsterdam: De Haan, 1985)

Simon Wiesenthal, *Justice Not Vengeance: The Test Case* (London: Weidenfeld & Nicolson, 1989)

Roses from the Earth

Cara Wilson, *Love, Otto: The Legacy of Anne Frank* (Kansas: Andrews & McMeel, 1995)

Wolf von Wolzogen, *Anne aus Frankfurt* (Frankfurt: Historical Museum, 1994)

Index

Index